Lite Sentence

Also by Charles W. Colson

Born Again

Life Sentence

Charles W. Colson

© 1979 by Charles W. Colson

Published by Fleming H. Revell
a division of Baker Book House Company
P.O. Box 6287, Grand Rapids, MI 49516-6287

Spire edition published 1999

Printed in the United States of America

ISBN 0-8007-8668-8

Unless otherwise indicated, Scripture quotations are from the King James Version of the Bible.

Scripture quotations identified JB are from THE JERUSALEM BIBLE, copyright © 1966 by Darton, Longman & Todd, Ltd. and Doubleday, a division of Bantam Doubleday Dell Publishing Group, Inc. Reprinted by permission.

Scripture quotations identified LB are from *The Living Bible* © 1971. Used by permission of Tyndale House Publishers, Inc., Wheaton, IL 60189. All rights reserved.

Scripture quotations identified NAS are from the NEW AMERICAN STANDARD BIBLE ®. Copyright © The Lockman Foundation 1960, 1962, 1963, 1968, 1971, 1972, 1973, 1975, 1977. Used by permission.

Scripture quotations identified NIV are from the HOLY BIBLE, NEW INTERNATIONAL VERSION®. NIV®. Copyright © 1973 by International Bible Society. Used by permission of Zondervan Publishing House. All rights reserved.

Scripture quotations identified RSV are from the Revised Standard Version of the Bible, copyright 1946, 1952, 1971 by the Division of Christian Education of the National Council of the Churches of Christ in the USA. Used by permission.

Information on the questions at the beginning of each chapter is given on p. 6. The quotations on pp. 274 and 276 from Dietrich Bonhoeffer, "Who Am I?" (translated by J. B. Leishman), are from *The Cost of Discipleship,* 2d ed. (Macmillan paperback), © SCM Press Ltd. 1959, and are used by permission of Macmillan, Inc.

For current information about all releases from Baker Book House, visit our web site:
http://www.bakerbooks.com

To

*An unknown prisoner
whose prayer made all
this possible.*

Bibliographical information on chapter beginning quotations

Epigraph, page 6. Oscar Wilde, "The Ballad of Reading Gaol."

Page 31. C. S. Lewis, *Mere Christianity,* New York, Macmillan, 1952.

Page 48. Karl Menninger, "Doing True Justice," *America,* July 9, 1977.

Page 81. Henri J. M. Nouwen, *Out of Solitude,* Notre Dame, Ave Maria Press, 1966.

Page 105. Alexis De Toqueville, *Democracy in America.*

Page 117. Jacques Ellul, *The Presence of the Kingdom,* New York, Seabury Press, 1948.

Page 128. Nicholas Wolterstorff, "Reflections on Patriotism," *The Reformed Journal,* July–Aug. 1976.

Page 161. William Barclay, *The Daily Study Bible, The Gospel of Matthew,* vol. 1, Philadelphia, The Westminster Press, 2d ed., 1958.

Page 174. Henri J. M. Nouwen, *Out of Solitude.*

Page 182. Philip Slater, *The Pursuit of Loneliness,* Boston, Beacon Press, 1970.

Page 191. Vernon Grounds, "Getting into Shape Spiritually," *Christianity Today,* Feb. 2, 1979.

Page 200. Rudyard Kipling, "If."

Page 220. Malcolm Muggeridge, "Living through an Apocalypse," speech given at Lausanne, World Congress on Evangelism, July 22, 1974.

Page 228. Carl F. H. Henry, *A Plea for Evangelical Demonstration,* Grand Rapids, MI, Baker Book House, 1971.

Page 240. Henry Fairlie, *Seven Deadly Sins Today,* New York, New Republic, 1978.

Page 252. Jacques Ellul, *Violence,* New York, Seabury, 1969.

Page 264. Soren Kierkegaard, quoted in Malcolm Muggeridge, *Third Testament,* Boston, Little, Brown & Co., 1976.

Page 275. Martin Marty, "A Taxonomy of the Born Again," *Christian Century,* Oct. 4, 1978.

Page 287. C. S. Lewis, "Christian Hope—Its Meaning for Today," *Religion in Life,* Winter 1952–53. (Reprinted as "The World's Last Night" in *The World's Last Night and Other Essays,* New York, Harcourt, Brace & World, 1960.)

Contents

Before We Begin

The decision to begin writing this book was made two years ago while on a short vacation in Oregon. It was supposed to be a restful time. The sound of waves lapping on the beach below was soothing, the smell of the salt air invigorating.

I was reading a book that had a thrilling personal story. Yet like so many Christian books the ending was happy and completely victorious, leaving the fairytale impression that the Christian life is simple and almost carefree.

Frustrated, I put it aside. When I began looking for heavier reading in my brief case, I came upon a newspaper report of the lastest Gallup Poll. One third of all adult Americans, 50 million people, claimed to be "born again." Church attendance after a decline of 17 consecutive years was increasing. That was good news.

Yet abortions were increasing, too, at a much faster rate, divorces were up, millions of couples were living together out of wedlock, pornography was rampant, avowed homosexuals sought the right to be ordained as clergymen, economic and racial discrimination continued. The crime rate had hit an all-time record high in 1976, a subject of special concern to me and the prison ministry of which I was a part.

"Religion up but morality down" was the paradox Gallup discovered. One out of three professed to have made a personal commitment to Christ and to be experiencing God's regenerative work, and yet the world around us was getting sicker and sicker. "Religion is not greatly affecting our lives," Gallup concluded.

The paradox was disturbing, even mind-boggling.

I began making notes of concerns I had about what it takes to live the Christian life: commitment, self-denial, Bible study, service—what it really means to be born again. There emerged the outline of a book, the determination to write it and prayer that God would use it to challenge His people to do His work on this earth.

My first draft looked like a long-winded, sometimes angry sermon. Leonard LeSourd, the publisher who worked so closely with me during the writing of *Born Again,* read it and shook his head. Soon I discovered that my own thoughts and values were changing so fast that what I wrote one month was outdated the next. I was studying avidly under the tutelage of Professor Richard Lovelace, eminent church historian at Gordon Conwell Divinity School, Professor Jim Houston, principal of Regent College in British Columbia, and Dr. R. C. Sproul at Ligonier Valley Study Center.

For six months I put the project aside, yet my concern over the need for a contemporary restatement of Christian discipleship grew more urgent in my mind. Jim Houston must have sensed this when we met one day at Fellowship House. "Simply tell the story, Chuck," he said calmly in his most charming British accent. "Tell the story of your own experiences as a new Christian and with the prisoners."

I began writing again in earnest, completing this manuscript in the early months of 1979.

Even before the manuscript was complete, a close colleague voiced doubts about whether I was ready for a second book. Had I earned the right to speak about Christian discipleship? After much prayer, I wrote to 20 trusted Christian friends, all with many more years in the trenches of Christian service than I. The overwhelming majority urged me to continue. It was a powerful confirmation that the decision to write was correct.

As this book is published, my prayers are simply these:

* That my own experiences—the triumphs and the failures, the questions with which I've wrestled and some answers I've learned, the challenges I see—may encourage others to grow in their faith and commitment.

* That the renewal in our churches turns them into mighty instruments for God's transforming work in our society.

* That many thousands of spiritually renewed people begin to visit the prisons of America, bringing light and hope into dark and despair-filled cells.

* That Christians might assault all areas of human need with the compassion of Him who died on the Cross for all mankind.

* That a doubting, cynical world will be drawn to countless examples of Christians living out their faith, caring and sacrificing for one another, and will see that this does make a difference in all of life.

* That Christians will reject shallow faith and will hunger and thirst after righteousness through the authority of Holy Scripture, the person of Jesus Christ, the power of the Holy Spirit.

Obviously these prayers go far beyond what this or any book can accomplish. These are nonetheless my prayers, and my hope is that this book can make some contribution to the revival so desperately and urgently needed.

I dare to dream great dreams because it is a great God we serve.

May 10, 1979   CHARLES W. COLSON

Prologue—Two Worlds

SEPTEMBER 13, 1971. My "hot" line, the direct connection to the Oval Office, was ringing.

"Chuck, the President wants you. Right away." The voice was familiar: Steve Bull, President Richard Nixon's aide-de-camp and scheduler. After two years on the White House staff the summons to the President's office several times a day was routine.

Stuffing papers into a folder marked "The President" and barking orders to an assistant, I walked briskly from my suite in the gray-turreted Victorian structure known as the Old Executive Office Building, where most of the White House staff was housed, across the narrow alleyway and into the basement of the West Wing of the White House. A blue-suited police officer, gold braid shimmering in the fluorescent lights, jumped to his feet as he always did when senior officials passed his desk. The more important one's rank in Washington, the less one is supposed to notice such things; I barely nodded at the ramrod-stiff officer as I headed to the narrow flight of stairs.

A somber-faced Steve Bull, a Secret Service agent at his side with radio plug in his ear, was waiting at the small curved door leading into the Oval Office. Steve grasped the handle, swung it open smartly and I entered without breaking stride. Presidents and their staffs put a high premium on split-second efficiency.

Every time I strode into this historic room, I was awed by the surroundings; the blue and gold of the oval carpet seemed so vivid, the walls so white, the light streaming into the room from the floor to ceiling windows almost supernaturally bright. My heart always beat faster as I walked toward the great mahogany desk where the President sat.

The President was writing in longhand on a yellow pad, the cap of his exquisite gold pen clenched between his teeth like a cigarette holder. I sat down in an arm chair to the side of his desk and spread my papers out.

"Coffee?" he asked, still not looking up. I barely had the "Yes, Sir" out of my mouth when Nixon slid his hand across the desk and hit a small black buzzer. Almost instantaneously, smiling Manola Sanchez, the President's Cuban-born valet, stepped through a side door, carrying a huge silver tray. Presidents can be as impatient over morning coffee as they are over those who steal classified documents.

The President leaned back, sighed, and tossed the yellow pad into a black briefcase. "Well, what do you think of Rockefeller now? Guts? I mean he's got real guts, right?"

By now I was used to Nixon asking questions which seemed to come out of left field. His mind moved like a triphammer and he assumed everyone on his staff was thinking of the things he was.

"The thing at Attica," Nixon snapped.

"Yes, Sir. Of course." An item in the morning news summary flashed into mind. At a New York State prison, rioting inmates had taken several hostages. Rockefeller refused to negotiate, sent state troopers in with guns blazing: 40 dead. I hadn't paid too much attention. Prisons were of no concern to me; besides it was a New York State matter.

"Rockefeller did the right thing, Chuck," Nixon continued. "He'll catch it though from all those liberal jackasses in the press. But he's smart. The public want no more nonsense from criminals. The public will cheer him on. 'Gun 'em down,' they'll say."

"No doubt about it, Mr. President. Our people out there have had enough of being soft on criminals." I swung my arm toward the Rose Garden as I always did when I said, "out there," though the Rose Garden is a long way from where people live.

For the next several minutes, as we sipped coffee, the President talked about our anticrime program. I took notes profusely so I could relay his instructions to others on the staff. "Must get tough," I under-lined at the bottom of one page. It was good politics. We believed that long sentences, increased police powers and tough prisons were the answer to the crime problem.

Neither of us mentioned the 31 prisoners who had been killed, but I suggested that the President send personal letters to the families of the nine slain guards. A nice gesture.

"Maybe I should call Rocky." Nixon reflected a moment; I sensed he was savoring the thought that Rockefeller, his one-time liberal tormentor, was being carried along by the strong conservative breezes we were doing everything we knew how to fan. "You agree?" He reached for the phone as he glanced quickly at me.

"Yes, Sir. It will be good if the Governor knows of your support."

I didn't realize it then, but my mind had become conditioned to weigh all events, big and small, even those in which people died, on the political scales. If what Rockefeller had done were politically dan-gerous, my instincts would have said no. Nixon knew that; that's why I had become his favorite political sounding board.

Nixon spoke brusquely into the phone: "Ah, yes, get me Governor Rockefeller. He's probably up at that place . . . uh . . . " He glanced at me.

"Attica," I whispered.

"Attica, that's it."

APRIL 3, 1978

"Attica, that's it." Bill Showalter, pastor of a Presbyterian Church in Rochester, New York, pointed through the car's front windshield. Each time the fast-swinging wipers pushed the late winter snow aside I could catch a glimpse of distant gray turrets atop massive concrete walls. I glanced at Paul Kramer, once my fellow prisoner, now released and working with me in our prison ministry. His face was somber. To us, all penitentiaries brought back painful memories.

Attica was like a ghost town, reflecting the drabness of the leaden sky overhead. Rows of look-alike white bungalows, the homes of prison staff and guards, lined the side streets, while the downtown area con-sisted of two blocks of soot-colored brick buildings. The quietness was strangely unsettling, as if Attica was still under a cloud of death, a place where a plague had once visited, leaving the people hiding in their homes in dread of its return.

The ancient fortress is on the southern edge of town. A 10-foot-high, gray stone spire rose up before the main gates, a monument erected by townspeople in memory of the 10 guards slain in the 1971 riots (one died later from injuries). Somehow the architecture seemed cold, memorializing not the glory of lives lived and lost in a noble cause but the horror of senseless death.

We parked in a large, ice-packed driveway and announced ourselves to a remote-controlled speaker box. From walkways atop the walls, blue uniformed guards peered down; the towers looked like angry porcupines, bristling with glistening steel gun barrels. Attica is a maximum security prison. It took us a half hour to clear the front gate.

"See that?" The black chaplain escorting us pointed to a small, fenced-off area just inside the gate that might have been a patch of garden. "That's where prisoners are buried." He added that more than 200 tiny markers were laid out there. When no family claims the body of an inmate who dies in prison, he is buried in this plot. No name is put on the grave: only the man's prison number is etched in the steel marker.

The thought of so many identities lost forever in this world sickened me.

"Worst thing about it," the chaplain continued, "was the monument."

"What do you mean?"

"The prisoners built a memorial to the guys killed in the riot." I noticed everyone spoke of *the* riot as if it were the only thing of meaning here, earning Attica its place of shame in history for all time. "The inmates wanted one like the people built outside. But the warden made them remove it after it was built. Guys are still pretty uptight."

Many of the slaughtered inmates had been bystanders who had had no part in organizing the riot. Why couldn't they have a piece of rock over their nameless grave plate, I wondered, something which said that they once lived and breathed and existed as part of the human race?

So the 1971 riot lived on like a curse. Memories were, I soon discovered, as vivid as if it had occurred yesterday. The massacred inmates and guards were its physical victims, but the emotional victims included 1,700 inmates, the staff, and a whole town. The present warden was the assistant warden then; he was considered a good man, but his very presence kept the memories alive for the prisoners.

The chaplain reported that prison officials were uneasy about having the men assemble together for our appearance but had agreed to allow all inmates who signed up 24 hours in advance to attend my talk. Eight hundred did so. Two hours were set aside for the meeting in a cavernous auditorium.

Bill Showalter had rounded up 20 Christians from community churches to join us. Our group was ushered into the auditorium through the backstage area, while the inmates were being marched through the front entrances.

"No contact is allowed between inmates and visitors," the lieutenant escorting us ordered. "You will sit here." He pointed at a row of chairs behind the speaker's podium. I tried to protest. In other prisons local people have been allowed to mix with the inmates; it eliminates the "we" versus "them" tension and builds relationships which can help their future ministry. But the lieutenant was adamant.

"Can't I at least walk down and talk to the men?" I asked.

"No, you can't. We are responsible for your safety in here, Mr. Colson."

"These men are going to have the wrong feeling," I insisted, "with me up here and them down there."

"No," he said again. "Maybe after you finish speaking. We'll see."

The concern for security was not unreasonable, I realized, but as the prisoners began to file in, the situation could not have been worse. One group at a time was marched in, the chairs down front assigned first. The inmates were beneath us—bad symbolism. They quickly became restless with nothing to do but stare at the nicely dressed people up on the platform. More than half of the inmates were black; I looked around and saw that our volunteers were all white.

I shifted restlessly in my chair and looked at my watch. It was 10:30 A.M.; delays had already chewed up a half hour of our allotted time and only 200 inmates were in the auditorium. The guards appeared to be in no hurry.

I leaned over and whispered to the chaplain sitting next to me, "What's holding us up?"

"That's the way things work around here," he shrugged.

The tramping of feet on metal grates every few minutes announced the arrival of each new group. By 10:45 only 400 restless inmates were in the hall; shouted obscenities shattered the quiet as the guards prowled the aisles trying to appear casual. But I sensed their tension. It wouldn't take much for this to explode, I thought.

By 11 A.M., 500 to 600 inmates were in their seats. Something had to give. "Let's start this thing," I suggested.

Nodding, the chaplain bolted from his chair, grabbed the mike, welcomed everyone, and turned the program over to Bill Showalter.

Bill is intelligent and articulate, and all went well until his closing line, "And so I present to you a man who spent seven months in prison and therefore knows how you men feel."

Bill's last words were drowned out by howling laughter and catcalls. Seven months seemed like a slap on the wrists to these men, many of them lifers, all doing long sentences. Guards moved quickly toward two inmates in back who stood up shaking angry fists in the air. I jumped up and took the mike from Bill; the noise was deafening.

I tried speaking but the words could not penetrate the wall of sound. I tried again, no use. "Lord help us," I prayed softly.

Suddenly a huge black man in the front row—he looked seven feet tall—bounded to his feet and turned to face the crowd. All I could see was the top and back of his clean-shaved head, as smooth as glass and shining in the glare of the overhead lights. His voice reverberated through the auditorium. "Let him speak, you monkeys," he roared. Then he turned to me and nodded as the din slowly began to subside. Still I had to shout to be heard.

"That's right, you guys, I spent only seven months inside. That's nothing." There was a roar of agreement. "But," I continued, "I have come back . . .

"And I'll keep coming back over and over to help you men as long as God gives me the strength."

There were a few jibes and jeers as I continued, but slowly the mood was changing. They listened, even remaining quiet as I explained certain Gospel passages. Afterwards I asked Paul Kramer to the microphone to help answer the more hostile questions. Paul was like a rock, imperturbable, his feet firmly planted on either side of the microphone as he patiently replied to the prisoners' challenges. The question and answer period was like a poultice placed on a sore, sucking out the remaining poison.

Our time was nearly over and I wanted to go down among the inmates and talk and shake hands with them. But the lieutenant was standing at the head of the small flight of steps, blocking the way down to the floor.

On an impulse, I moved suddenly. "Okay, lieutenant, the speech is over," I shouted and then, not waiting for him to answer, jumped from the platform and headed down the center aisle. Quickly I was surrounded by inmates, six and seven deep. The guards, startled at first, left us alone. Rich dialogue followed with a variety of men, some Christians, others earnestly seeking, many simply in need of a word of encouragement. Perhaps a few inmates this day saw a small flicker of light in a canyon of darkness.

September 13, 1971 . . . April 3, 1978: two worlds, and a journey traveled, some things learned.

*When I was converted, I made this mistake: I thought
the battle was already mine, the victory already won,
the crown already in my grasp. I thought the old
things had passed away, that all things had become
new, and that my old, corrupt nature, the old life,
was gone. But I found out, after serving Christ for
a few months, that conversion was only like enlisting
in the army—that there was a battle on hand.*

D. L. MOODY

1. Release

The sensations I felt upon my sudden release from prison on January
31, 1975, are as vivid to me now as if it all happened yesterday.

The message that I had been freed was telephoned to my lawyer,
Dave Shapiro, shortly after 5 P.M. He reached me immediately. "You're
free," he shouted, "free!"

For a moment I could not reply. Months of frustration had left
my emotions paralyzed. "Don't kid me, Dave. I can't take it," I said
at last.

"You're free, I tell you, you're free," he kept barking as my mind
and body slowly relaxed. Tears flowed, not of joy so much as relief
as tensions collapsed like air escaping from a balloon. Even then,
something deep inside kept callously insisting, "Don't believe it until
you see the judge's order."

My senses were still numb four hours later when a smiling U.S.
marshal handed me the signed release form. We stood at the front
gate of the barbed-wire enclosed prison compound at Fort Holabird
in Baltimore, where I had spent the last part of my sentence. My
wife, Patty, her eyes reddened, was there to drive me home. The
protective mechanism inside me gradually released its iron grip. The
shouts and waves of the 18 other inmates, mostly prized government

catches from organized crime, told me that my prison ordeal was really over.

I climbed into the front seat of our red station wagon and rubbed my hand along the smooth vinyl upholstery. Patty had to drive since my driver's license had expired. I became suddenly aware of other deprivations. I would not be able to vote, hold public office, practice law or obtain a number of state licenses denied to ex-prisoners. Some cities would require that I register at the local police station, as all felons must, when visiting. All this could be for the rest of my life unless the appropriate state governor chose to waive the limitations. Tonight that didn't matter. I was going home.

The thought started my heart racing. As Patty drove us through the iron gates of the old army post, the night sky, always smoke-laden from the belching stacks of nearby Baltimore factories, was suddenly brighter. The air seemed clean; the drab, winter surroundings almost pristine.

Exhausted from the emotional roller coaster of the past months, my body aching even as my spirit soared, I leaned my head back on the seat. Patty was talking so excitedly she sounded like a chirping bird. The adjustment from prison to freedom, I had read, was as hard as the adjustment going in—like suddenly walking into sunshine after days in inky darkness. Prison *is* darkness, under the spell of the Prince himself, I'd come to realize. Now the light was blinding, painful to my dilated pupils.

"Life will be different for us from now on," I promised Patty as we sped south along Interstate 95 toward Washington. "We'll have more time together. We'll travel. No more harassments because I'm no longer a public figure."

Patty glanced at me with a skeptical look.

"I mean it, Dear. You just wait and see. I've learned what's important in life."

More than anything else, I wanted to take a long walk through the woods, gaze at the birds, sniff fresh flowers, feel quietness. For seven months there had been constant noise, radios blaring rock music, people shouting, locker doors slamming, steel biting steel, like a harsh and discordant symphony. Now I yearned for peace and stillness. The seemingly little things most people take for granted had become terribly important.

I vowed, for example, to throw away the clothes I was wearing which had been kept in a prison locker. The stale odors permeated the fabric. How the stench, day in and day out, haunted me. Rolling the window down I breathed heavily of the chill, damp, night air.

Short-lived was my vision of peace; the front yard of our Tudor-style country home was ablaze with television lights as Patty and I drove up about 10 P.M. Trucks with humming generators were parked everywhere, long black cords snaking out of their rear doors. Fifty or more shivering reporters waited near the front door.

The press had been camped in front of our house countless times during the long Watergate ordeal. Judge Gesell's surprise order releasing me because of "family problems" was, I imagined, the final chapter. One last encounter with the press this night and it was over.

Mikes were shoved in our faces, questions bombarded: "How do you feel?" "Will you see former President Nixon?" "Are you bitter?" There was nothing newsworthy to say. I made a few comments, thanking Judge Gesell and the Lord, and then we darted through our front door.

The headline the next day might well have irked the judge.

"Gesell frees Colson; Colson thanks the Lord."

"Hi ya, Brother." It was Doug Coe, arms outstretched, standing in our hallway wearing a blue ski parka and the broadest grin I've ever seen on any man's face. They were the same words with which Doug greeted me when we first met 18 months earlier, words which seemed to me then ridiculously familiar.

But in the months that followed, Doug had showed me the reality behind the term "brother." It was his daughter, Paula, who had stayed with Patty all through my months in prison. Now Doug, Paula and Doug's wife, Jan, were on hand to greet us, having arrived at our home as soon as the first reports of my release were broadcast. They had placed flowers throughout the house, started a roaring blaze in the living room fireplace, prepared snacks.

In the year and a half since I had made the most important decision of my life, I had learned that Christian fellowship did not mean light-hearted fraternal gatherings but caring men and women "bearing one another's burdens."

Later that night I lay in bed, staring at the ceiling, talking half to myself and half to the Lord. "I did my time . . . I paid my debt . . . now I'm free, ready to build a new life, a more simple life. No more politics . . . maybe a good job in business . . . perhaps some writing . . . time with my family."

I liked the sound of it. I wanted to put the hate and anger of Watergate behind me and forget the grimness of prison life.

But sleep would not come. What was wrong? Though I kept shaking them off, the images which crossed my mind were not of peace and order and the simple life. I tossed and turned. The softness of the bed felt strange. Finally, I drifted into a fitful sleep.

Suddenly I was back in Dormitory G of Maxwell Prison, Alabama. The air was stifling; there were groans, body noises, locker doors clanging, odors—and faces of men with no hope, life sucked out of their yellowish skins.

I awoke with a start, shivering, yet sweating. Patty sat up and put her arm around me. The dream faded and I lay down again. But sleep did not return. I remembered once sitting in the crowded day room at the entrance of my prison dormitory; the old black and white television set was presenting a melancholy serial. There were two noisy card games going. I was trying to read despite the clamor.

"Hey, Colson." A tatooed prison veteran, Archie, stood in front of me. "You'll be out of here soon. What are you going to do for us?"

The room was suddenly silent, all eyes on me.

"I'll help in some way. I'll never forget this stinking place or you guys," I replied.

"They all say that," Archie sneered. "I've seen you big shots come and go. They all say the same thing. Then they get out and forget us fast. Ain't nobody cares about us. Nobody."

"I'll remember, Archie."

"Bull!" he shouted with a defiant gesture. The scene faded, but Archie's angry face stayed with me.

The next morning I knew that our first order of business had to be a visit to our son Chris in Columbia, South Carolina.

An 18-year-old college freshman, Chris had become bitter because of what had happened to me. Constantly broke, unable to stay within his spending allowance, he had been shown a way to make some quick, easy money. Foolishly, he had purchased a few ounces of marijuana, then was arrested in a campus raid along with 40 others. Because his name was Colson, his case made front-page news. A lawyer friend of ours bailed Chris out of the "tank" in the city jail, but Chris' problem was the main reason, along with the release of other Watergate prisoners, that prompted Judge Gesell to free me early. For Chris faced criminal charges.

The following Friday morning our DC-9 descended through thick layers of menacing gray clouds, landing at the rain-drenched Columbia airport. Chris, looking pale and still shaken, was waiting at the terminal gate. My resolve to be stern so that Chris would not quickly forget the lesson, dissolved the moment I saw him.

"You'll be all right, Son," I said, embracing him.

"I'm going to try, Dad, honest I am," he replied earnestly.

Hours spent in the "tank" at the century-old city jail had chastened Chris; together we would find an answer, I assured him. Remorse then flooded me as I realized how much four years in the White House, two years of embroilment in the Watergate upheaval and seven months in prison had kept us apart. I had not been the father I should have been. That would have to change.

During our visit we discovered one shaft of light in a dark situation. Chris' lawyer explained that if he got into no new trouble in the months ahead, he might be eligible for a state counseling program that could lead to charges being dropped and his record cleared. Chris vowed to stay out of trouble. Whatever was ahead, we would face it together. It was a great visit.

Since we were in South Carolina, Patty and I decided to fly the short distance to Montgomery, Alabama, and visit my friends at Maxwell. Just seven days after being freed from prison, I was back again— this time as a visitor. The main reason for our decision was Paul Kramer, a 27-year-old ex-marine, drug offender—the young man I met my first lonely and frightening night at Maxwell. Together we had formed a small Bible study in prison. It had grown as God's Spirit moved through the prison, and we had become close as brothers. Leaving Paul behind when I was transferred to Holabird for the last two months of my imprisonment was one of the saddest moments of my time behind bars. Hopefully this visit would provide him reassurance since he still had another year to serve. I wanted Paul to know he was expected in our home when his sentence was up.

To my chagrin I saw that a TV camera crew was set up at the front door of the prison administration building. Word had leaked out about my visit. Two blue-jacketed guards escorted me to the familiar open compound, surrounded by the four, one-story, white stucco dormitory buildings. The setting was unchanged from that day many months earlier when I had been ushered in as prisoner number 23226.

Then I saw Paul walking toward the glass-sided control room from which all movement inside the prison is monitored. When he saw me, a broad grin spread across his face. He started to jog towards me. Without giving it a thought, I wrapped my arms around him and hugged him warmly.

The cameras had been turning and this irked me. Physical contact between inmates is prohibited in all prisons; any sign of affection is viewed with suspicion in places where homosexual behavior is such a pervasive problem.

"They'll show that on television tonight and half the world will believe we're queer," I lamented to Paul.

"Who cares?" Paul replied, as we walked slowly to the visiting area. "It's all in the Lord's hands."

He was right. Weeks later I learned that a stubborn nonbeliever in western Pennsylvania was alone watching the late news when the footage of Kramer and me greeting each other was flashed on the screen. The man later wrote me: "For years I have resisted church and every sermon my wife forced me to listen to. But seeing a once powerful White House official embracing that poor prisoner got to me somehow as none of the other arguments ever did. I knew Christianity had to be real." He then said that he had become a believer that very night.

I was being taught never to second-guess God's ways.

The big letdown came after our trip to South Carolina and Alabama. Senator Harold Hughes, Minnesota Congressman Al Quie, former Texas Judge Graham Purcell and Doug Coe, my close friends at Fellowship House, whose prayers and wisdom had helped me so much during the desperate Watergate days, were prodding me to commit myself to Fellowship projects. I found myself resisting. Even worse, I was becoming angry at Patty without provocation, especially when she talked about my going back to law practice someday. Irritation was always just under the surface, it seemed, as the euphoria of freedom began to wear off.

While in prison I had disciplined myself never to sleep during the day as I watched other inmates become dulled and lifeless, their bodies atrophying as they tried to sleep away their sentences. Now I found exhaustion creeping over me almost every day. Sometimes it was a chore just to walk about the house.

When Barbara Walters invited me on the "Today Show," my first reaction was to refuse. Mentally gearing up to relive all the Watergate horrors was a depressing prospect and I was not up to the pressures. Publicity was the last thing I wanted or needed. But Barbara had been very sympathetic and friendly to Patty and me when I entered prison. Reluctantly, I agreed to appear.

During the interview Barbara's questions were prickly as always, especially about my relationship to Henry Kissinger. I found myself being critical of Henry which was not a comfortable position for an ex-con to take about the Secretary of State.

"The same old 'hatchet man,' " was one comment in the press. The *Washington Post* in a front page article assaulted my credibility, an article which breathed fresh life into all the pent-up, anti-Nixon, anti-Colson passions. Even my Christian friends chided me about the negative position I had taken, the lack of love shown. I had allowed Barbara to dominate the interview and therefore said little about my new faith. In short, I had blown it.

Some days later we were ending an early dinner when the telephone rang. Patty answered, then called me to the phone, clasping her hand to the receiver. "It's the President," she said in hushed tones.

"Who, Jerry Ford?" I asked, stunned for a moment.

"I guess so. It's the White House operator. She just said, 'The President.' "

I grasped the receiver, reviewing my many encounters with him when he was a congressman and I was Nixon's assistant. We were good friends once, but now he would be running for election and so far had studiously avoided any contact with the Watergate fallen.

"Mr. Colson, the President is calling." The familiar crisp voice of the chief operator on the White House switchboard repeated the phrase so common to me through all those years.

There was a click, then, "How are you, boy?" It was the voice I had heard so many hundreds of times. Richard Nixon was in San Clemente exile, but the White House switchboard had placed this call. His voice was strong, his tone sincere; I had learned to tell when it was or wasn't.

Few historians will credit Richard Nixon with having a warm heart, but I believe otherwise. The former President had written me an especially friendly and moving letter on my last birthday. Patty had brought it to me in prison. Now as we reminisced, I knew he cared.

Then he came to the point. "I, uh, caught some excerpts of your interview on the 'Today Show' and, uh, well, Henry called me . . . You know we only have one President now. One Secretary of State. So we need to support them, you know, Chuck. They are all we have. I mean, you and I know Henry's faults, but as Americans we support our leaders and our country, right?"

This was Richard Nixon at his best. For all his faults, including those which had toppled his presidency, he deeply loved his country.

"Yes, Mr. President, I understand."

I never publicly criticized Henry Kissinger again and in fact wrote him later to apologize. Nixon was right. More important was the lesson painfully learned that when I let my old political nature emerge, my witness for Jesus Christ was hurt.

Nixon had a final word of advice. "One thing, Chuck. You aren't seriously thinking of getting involved in religious work, are you? I mean, you are going to do something else with your life, I would think."

My answer was evasive.

"You have a great future," he continued. "You can do big things in business. Remember, you aren't beaten. You have tremendous abilities. I know it. Go out now and make some money for your family."

When the conversation ended, I checked my watch. We had talked more than 20 minutes.

"It was like the old days," I told Patty. For an instant my heart skipped as the longing returned for the old relationship, to advise a President, even a discredited one. Just as a reformed addict continues to crave dope, I felt the need again to be near power as I remembered it in the White House. How easy it is, I realized, to fall back to one's old ways. Then a verse of Scripture surfaced and I was instantly aware that all the glory of the White House was as so much "loss compared to knowing Him." More and more these passages were appearing to help me at times of need.

I knew too that Richard Nixon and I would have more contact in the years ahead, but the relationship would be different. My affection for him was strong; what had happened to him and his presidency wouldn't change things between us, but what had happened inside of me would.

Nixon's call made me wonder. What was my future? Law had lost its allure. But I was no evangelist. I had proven that on the "Today Show." During one hour of interview I had barely mentioned my conversion. No, I was not one to be in full-time religious work. Business, perhaps. Nixon, who knew me well, seemed to think that was where I belonged.

So had another friend, a man whose opinion I greatly respected. After the "Today Show" he was quite blunt with me. "If you remain in the public eye, Chuck, you'll be under constant attack. To millions of people you are the enemy, the symbol of their frustration and anger. They think your new religion is a cop-out, a tricky 'hatchet man' device to avoid punishment. For you, they'll always have a blind, unreasoning hatred, just as they have for Nixon and the others on his staff. Get out of sight, Chuck. Keep a low profile. Go into a quiet business. You're good at that and you'll make money. Five or 10 years from now the climate will be different and you can re-emerge. But for the sake of your sanity and the peace and tranquillity of your family, I would say a firm good-by to television, the reporters and the whole media scene."

It was good advice. For too long I had been in the line of fire, buffeted in headlines, an object of so much of the hate and fury which Watergate unleashed upon the nation. If the country was not weary of it, I surely was.

There was something else almost as certain. Though I often anguished for the men I'd left behind in prison and was angered over the injustices to which they were subjected, prison work was not for me. Several friends had suggested that I develop some kind of ministry to inmates. But the thought of going back into prison chilled me; the stench was still pungent in my nostrils. Maybe I could give a few talks about prison reform, perhaps prod friends still in politics into doing something. But it was not my career.

As winter passed and the cherry blossoms came to Washington, indecision about my future deepened. I wondered: Was this only a part of something much deeper? Old values were being assaulted and rethought, always an uncomfortable process. Gone for a time at least, was the passionate partisanship and political zealotry which had burned in me for so long. Was I simply worn down from the long ordeal, reacting against what I'd been through? Or was there something more significant taking place inside me?

I struggled with questions about my faith. Jesus Christ was very real to me, but what did that mean from this point on? He had strengthened me through the Watergate and prison crises, but now all that was over. What was next? I felt I had received salvation and would go to heaven, but is that the only purpose of the Christian life?

What does a new believer do? Attend Bible study, church and prayer meetings, of course. Follow the commandments, indeed. But what else? What is the real goal of being a Christian?

I felt restless and confused.

Imagine yourself as a living house. God comes in to rebuild that house. At first, perhaps, you can understand what He is doing. He is getting the drains right and stopping the leaks in the roof and so on . . . But presently He starts knocking the house about in a way that hurts abominably and does not seem to make sense. What on earth is He up to? The explanation is that He is building quite a different house from the one you thought of—throwing out a new wing here, putting on an extra floor there, running up towers, making courtyards. You thought you were going to be made into a decent little cottage: but He is building a palace. He intends to come and live in it Himself.

C. S. LEWIS

2. Indecision

During the next months I began an intense search to find out what God wanted me to do. Give Him your life and He is in charge, I had been told, but it was not as simple as snapping your fingers and receiving an instant sign from heaven.

I felt pulls from many directions and had no way of being sure what was right. Richard Nixon and other friends had urged a business career. One opportunity resulted from a meeting with a small group of businessmen in a western state for a breakfast of fellowship and prayer.

As we were taking our places around some tables pulled together in a U-shape, a latecomer strode through the door. Tall and distinguished, the man's commanding presence silenced all conversation. Our host rushed over to greet him. "Jim Fuller, we're so glad you could come."

Fuller's sharp, stern features didn't relax. He nodded to the host and the others, then began drumming his fingers restlessly on the table the moment he sat down. Because of the sudden tension in the room, I concluded he was not a regular participant in these fellowship meetings.

"Who is he?" I whispered to the man on my left.

"The biggest industrialist in our state and one of the wealthiest men in the country." I shook my head; the name meant nothing.

After breakfast, I talked for perhaps 20 minutes about some of the faith principles I had learned working with the men and women of the Washington Fellowship. Mr. Fuller stared at me intently, expressionless. Whenever our eyes met, his frown increased and his brow seemed to furrow more deeply. At least I had his attention, I thought to myself.

When I finished, Fuller walked brusquely toward me as the other men stepped back to let him pass through. "Are you through talking?" he asked abruptly.

I was nonplused: Was he complaining that I had spoken too long? "Yes, that's it for today," I stammered.

"I would like to hear more sometime." He smiled, shook my hand, turned and marched with military-like bearing to the door, picked up his coat and disappeared.

The room buzzed with conversation. Jim Fuller had never before shown any interest in spiritual matters though regularly sought out by religious groups of every kind. One man shook his head in surprise.

"I invited him, never expecting him to accept. If only . . ."

"If only what?" I asked.

"If only you'd given your testimony. We might have won him. We missed our big chance."

On the flight back to Washington, I pondered those words, vaguely troubled. He had acted as if Fuller was some kind of rare animal to be trapped and brought back alive to the zoo. Are we Christians so obsessed with winning souls that it has become like trophy hunting? I stored this question away in my mind for later examination.

Two weeks later Jim Fuller called me to say he was coming to Washington on business. Could we get together? We arranged to meet at Fellowship House, scene of so much Christian activity in the Washington area. At the appointed hour I escorted my visitor into the library where our prayer group met every week. We sat in two of the comfortable, down-filled chairs, the large, round coffee table between us.

Fuller was as brusque and businesslike as he had been in the hotel. "Mr. Colson, I'll come right to the point. That breakfast was most important to me. Let me explain . . ."

I studied him as he talked. He was nearly 60, but he was so physically fit he looked many years younger. His stoic expression never betrayed a hint of emotion as his well-organized mind clicked off points like a computer. Everything about him from his conservative suit to his neatly parted sandy hair evidenced a rigidly self-disciplined life.

Jim Fuller had amassed a staggering array of assets in his conglomerate, but in the tight money market of the previous year he had found himself squeezed for ready cash. "It's working out all right," he quickly added. "But the experience made me rethink some things."

He paused and for the first time seemed a bit uncertain. "Some of the things you said indicated an unusual kind of strength. Well, frankly I was a little envious. For the first time in my life I felt the need for that."

He looked at me directly now, but his words had softened. "What I'm getting at, Mr. Colson, concerns you. What are you going to do with your life?"

I answered as honestly as I could. "Right now, I'm simply waiting to see what God wants for me. I've made no plans."

Fuller had turned numerous bright young men into millionaires. I'd heard about his remarkable success story and sensed that he was getting ready to offer me a position that would be hard to refuse. Yet something inside said I had to turn it down—and quickly. And so I replied: "You can have what I have, Mr. Fuller. You don't have to hire anyone. It's free. It is Jesus Christ." It wasn't said glibly or piously; the words came naturally. But I wasn't prepared for the response.

"Don't ever talk to me about Jesus Christ," he shouted, slamming his fist on the coffee table so hard the cups rattled.

I nearly jumped out of my chair at the outburst and he looked as surprised and embarrassed as I must have. Such an emotional response was not in his carefully programed temperament.

"I'm sorry," he quickly retreated. "It's just that I can't be a hypocrite. I don't believe . . . I can't say I do if I don't. And besides," he added, "if I were to seek God, I'd want to get my own life in order first."

"That's not the way," I interrupted, still rattled by his explosion, but his explanation continued. And now for the first time he was rambling, his voice softened, almost mellow.

"I grew up in a strict home. It was stifling: don't drink, don't smoke, don't swear, don't play cards. I broke away from all that and made it on my own. I don't need religion, don't want it. It would be hypocritical just because I now have a few temporary problems."

I wanted to reach across the table, put my hand on his arm and tell him how his pride was in the way—consuming him in fact—just as mine had done to me. I ached for this man because he was building his defenses, just as I had done the first time my friend and business associate Tom Phillips had explained to me what it meant to ask Christ into one's life. But there was nothing I could say; only God could penetrate the armor.

"Can we be friends?" he asked, his voice still soft.

"Of course," I replied, "and if you don't want to talk about the Lord I won't bring Him up. If you do, however, tell me. It's up to you."

With a big grin he stood up. "That's a deal." Just like many hundreds he had made in the business world. With that he was gone.

Did that inner nudge to turn down Fuller's business offer mean that a business career was not for me? I wasn't sure. A short time later there came an interesting offer for an executive position in communications. Something inside led me to say no to that too.

Meanwhile my longtime friend and law partner Charlie Morin assured me that though I was disbarred from practicing law in the State of Virginia, this would not be so in Massachusetts. Charlie argued my case and the State Supreme Court voted not to disbar me, instead leaving a suspension in effect. But the prospect of going back to law did not excite me.

Much was owed to those in my prayer group at Fellowship House—Doug Coe; Harold Hughes, recently retired from the U.S. Senate; and Al Quie and Graham Purcell—who understandably assumed I'd be spending my time working with them. At one meeting in the basement room of Harold's home, Doug spread out before us calendars with the year ahead blocked out: "We'll schedule August for a retreat in Northern Michigan, October will be set aside for speeches to governors' breakfasts." So it went.

I gently protested, explaining that there had been so much adverse publicity about John Dean and other Watergate figures getting rich on the lecture circuit that I had written Judge Gesell promising not to do it. It didn't look right anyway. The public justifiably would say that "crime does pay" and in my case it could compromise my witness. We agreed that I would do only a few prayer breakfasts each year with any remuneration to go into a special fund for use in prisons.

Despite my reluctance to make speeches, I deeply wanted to be part of this fellowship, knowing only too well that I would have been lost without their help back in those first days after my conversion. I didn't know then how to study or read the Bible or even pray intelligently. But for these caring people, I might well have been one of those who makes decisions through evangelistic efforts but then never attends church or grows in the Christian faith. The casualty rate of new converts is much higher than most people realize.

With business, law and public speaking ruled out for now, I decided to spend nearly full time finishing a book on my conversion experience which I had started writing in prison. There had been some extravagant offers from secular publishers, but knowing that their main interest was to have an exposé of Richard Nixon, I turned them down and accepted instead a small advance from a Christian publisher, Chosen Books, to tell the story of what God had done in my life.

Patty meanwhile was her usual patient self with me, but I knew she was increasingly uncomfortable about my becoming involved too much in religious work. The aggressive Christians nettled Patty, made her feel that her own quiet, Roman Catholic beliefs were inadequate. I sensed her fear that if I became ardently evangelistic, it could draw us apart.

One morning at breakfast, Patty came right to the point. "Honey, let's talk about the future. What are you going to do with *your* life?"

"I've got to finish the book first."

"But what comes after that?" she pressed.

"I honestly don't know."

"I hope you will practice law, maybe in Boston—that would be a good life for us."

"Someday, maybe. Someday." My heart ached for Patty. So loyal and loving during the long ordeal, she had been through as much as I had, maybe more. A part-time secretary was working in our basement. Both phones were always busy. My book editor, Leonard LeSourd was spending many long days and nights with me. With never a complaining word, Patty would make lunches for us every day and often dinners.

But for her the fear, usually unspoken, that I'd spend my life in Christian service—and maybe working in the prisons—was the most difficult. Patty, a private person, could see what that would mean in our lives: our home disrupted, constant travel, back in the public light again. On several occasions I assured her that if I should get involved in any prison work, it would be a sideline; it would have to be since it couldn't possibly provide us a living.

One of the best decisions I made during this period of confusion in my life was to ask my friend, Fred Rhodes, to become my working partner. Correspondence was piling up, requests for speaking dates had become more than I could even acknowledge. If I was ever to get my book written, I needed to be freed from paperwork.

Fred was not only a good administrator, he was a loyal friend. After having served such high government posts as deputy chief of the Veterans Administration and chairman of the Postal Rate Commission, he elected early retirement at the end of 1974 and wrote me in prison that he would be available to help me in the Lord's work whenever I was released.

As we worked together, he would find occasions to talk about prisons and remind me of my friends there. "Have you heard lately from Paul Kramer?" "Did Lee Corbin get his release?" "What can we do to help those poor guys behind bars?"

While we wrote letters and prayed for these men, we agreed that there didn't seem much else we could do. Yet every few days Fred brought up the subject. I don't think he was aware of how subtle this pressure was.

Others were adding to the pressure. One day when Harold Hughes and I were together at Fellowship House studying Scripture, I made a comment about the "lousy prison system."

Harold scowled at me; he can look fierce even when mildly annoyed.

"What's the matter?" I asked.

"That's about the twentieth time you've said that. I'm sick of hearing it. If you think it is so bad, it's time you got busy and did something about it."

"Yeah," I replied. "Well I've been thinking about it."

Harold's words stung me hard though I tried not to show it. What could anyone really do? I wondered. To tackle the prison system would require a tremendous undertaking. Such staggering, overwhelming thoughts were quickly shoved to the back of my mind.

Pressure upon me was gradually building in other ways.

At Fred's urging, I had accepted one major speaking invitation. This was to the Pastors' Conference at the Annual Southern Baptist Convention which was to meet in June 1975 in Miami Beach. Fred had suggested it while I was still in prison, the inspiration coming to him because a rawboned Southern Baptist country pastor, Edmond

Blow, had had such a meaningful ministry to those of us at Maxwell.

"The way things stand, I won't even be eligible for parole until July, but if your faith is so strong, go ahead," I had written from prison.

After my early release, I'd almost forgotten about this speech. Fred, who once served as vice president of the Southern Baptist Convention, reminded me of it in late April. He urged me to begin preparations, explaining that about 20,000 pastors would attend at the Miami Convention Center. That is a frightening prospect for an accomplished speaker, let alone one who had never given his testimony before a large crowd.

As the date approached, I could tell that Fred was getting more and more nervous. There had been vigorous vocal opposition by Baptists to my speaking when it was first announced. "Who would believe anything that criminal Colson has to say?" was one comment.

A number of pastors urged the program committee to cancel me out, but the head of the committee took a stand. "He professes Jesus Christ. Let's hear what he has to say." Though rumblings continued, the opposition slowly subsided. At Fred's suggestion, Brother Blow would introduce me.

I wrote out my speech in advance, then rehearsed it with Fred, wanting to be sure I stayed within the 23 minutes allotted. Fred had warned that the convention was always tightly run. We even agreed on a signal: Fred would sit in the front row with a copy of the speech. If at key points I was running over my time limit, Fred would take off his glasses and I would skip over certain paragraphs.

The Miami Beach convention center was an awesome sight. But for the missing red, white and blue bunting and balloons, it might have been the 1972 Republican Convention. Almost exactly three years earlier, I had walked into the same hall at the side of the President of the United States. This time I walked alongside a gangling, wide-eyed, rural Alabama preacher, Edmund Blow.

When we arrived, Brother Blow took one look up at the bleachers rising on three sides with crowds filing in, and said, "Excuse me, I have to find the bathroom."

I knew exactly how he felt. The thought of a new Christian like myself trying to talk about faith to 20,000 preachers now seemed like an absurd assignment. What had I gotten myself into?

The convention keynoter preceeded me on the platform. He was an eloquent speaker, but many were not listening as they walked in the aisles and visited in small clusters; in fact, the crowd noises were almost drowning out his speech. With perspiration streaming down his face, he tried every known oratorical gimmick. It was actually a good speech, but the scene reminded me of the early hours of a political convention when speakers drone on endlessly to unhearing delegates who are milling about in feverish pursuit of last minute votes. When the speaker finished, there was a smattering of applause.

While Brother Blow was being presented by Dr. James L. Pleitz, chairman of the conference, I was near panic. *These people won't even listen,* I thought. I had been in politics long enough to know audiences; this one was anything but friendly.

When Blow mentioned my name in his introduction there was a murmur. No applause. Then a hush fell over the crowd.

As I stood on the rostrum, the lights in the giant hall were gradually dimmed. Then there was total blackness. In front of me the television lights were so bright that I couldn't see a single face, including Fred's. Tense, rattled and confused I silently sought help from outside myself.

I began talking, the words coming out woodenly. Then I lost my place in the speech. Perspiration was running down my neck. The hall was absolutely silent. As I searched my notes, I could see that my hands were trembling. *What in the world am I doing on this platform?* I angrily asked myself.

There was nothing to do but forget about everything and simply trust the Holy Spirit. I wasn't sure of what I was saying and I certainly couldn't see Fred's signals. As he later told me, when my speech began to run long, he was frantically taking his glasses off and putting them on again until people around him probably wondered if he was having some kind of seizure.

I began with the text, "That which we have seen and heard declare we unto you" (1 John 1:3). Then I described how empty my life had been, even when I had all the world's power and riches in my grasp, how pride had tripped me up and helped bring on the horror of Watergate and prison. Then I described the joy and fulfillment which came through my new faith in Jesus Christ.

When I finished I did what the speaker before me had done, folded up my notes and walked away. Suddenly there was a deafening sound: a rumbling noise that sounded like an airplane crashing through the roof. I could see nothing through the blinding television lights. Then as the hall lights were turned up, I saw the people standing on their feet: the noise had come from folding seats snapping back behind them. I stood in the middle of the platform dumbfounded.

Brother Blow threw his arms around me and even in that moment of joy ministered to me just as faithfully as he did in prison. "Careful, boy," he whispered, "Satan is on your back." To this day, I hear his words rising over any applause I receive when speaking.

When we got back to our hotel, Fred stood solemnly in the center of the room, shaking his head.

"What's the matter, Brother?" I exclaimed.

"We've got to pray, right now," he said somberly. "This is the kind of heady experience that could really get us off the track."

As we knelt by the coffee table, Fred took off his glasses: "I don't need these to look to Heaven."

Fred's voice cracked with emotion, but I doubt if the Lord heard any more grateful prayers from anywhere else around the world. And from that moment I've never prayed with my glasses on.

The press conference the next morning was one of the friendliest I had ever attended. There were the usual questions about Nixon, Watergate and my conversion, but the reporters were with me. One query took me by surprise.

"Mr. Colson, have you joined a church?"

"Well, I've been an Episcopalian, but I go to Catholic mass occasionally with my wife and sometimes we go to different churches."

It was a lame, unsatisfactory answer. Seeing disappointment on the faces of friendly Christian journalists, I tried again by explaining that it was as a youth that I had attended the Episcopal Church, that I was trying to find the right church. My words lacked conviction. What came out was that church was not important to me.

Reporters probed me on other subjects, but later my thoughts returned to that one question: What did I believe about the Church? My indifference had been exposed. Here was another area of my life to which I had given little thought. What had once seemed so simple—accept Christ and enjoy a new life—wasn't simple at all. In fact, more questions were being raised than were being answered.

. . . I will appoint you as a covenant to the people,
As a light to the nations,
To open blind eyes,
To bring out prisoners from the dungeon,
And those who dwell in darkness from the prison.
Isaiah 42:6–7, NAS

3. One Saturday Morning

It began like any Saturday morning. Through habit Patty and I usually allow ourselves an extra half-hour sleep on weekends. This day was bright, an April sun streaming through the French doors and into our bedroom. Sleepily I glanced out the window looking for the first green shoots on the bare tree limbs.

I've never been a morning person. It takes me an hour or so—and two cups of coffee—to think clearly and function normally. I stumble about looking for slippers and a robe, bumping into the furniture.

On this Saturday I plodded to the bathroom, stared through sleepy-eyed fog into the mirror and reached for the shaving cream. Then suddenly startled, I stared back at my reflection. A series of pictures flashed across my mind. Men in prison gray moving about. Classes. Discussions. Prayers.

"Of course, of course," I whispered as if in response to obvious commands. "Take the prisoners out, teach them, return them to prisons to build Christian fellowships. Spread these fellowships through every penitentiary in America."

I was now wide awake, my heart racing, every nerve in my body alert and exhilarated. I can still remember how vivid and lifelike it was. Before my eyes was a simple plan with every detail fitting into place. More than thoughts, I saw sharply focused pictures—of smiling men and women, streaming out of prisons, of Bibles and study groups, of fellowship around tables. Then I realized something else: I had never thought of anything like this before. It was not my idea, but something I was reacting to.

These mental images lasted but a few seconds, then they were gone. I had never experienced anything like this before or since.

Was it of God? Or just a flash inspiration, like any good idea which pops suddenly into one's consciousness? Even as I splashed cold water on my face, I felt an unusual assurance. Excitedly, I dried my hands and face and raced to the telephone.

"Harold . . . this is Chuck . . . sorry to bother you, but can we get together?"

I had made similar requests of Harold Hughes often during the Watergate crisis. Harold's blunt honesty and deep faith made him a superior counselor and a true friend.

Twenty minutes later Harold was sipping coffee in my makeshift basement office in front of a desk piled high with chapter drafts of the book I was writing. "Brother, you may think I'm crazy," I began. Then I outlined what had appeared to me.

As I spoke, the details became even more clear: the inmates would be furloughed out of prisons in twos, probably for two-week periods, maybe three. The principles of discipleship would be taught at Fellowship House; the prisoners could be quartered nearby.

Harold was intent, though I wondered if he thought I had eaten something too rich the night before. My words, as I heard them, were describing a very radical idea.

When I finished, Harold leaned back in his chair, arms folded across his expansive chest. "It's of God, no doubt about it," he declared.

Then he heaved a sigh and added, "Of course, it's also impossible. We couldn't get inside prisons much less take men out."

" 'With God, all things are possible,' " I quoted back at him one of his favorite Scripture passages.

Harold was scowling. "But where would we begin? There are hundreds of prisons; wardens are a hard-nosed bunch." Harold then recounted how as governor of Iowa he had tried to bring about prison reform and had run into every possible obstacle.

We spent the morning praying and discussing strategy. Having been in politics so many years, we both thought we knew how to press buttons and make things happen. But this was an awesome challenge.

It was Harold's suggestion that we begin with a visit to James Eastland, respected senior member of the U.S. Senate and chairman of the Judiciary Committee which handles all laws relating to prisons and criminal justice. One call from the chairman and attorneys general have been known to stand at attention. His power was legendary in Washington and he used it, quietly but always effectively. His support would be crucial.

Despite their political differences—Harold, younger, liberal, and a maverick; Eastland an older Dixiecrat and conservative—the two men had a warm personal friendship. Two weeks later we were in Eastland's spacious Senate office.

Always the courtly, southern gentleman, Senator Eastland listened while patiently twirling an unlighted cigar in his mouth as I detailed the horrors of prison life. At one point, he leaned forward, peered through his silver-rimmed glasses and smiled: "You didn't mind it at Maxwell, did you? That's a nice place." His drawl was so gentle, his round face so kind, I restrained a sharp reply.

"Have you ever been there, Senator?"

"No. Maybe I should some day. Got a lot of my constituents there," he chuckled.

"Have you ever visited any prison, Senator?" I asked.

"No . . ." He looked reflective, rubbing his chin. "No, I haven't. Pretty busy in this job, you know."

Over and over in the months ahead I was to discover the same pleasant indifference in men who had the fate of thousands of prisoners in their hands. They pass the laws, provide the money, express appropriate horror about the rising crime rate, but beyond that, they just don't care. But then, I reminded myself, I had possessed this kind of power once and I hadn't cared either.

Senator Eastland listened politely for almost two hours, then suggested we meet with his staff. "You talk to my boys here, then we'll certainly look into doing something like you fellas are talking about. Mighty interesting—and mighty nice seeing you. Keep up the good work, Harold." He slapped his colleague on the back.

That was it. The weeks passed by. We heard nothing further from Senator Eastland or his staff. We called several times. His staff was always polite; the matter, we were told, was being considered.

I talked with other old friends in Congress. Most of them thought it was a "nice idea" to do something for men in prison. We didn't hear anything further from them either.

Patty knew that something was moving me toward prison work and it made her restless. I had been back to visit Paul Kramer again in June, and we corresponded regularly. Often in the evenings I'd talk about him and the others.

Though I never told her, I suspect Patty knew that my nightmares were continuing. Faces of the men I was with at Maxwell would parade past me. The sensation of helplessness, of time standing still, walls closing in, fears of assault, were memories which stubbornly refused to be erased by the passing months.

It may have been unfair of me but I sloughed off all of Patty's concerns. Wives worry about security and finances; I should have too, I suppose, having grown up in the depression, scraped through college on a scholarship and graduated with a net worth of minus $300. But surely we could live for a while on what I had saved from my law practice, and there were always good business offers waiting.

My mother, living alone now since my dad's death, was more direct with me. "When are you going to get a job?" she asked during my next visit. Several of mother's friends were with her at the time, and I'm sure they pictured me trotting off to the welfare office each week to pick up a check.

It was difficult for even those closest to me to understand my situation. I wasn't sure I did myself.

Though the future seemed uncertain, other pieces of my life were coming together. We learned that the charges against Chris had been dropped. His record was cleared in South Carolina. For Chris, it had been a sobering experience and surprisingly had brought us much closer together.

Wendell, beginning his senior year at Princeton, was elected captain of the crew and was doing well in his studies. My conversion had been hard for him to accept. During our long talks together, he poured out the most convincing humanist doctrines the Ivy League has to offer. But every now and then in his eager young face I caught a glimmer of understanding that there could be an honest alternative.

Our daughter, Emily, captain of her high school cheerleader squad, had been strong throughout my prison ordeal. The scars, if there were any, weren't showing.

As the weeks passed, my conviction deepened that God had indeed given me a vision for a new work in the prisons even though nothing had happened and the doors seemed closed. During one of our regular

Monday morning fellowship breakfasts Harold shook his head: "I don't think we'll get any help from Congress. Politicians are wary of prison work. They know that 80 percent of the public wants to hang criminals. Why should they do anything?"

"What if we went right to the head of the Bureau of Prisons?" I asked, realizing as I said it that it was a foolish idea. Government bureaucrats wouldn't risk giving prisoners furloughs unless there was political heat on them to do so.

"Nothing to lose," Harold mused. "Who is the director?"

"Norman Carlson. He's a career man, nonpolitical, tough, respected. That's all I know." We all agreed with Harold. What could we lose?

Harold beckoned for Doug's secretary, Jo Adamson, to come into the library where we were meeting. "Please call Norman Carlson at the Bureau of Prisons and ask for an appointment for Mr. Colson and me," he instructed her.

Jo is a perceptive young woman. "His secretary will want to know what it is about," she warned.

Harold looked at us, then shrugged. "Tell her it's about bringing Jesus Christ into prisons," he roared. Jo laughed nervously, then realizing that Harold was serious, nodded and quickly departed.

Jo repeated the message verbatim to a secretary in Norman Carlson's office. We got the appointment for the next day.

On a sunny June morning Fred Rhodes drove us to the Bureau of Prisons, located in an aging gray concrete building just a few blocks from the capitol. Fred stopped the car outside the entrance, and we prayed together that God would touch Norman Carlson's heart. Fred prayed with such emotion that I hardly heard the horns blowing behind us.

The office building seemed appropriate for the Bureau of Prisons, I thought, as we walked down a long, dimly lit corridor past walls painted drab government green, over floors covered with a well-worn, mouse-colored carpet. To Washington veterans the physical appearance instantly signals the relative importance of an agency. Then I remembered Senator Eastland's admission about never visiting prisons. Most people, even in government, probably know the Bureau of Prisons only as a box on the Justice Department's organization chart.

Seven months in prison had created in my mind a stereotype of wardens and prison officials: unfeeling, tight-lipped, hard-nosed bureaucrats. At first glance Norman Carlson fitted that description. He is a tall, muscular man with a strong, stern face and close-cropped blond hair.

We saw him from his outer reception area, standing in the doorway of his office in shirt sleeves. Suddenly his face relaxed with a friendly grin. "Hi, fellas. Come on in." Then he led us to comfortable, orange-colored sofas in the corner of his large, attractively furnished office.

To our surprise we learned that Carlson had grown up in Iowa, Harold's home state. He knew and approved of the work Harold had begun in the state prisons while governor.

I studied Carlson as the two began swapping tales about Iowa prisons: he looked efficient, open, a man who'd risen fast through the system. In 1972 he had received a coveted award as one of the 10 outstanding persons in government service. But he still was no risk-taker, I figured. Government officials have to go to Congress once a year and justify adding millions to their budgets by telling what a good job they and their agencies do. No matter how I phrased it, I was going to be critical of Carlson's prison system and he could well take it personally.

Harold asked Carlson if he objected to beginning the meeting with prayer. Carlson indicated he did not and Harold led us. Then he set the stage. "Mr. Carlson, we came here today to tell you of a dream we have for a new work in the federal prisons. We need your cooperation. Chuck will explain."

I developed the case slowly, depicting my own experiences inside the prisons, what had happened with our little fellowship at the Maxwell facility, and how Jesus Christ can touch and change the lives of men in prison. Then I covered point by point what I felt was wrong in the system.

"More than half of those who come out of prison commit new crimes. The repeat offender rate is 80 percent in some states. Prisons simply do not rehabilitate, Mr. Carlson," I said at one point, pausing to give him a chance to reply. He nodded but didn't say a word.

"We're spending billions on prisons but four out of five crimes are committed by ex-convicts according to one study. It's futile and a horrid waste. We must do better, do things to turn lives around. It's the only answer," I said, pausing again. Still no response.

This man's career was to run the prison system, and I was describing it as futile and wasteful. But if he was angry, he didn't show it. He remained silent, his expression inscrutable.

I felt like a man walking through a mine field sticking one foot out waiting, then gingerly testing the next step but always dreading the explosion that ends it all. With each safe step my confidence increased. I was now hammering hard at certain prison horrors.

I glanced at Harold; his head was down. I hoped he was praying.

As I continued, Carlson remained attentive. But at any moment I was ready for him to raise his hand and stop me cold. In the system for 20 years, he could easily dismiss my advice and show me the door.

Then I drew a deep breath, wondered momentarily about Carlson's faith, and moved headlong into my final point. "Mr. Carlson, the prisons—your prisons—aren't helping these men. Everybody there, even the best of your staff, are looked upon as cops. But one Person can make a difference: Jesus Christ. His love and power to remake lives is the answer. He will heal and reconcile. I know it. I saw it happen. Give us a chance to prove it."

Still not a muscle moved in Carlson's face.

To activate our program I asked Norman Carlson if he would issue an order allowing Harold and me, or our representatives, to go into any federal prison in the country and select prisoners to bring out for training. In the moment of silence which followed these words, I nearly laughed. It sounded preposterous.

"Is that it?" he asked brusquely.

"Yes, Sir."

"Well there's much truth in what you say, gentlemen. I know prisons are not good places—not even the best of them . . ." He paused and I waited for the "but" to be followed by six reasons why it could never be done.

Carlson's face remained enigmatic. "Let me ask you a question. A few weeks ago my wife and I were at the Terminal Island Prison in Southern California. On Sunday we went to chapel. At one point in the service the chaplain asked the inmates to join in with spontaneous prayers. In the back—I couldn't see him—a man prayed for my wife and me. I was surprised that he did that."

Harold and I were so startled by this story that we were silent for a long moment. "Well, Mr. Carlson, he's a Christian," I finally said. "We're taught to pray for those in authority. I did for the warden at Maxwell."

"I know that," Carlson replied, his eyes bright with emotion. He raised both hands and then pointed all his fingers into his breastbone. "But I'm the one keeping him in prison."

It was an electric moment. "Mr. Carlson," I said, "that man prayed for you because he loves you."

Carlson stared deep into my eyes, then shook his head in bewilderment and the conversation moved back to the prison program.

I expected Carlson to evade my request, knowing from long experience that no government bureau chief would take such a bold step without consulting his staff, weighing the pros and cons and at least thinking about the impact of his decision on his career. The best I could hope for was that he'd leave the door open just a crack.

I was stunned, when moments later, Carlson gave us a terse, three-sentence answer.

"Go ahead with your plans, Mr. Colson, Senator Hughes. I'll issue the order. Get together with my staff and work out the details."

Harold said later that my feet were barely touching ground as we retraced our steps back along that same drab corridor.

I did not then fully understand all that had happened in Norman Carlson's office that June day. And it would be months before I'd even think again of the unknown inmate in the back of the prison chapel who had prayed for Carlson and his wife. I still had much to learn about the way God works in our lives—and what He wanted from mine.

To a committee studying prisons:
   Have any [of you] tried to live for a time with the smells, the sweat, the urine, the mice, the accumulation of bad breath? More—the debilitating heat, the fetid air, the broiling summer sun? Have any [of you] looked closely at one of the soiled, torn, lumpy mattresses infested with insects and vermin from which there is no relief through the long nights?
   I will not ask if any member of the committee has ever seen blood running down a trouser leg, or heard the sobs and screams of a boy being chain-raped, with accompanying grunts and raucous shouts.

                                                          KARL MENNINGER

4. Discouragement

We quickly learned that when Norman Carlson agreed to do something, he meant it. After our meeting he issued several executive orders to open the way for us to invite the first group of prisoners to Washington, D.C., for two weeks of training.

Carlson's directives emphasized that this was to be a "pilot" program—an experiment. That was fine with me because I was a long way from committing myself to full-time involvement in prison work. Since we would need four months of planning and preparation, we set early November 1975 as the date for the first class. Although contributions would be needed to defray expenses, we concluded that I must maintain a low profile and we would not seek publicity. As it turned out, we weren't quiet enough.

The *Washington Post* of August 10, 1975, carried a major, "Where are they now?" article about the Watergate fallen. Buried in the section about me was this seemingly harmless sentence: "They (Colson and Hughes) will soon bring a small group of federal inmates to Washington for a religious retreat under the auspices of Fellowship House."

In the interview I had mentioned our prison project almost as an aside. I skimmed the *Post* article quickly and concluded that it was not important enough to clip and save. But then I didn't need to. I was suddenly deluged with copies attached to angry letters from the neighbors around Fellowship House.

This focal point of Christian activity in Washington is located in one of the more affluent residential areas of the capital, surrounded by embassies and grand old homes of the city's establishment. The large, three-story stucco home, once the Danish Embassy, was acquired back in 1962, a gift of one of the Fellowship's backers. Believers in Jesus Christ come there from around the world—ambassadors, businessmen, church leaders, politicians.

The neighborhood hadn't been so stirred up since rumors early in World War II about German submarines in Chesapeake Bay. A neighborhood association was formed to protest the action and retained Tommy Corcoran, legendary New Deal brain-truster for Franklin Roosevelt in the 1930s.

"Listen, Chuck, you've gone too far," Corcoran told me in an angry call. "Have you considered what this will do to our property values? What about the women and children who will be afraid to go outside their homes if you turn these criminals loose?"

I reminded him that he had served a President who had taken a strong stand on civil liberties including prison reform.

His reply was icy. "We'll see you in court."

Doug Coe agreed to serve as peacemaker and began scheduling meetings with irate property owners. Fred Rhodes had taken on the task of inviting to Washington key leaders of the Fellowship from around the country, responsible business and professional people who were Christians and had community respect. They were taught how to visit prisons near their homes, interview prisoners and recommend to us those they felt were stable Christians and could be trusted with freedom. We would pass their recommendations on to the wardens who could approve or veto our selections.

Meanwhile expenses were mounting. Renovations were needed in the basement of the Good News Mission, a halfway house 20 minutes from Fellowship House, where the prisoners would be quartered. We promised a $1,000 gift for this work. Transportation was necessary to move the inmates around Washington. The program would require several thousand dollars.

We encountered some obstacles from prison chaplains as well. During my first meeting with Dick Summer, chief of federal chaplains and a 20-year veteran in prison work, he insisted that his men select the inmates who would attend the training seminars. I argued that prisoners would distrust the program if the government-employed chaplains did the choosing. Knowing that Norman Carlson agreed with this principle, I held firm and eventually Dick Summer and I reached an agreement. The friction in the prison system that came to light during this opening skirmish should have alerted us to the much more serious problems ahead.

In September, another newspaper article brought new havoc into our lives and revived the Watergate drama in a terrifying way. The banner headlines of the Sunday *Washington Post* proclaimed, "Hunt Told Associates of Orders to Kill Jack Anderson." I stared incredulously at the front page. Any reference to Howard Hunt, the Watergate burglar I had originally recommended to the White House, always implicated me, at least by association. As for columnist Jack Anderson, he had been the arch nemesis of President Nixon—and of all recent Presidents. But I could not believe that anyone in the White House had ever seriously considered killing him.

My eye glanced at the by-line; the story was written by Pulitzer Prize winner Bob Woodward who, with Carl Bernstein, had become a Watergate celebrity through the best-selling book and motion picture, *All the President's Men.* Woodward had called me a few days before; I thought he was joking when he asked if I knew anything about a plot to kill Anderson. As I read on, the story was too bizarre to be believable; yet so were a lot of other things which eventually crawled out of the mire known as Watergate.

The article referred to a senior official who, it was reported, had ordered Hunt to do Anderson in. That narrowed it to a few of us. Then came this sentence: "Charles Colson, the former White House special counsel who recruited Hunt for White House work, said yesterday that he had never heard of the plan." I slammed the paper on the kitchen table. That was the same as naming me; readers would draw only one inference.

Patty couldn't cheer me up. "What do you mean 'smile'?" I growled at her. "I've been accused of a lot of wild things but not murder!"

Reporters sought out Howard Hunt, now in prison, for more details: Howard shrugged it off: "Well, it wasn't really an assassination that was ordered . . . I was supposed to drug Jack Anderson so he would become incoherent before a radio program and embarrass himself publicly . . . When I told Charles Colson about it, Colson nodded . . . and (Hunt) was certain Nixon wanted it."

When I read this story, I shook my head in disbelief. Hunt was a writer, author of 40 novels, with a lurid imagination. Had we been dumb enough to talk about such a stupid idea even in levity? Or did our arrogance dull our sensitivities to common sense?

Whenever an exclusive story is featured in one of the major news outlets in Washington, it spreads like a flu epidemic. Accuracy is not always checked as competitive zeal sends reporters scrambling for new angles. The major newspapers and TV stations are all profit-making businesses, big and successful ones at that. One reporter topping another means dollars as well as journalistic prizes. So I was right back in the middle of another round of preposterous headlines.

Dave Shapiro, my friend and lawyer during the long investigations and trials, telephoned me that morning. "Get in here. You need a lawyer," he said sternly. For all his ability, Dave often panicked over newspaper stories. Yet memories of the dark days returned and my stomach churned.

The next day I spent hours reviewing old files and notes with a worried Shapiro and his colleagues. Dejectedly, I girded myself for a new round of questioning, grand juries, and batterings in the newspapers.

"When the grand jury is convened, you'll refuse to testify, of course," Shapiro said crisply. "Conspiracy to commit murder is a serious business." My lawyer's face was a mass of wrinkles as he rehearsed the worst that might come.

"Wait a minute, Dave, this is crazy. There was never a conspiracy. I don't even remember any kidding around about it."

But Dave kept right on talking, ignoring my protests.

When I met with Doug, Harold, Al and Graham, we considered one basic question: How does a Christian handle false accusations? My inclination was to battle back, protest, proclaim my innocence.

The others shook their heads. "Anything you say, Chuck, will be twisted," noted Harold. "Let's find out how Jesus handled these situations. He was falsely accused more times than any man in history."

The minute Harold spoke, I knew the answer. I had been reading the Beatitudes only a week before. Jesus had told His disciples: "Blessed are you when men revile you and persecute you and utter all kinds of evil against you falsely on my account. Rejoice and be glad, for your reward is great in heaven" (Matthew 5:11–12, RSV).

Did this statement apply to me? Was I being falsely accused because of my stand for Christ? Far from it. Still, as a Christian, shouldn't my response to unfair accusation be the same? I was to accept the attack without defending myself. While I wasn't quite able to "rejoice and be glad" in the situation, I did turn it over to the Lord. But it was tough to do, I discovered.

Weeks passed with no word from the prosecutors. We learned only that a congressional committee was looking into the matter. Like so many exposé type stories that create national attention, when there is no followup investigation or presentation of hard evidence, the story fades out of the news, relegated to newspaper morgues, while in the minds of millions the implied accusation remains.

It is a terrifying experience to be associated with a "murder plot," yet I see now that this episode was used to prepare me for even more difficult testings.

One of my former law partners, Myron Mintz, a warm, ebullient, handsome man in his late 30s, and his attractive, blonde wife, Nancy, had become close friends during my trial and imprisonment. In August, Nancy gave birth to their first child, an especially joyous occasion because they had wanted children for many years.

Myron and Nancy had virtually remodeled their house in preparation for this big event. Modern baby equipment had been acquired and put in place. When Meredith was born and brought home, Myron would gape at her and chuckle giddily as he showed her to visitors.

One night, when Patty and I were home alone, the phone rang. It was a friend of Myron's. "The Mintz baby is dead," came the chilling report. "A crib death. He needs you." For a moment I was frozen with shock.

Myron was not only a friend but a political disciple. He told me once that I'd been something of a hero figure to him in the White House, Watergate notwithstanding. My conversion however stunned him. Ever since, I was conscious that Myron, a nonpracticing Jew, had been studying me, struggling to see what the conversion meant in the way I lived.

As Patty and I drove over to the Mintz home, my heart ached for them. I'd been with people in tragedies before and always felt inadequate. But now there was an added dilemma. They were probably angry at the God whom I had come to love. *Why would a loving God take away our child?* That would be a fair enough question for them to ask. And I, their friend, represented the God they believed had wronged them, wearing it on my sleeve in fact.

When we pulled into the driveway, now crowded with cars, a friend grabbed my arm. "Don't talk about God or give them any of the pious stuff," he whispered. I knew it was good advice.

Myron and Nancy were overwhelmed with grief. When I came face to face with Myron, I looked straight into his swollen, bloodshot eyes and said simply, "I'm sorry, Myron. I'm your friend and I love you." Myron then hugged me so hard my ribs ached and his tears soaked my shoulder.

Patty and I stayed throughout the evening waiting for their parents to arrive from Philadelphia. Such times are always filled with pain. Nancy, a Lutheran churchgoer, was indeed angry at God and didn't try to hold it back in front of me. "I never want anyone—you, Chuck Colson—or anyone else to talk to me about your God."

"I won't, Nancy, unless you ask me to," I promised.

It was such a helpless feeling. All Patty and I could do was to stay near Nancy and Myron and silently share their suffering. Later that night I tossed in bed as my mind grappled for answers. How does a Christian respond to the charge that a loving God would never permit senseless tragedy? The same agonizing question must have been asked at the time of Herod's slaughter of the babies of Israel and also in the aftermath of the massacre of the Canaanites. It has echoed over and over down through the ages.

The obvious response is simply to dismiss the question; after all, finite man cannot be expected to understand the ways of an infinite God. But that didn't satisfy me. God gave us minds to search out the answers to tough questions. I was getting my share. There was the question of church membership. What was the answer for Patty and me? And businessman Jim Fuller's anger at the mention of the name of Jesus. What should have been my response? And now the death of the Mintz baby.

There was something very wrong with the concept that all problems would be miraculously solved once a man invited Christ into his life. My problems, indeed, seemed to be on the increase.

The fall of 1975 continued to produce a series of setbacks. Invitations to speak had flooded in after my address to the Southern Baptist Convention. My conviction not to go the public speaking route soon got me into all manner of sticky situations with fellow Christians.

"We knew you were a phony all along," one man wrote after I had declined his invitation to come to his church. When I turned down another man he wrote back, increasing the fee I would receive. Since I hadn't asked for a fee and wouldn't decide on that basis anyway, I refused again. He angrily wrote a letter to his local newspaper, denouncing me as a money-hungry fraud.

Seeing that these refusals were giving me a bad image, I began accepting some requests asking that compensation be made to our prison project through Fellowship Foundation. A few were happy to do this; others promised a contribution and never followed through after I had given the speech. It was disillusioning.

"Some Christians are as double-dealing as pagans," I complained gloomily to Harold and Doug one day.

"Christians are sinners like everyone else," Doug agreed. "The main difference is that we know the way; we just don't always follow it."

"You'll discover another discouraging fact about us Christians," said Harold. "We sometimes exploit one another in the name of good works."

I shook my head sadly as another chip flaked off of the image I held before me of Christians being a superior brand of people.

With the first prison class scheduled and plans being made for additional ones, Fred and I decided to begin visiting penitentiaries during these speaking trips. In this way we would get to know any Christian wardens, guards and inmates who might work with us. One such visit was vivid and unforgettable: the 65-year-old maximum security prison at Stillwater, Minnesota. On a raw, blustery day, Fred Rhodes, three Minneapolis friends and I pulled up to the front gate of the massive brick fortress.

For any ex-convict, to re-enter a prison is to relive the first day of confinement. The clanging of the heavy steel gates is a nightmarish noise, triggering a whole flood of feelings: fear, helplessness, uncertainty.

I felt these emotions as we stood before a caged area. The guard tripped a lever and the first barred door before us slid open. We were ushered inside, the door electrically closing behind us. The five of us were closeted in there for perhaps a minute. The second barred gate then slid open, and we walked straight ahead into the main, granite-walled walkway which connects four cellblock wings.

We knew that only three days before there had been a riot in Cellblock A of this prison; several guards had been taken hostage. Though the uprising was quickly squelched and the guards released, for the inmates it was a success. Their grievances were all over the local papers. For the state it was another in a string of embarrassments over Stillwater. A legislative committee had announced hearings.

Our husky guard grudgingly agreed to take us into the troubled cellblock. I could understand his reluctance. His right eye was nearly closed by purplish-black welts; he had been one of those caught in the melee of swinging fists and clubs.

We were ushered through a barred steel gate into the cavernous housing area; the concrete cellblock stands five stories high, containing 300 men in 6-by-10-foot cages. The inmates were on free time, some standing in line for telephones or showers, others drifting about aimlessly, still others lying on their bunks, staring vacantly at the ceiling. Over the vast expanse of damp, cold concrete was a blue-gray fog of dust and smoke; there was a sickening stench in the air.

Our escort was unarmed. That is standard procedure; the risk of the men overpowering the guard and seizing his gun is too great. If I'd thought about it, I might have been frightened. Since seizing of a few guards made headlines in the state, taking our party hostage would be national news.

The guard explained the odor; it came from the still pungent smell of burned cloth in the air since many mattresses had been ignited during the riot. We stopped to inspect one cell, its charred, water-logged mattress on the floor. The walls were plastered with layer after layer of thick paint, the chipped areas ringed by the faded colors of decades past.

"This place could go up like a gasoline tank," I exclaimed.

"Almost did; we got the fire out just in time," the guard agreed. Walking over to the cell door, I asked him about the procedure for releasing the men when all 300 were locked up. There was a long pause.

"Each cell has to be opened one by one," he replied.

"How many men could you get out of here in case of fire," I persisted.

He lowered his eyes to the grimy cement floor. "Maybe 50 . . . if we were lucky."

During the tour I looked for signs of the believer: a Bible, religious literature, a cross. We found only a handful who admitted to any faith. While eating lunch in the prison cafeteria, I noticed an inmate sitting alone several tables away. For some reason I asked the warden to invite him over.

He joined our table but at first seemed too nervous to speak. I don't usually ask this question, but here I did: "Are you a Christian?"

"I sure am," he replied, his eyes brightening. He was so nervous, he explained, because he had been praying silently that I would sit at his table.

Kirk Schenk was his name; his age, 25. His father was a businessman. Kirk had been in prison six months. I studied his pale, youthful features as, slowly gaining confidence, he told us about himself.

Kirk admitted his problem was alcohol. Arrested for a string of minor offenses, a tough judge heard his case and decided to teach him a lesson. He sentenced Kirk to 10 years for an unarmed robbery of $20.

"That is not as rare as you would think," he said, trying to force a smile. I knew he was right. Men being sentenced can face good judges on bad days or judges who want to placate editorial writers or simply incompetent judges who have been appointed as a reward for political service.

One cellmate can be doing 12 months for rape or armed robbery, another seven years for tax evasion. Such disparities create much of the bitterness which poisons every prison. There is no rational sentencing pattern in the United States and, except in a few instances, no review of a judge's broad discretion. The gavel swings with deadly finality.

What Kirk did not tell us—but what we heard from another inmate—was that he was denied parole because he would not cooperate with the state prosecutors. Kirk had been an eyewitness to the killing of an inmate; he had refused to support the state's case against the inmate accused of the murder because he believed the man had acted in self-defense. On the day Kirk testified for the defense, the state parole board notified him he was not eligible for parole.

The warden described Kirk Schenk: "Strange fellow sometimes. He lives what he believes, I guess. Breaks up fights. Speaks up for the underdog. Should have had his skull cracked, but somehow it hasn't happened yet."

We visited the segregation unit that afternoon where more than a hundred men were kept in rows of cages separated by narrow walkways. They were permitted to exercise on the walkway only one hour each day.

Every prison makes its own "law." At Stillwater, the "law" was unusually tough. Twelve months was the minimum sentence to the segregation cells. If during the 12 months an inmate broke a single rule, the clock went back to zero and the 12 months started running again. To some violators time soon didn't matter; many went berserk.

The air about us this day was filled with screams, moans, obscenities. The guard cautioned us not to walk in front of the cells; the men, he explained, were given to hurling their own excrement at visitors and guards. It was my first experience in a segregation unit; already I knew I could never forget the smells, sounds and sights. I prayed that somehow something would be done about "holes" like this.

The warden allowed Kirk to see us off. As I grasped his bony shoulder in farewell, I wondered how this scrawny young man could survive the horror I'd seen and heard.

After we drove away from Stillwater to the airport where I would catch a flight back to Washington, other questions pelted my mind: How many more Kirks were there? How many other states like Minnesota, proudly progressive on most social issues, maintain wretched pits of violence, filth, and despair like this? Many, I was discovering.

Winston Churchill once said that "the mood and temper of the public with regard to the treatment of crime and criminals is one of the most unfailing tests of the civilization of any country." How do we Americans rate?

Poor, I'd say.

No one cares—or do they? Who is going to do something about the thousands of Kirks trapped by circumstance, about the horrid conditions of caged men? Christians ought to be working in places like this.

Like the muffled drumroll of distant artillery, the words of the prophet Amos rumbled in my ears:

> Hate evil and love the good;
> remodel your courts into true halls of justice.
> Perhaps even yet the Lord God of Hosts
> will have mercy on his people . . .*

---

* Amos 5:15, LB

> *So this is now the mark by which we all shall certainly know whether the birth of the Lord Jesus is effective in us: if we take upon ourselves the needs of our neighbor.*
>
> MARTIN LUTHER

5. Twelve Disciples from Prison

Tension built as Sunday, November 2, 1975, drew closer. This was the arrival date in Washington of the 12 prisoners furloughed for two weeks to be trained by us as disciples. Then they would return to their federal penitentiaries to minister to fellow inmates.

In the middle of the selection process was the chief chaplain, Dick Summer, a tall balding man in his late 40s who looked more like a kindly school teacher than a prison official. There was usually a lilt in his voice and a warm sparkle in his eyes. But when we got together three days before the prisoners were to arrive, his brow was deeply furrowed as he thrust a piece of paper into my hand.

"Take this. It's my home number and an emergency number at the bureau. Call us, not the police, *when* . . . I mean, *if* there is trouble."

The main issue was now in the open. How would these prisoners react to their sudden freedom? Were we being foolish, or would they respect the trust? Dick's concern was understandable. A U.S. senator had just complained to Norman Carlson about the inmates coming to Washington, prompted no doubt by one of the protesting neighbors. With sinking heart, I realized that Carlson's job might be in jeopardy if there was an incident.

Meanwhile, the threat of legal action by Tommy Corcoran still hung over us despite Doug Coe's peacemaking efforts with Fellowship House neighbors. I tried to anticipate all the possible moves that could cancel out the program.

The 12 inmates (six blacks and six whites, including two women) had been selected from six eastern federal prisons: Alderson, West Virginia (for women); Allenwood, Pennsylvania; Danbury, Connecticut; Lewisburg, Pennsylvania; Petersburg, Virginia; Morgantown, West Virginia.

Would the selection process work? We knew we were bucking the institutional system and could do so only through Norman Carlson's support. Everything rested on the quality of the prisoners chosen.

Even among our own staff members there was some disagreement. The Fellowship was already sponsoring prison work at Lorton Penitentiary just south of Washington. The program was administered through John Staggers, a gifted black leader, whose round face can flash a cherubic smile one moment and the fierce look of an angry prophet the next. Staggers led the Lorton prisoners in Bible study classes and conducted visitation programs. We asked him to join our team.

At one of the planning sessions, I could sense he had some questions. "John, something bothering you about the program?" I asked him one day.

Staggers shook his head. "I don't know what you're trying to do, Chuck," he answered. "You bring a few prison cats here for talk and fellowship and then expect them to go back to prison and set up prayer groups. Man," the word was a low, drawn-out exhalation, "that's expecting a lot from people whose lives are in a mess. What's to keep them from taking off?"

"There are good men and women in prison who've made just one bad mistake," I answered. "They're no different from most of us. Let them know we trust them, and I'll guarantee they'll not try to escape."

John was not convinced. "We've already got a prison program here for the Fellowship. Let's do what we're already doing—only better."

"John, your program involves one state prison. If this succeeds it will cover the whole country," I answered, realizing my mistake the moment I spoke.

Staggers bristled. "This is not the White House, Chuck. Those cats in prison won't touch your program when they hear it comes from a big shot."

"You forget, John, that I'm one of those prison cats too."

John quieted down. "What do you want from me?"

"Teach for several days. Lead the music and worship."

Harold spoke up. "John, you know I've been a hundred percent behind the Lorton work you're doing. It's been great. That's why we need your experience in this new program."

John's resistance turned out to be healthy as he helped us think through every aspect of the program: house and feed the prisoners at the Good News Mission in nearby Arlington, Virginia, then bus them to Fellowship House for classes and social events; invite neighbors in to meet the prisoners; take the inmates to Capitol Hill for a visit with members of Congress; work in a softball game if weather permits; plan for good food, music, times for prayer and general sharing, solid teaching, even a graduation ceremony.

Sunday, November 2, was one of those perfect autumn days in Washington when the air is fresh and the foliage vivid. A good day to walk along the Potomac River; which I did that morning as much to calm my uneasiness as to enjoy the beauty.

Six friends of the Fellowship were each driving two prisoners from the six penitentiaries. They were due at the Good News Mission for a 7 P.M. dinner. We had prayed they would arrive without incident, but all day we half expected the phone to ring. No guards or marshals were to be on hand at any time during the two weeks unless there was trouble.

Bill Simmer, dynamic head of the Good News Mission, had begun this project as a halfway house for prisoners. Located in a semicommercial neighborhood of Arlington, Virginia, the mission contains two renovated old brick homes, plus a long, two-story, barracks-style building which houses most residents and provides a classroom and offices. Repairs were made in the basement of one of the houses where the men were to sleep. The two women prisoners would be given an upstairs room adjacent to that of the mission chaplain and his wife.

The first prisoners arrived about 4 P.M. Three hours later all but one group had checked in: a pastor and two inmates from Allenwood, Pennsylvania. Surely he would call if there had been trouble. Those who had arrived—Betty and Fran, Jimmy and Nick, Nat and Clay, Peter and Bob, Mike and Chris—had struck a congenial relationship almost immediately. This group, plus sponsors and a few from Fellowship House, ate dinner and then gathered in the main classroom of the Mission. Underneath the warm fellowship was a shaky feeling, part apprehension, part excitement.

For the prisoners, this was an unexpected bonanza. Two weeks of freedom: no guards, no iron bars, no institutional routine. But I could sense their uncertainty as well. What was it all about, really? How are we supposed to react? What is required of us?

Those of us in the Fellowship were equally uncertain. Had we undertaken too much? Were we adequately prepared? Where was the missing car?

At 7:45 P.M. the last car pulled up outside! Troy and Bill had arrived to join their fellow inmates. Their delay was due to nothing more serious than their driver-pastor taking a few wrong turns.

After an opening prayer, I briefly explained the vision for these seminars. Then Harold, dressed in a lumberman's jacket and baggy brown pants, a man's man in every way—voice, dress, rugged physique—stood up at the end of the table. He charged them first with their duty: "You men and women are here not to play or have a rest. You are here to learn what it means to be disciples who deny everything else in the world for the sake of Jesus Christ. If you have any other thoughts in your minds, get rid of them. I know what it's like to be a prisoner. I was thrown in jail in six states when I was an alcoholic and should have been in 20. Chuck has been there too. So we're no better than you, but we are going to teach you."

The prisoners were mesmerized by the booming voice and intense convictions of this man who had been a truck driver, alcoholic, combat soldier, governor of Iowa and a U.S. senator.

I studied the men and women as they sat around the table, and wondered if their commitment to Christ was strong enough for them to resist all the temptations they would encounter. One huge, muscular black with a squashed-in nose was called "Soul." He had already been behind the 35-foot-high wall of Lewisburg Penitentiary more than seven years on a 25-year sentence for armed robbery. Was his commitment real enough to keep him from just walking away during some free moment in the next two weeks?

I remembered dusky evenings at Maxwell Prison in Alabama when I stared longingly through the wire fence, seeing free people walking along a distant road. I had to fight back the devil's words: "Go ahead, run. You can get away from this place. Even a few minutes will feel so good." Every inmate thinks about escape. It is a reflex buried deep within the human psyche which urges him to battle for freedom and survival and sanity. It can overpower rationality, which is why some prisoners have tried to escape with only a few days left of their sentences.

Others around the table besides Soul caused me momentary concern. Two young men were tough-looking Italian-Americans. I assumed—unfairly, just as most people do—that they were part of organized crime.

Then another fear raced through my mind: Supposing we were conned? What if one or more weren't really Christians? We'd instructed our community people to be careful, but it is not easy to look into someone's soul.

There was no security at the Mission. Only two blocks away was every imaginable temptation—bars, pool halls, massage parlors. We believed these 12 were our brothers and sisters, and we would trust them as such.

Harold finished his remarks and it was again my turn. "One final thought. You men and women are here representing three hundred thousand other prisoners throughout the country, most of whom have no hope. You are trustees for them. If this experiment works, I can promise you that life will get better for all others behind bars. If you fail, their hopelessness will continue. You are on the spot; other inmates are watching. Your actions will affect how thousands of our brothers and sisters in prison live."

Nodding heads around the table told me they cared for their fellow convicts—and probably understood that other inmates back in prison would administer harsh discipline if one stepped out of line and spoiled it for the others.

Fred Rhodes had volunteered to be the driver for the prisoners for the next two weeks. When he delivered the 12 inmates to Fellowship House in the borrowed van the next morning for Bible study, his face was beaming: "These folks are great. We sang hymns all the way over."

I looked at Fred and broke out laughing. One year earlier he was being chauffered in a black limousine as the number two man in the Veteran's Administration, a $10 billion a year agency. Now he was driving a van filled with convicts.

"Go ahead and laugh. I love it," he smiled, scurrying up the stairs to join the group.

During the first day of teaching we passed out Bibles and notebooks to each prisoner (most of them already had a Bible). My topic that first morning was "What is fellowship?" This basic question had to be understood if the men and women were to go back to prison and spark a fellowship program among fellow inmates.

John Staggers gave the prisoners a look at the balanced Christian life through the visual device of a wheel, with Christ at the hub and four spokes representing the Word, prayer, fellowship, and witness.

Doug Coe then had a session with the prisoners on "Who is Jesus?" Most of the inmates had some knowledge of the trinitarian relationship of God the Father, Jesus the Son, and the Holy Spirit. Did they really know Jesus personally? Most said they did and the others would before the two-week course was completed.

I deliberately sat next to Soul at the first day's lunch. We all understood the unwritten code: Never ask inmates why they were imprisoned. But Soul volunteered.

"I used to be in the moving business," he said without a smile.

"You . . . look like you could pick up a grand piano single-handed," I commented.

"No, not that kind," Soul continued, still not smiling. "I moved money out of banks."

I quickly discovered that Soul had a keen sense of humor to go with a fine mind. The nickname had come both because of his singing voice and his leadership in helping scores of inmates and even some guards find Christ inside Lewisburg. One of the toughest prisons in America, eight men had been murdered in Lewisburg during two bloody years.

We were served butterscotch sundaes for dessert. I noticed that Soul hadn't touched his own. I asked him what was wrong.

"I'm too excited. I can't eat. Anyhow after seven years I don't think I could handle it."

I looked at Soul again, aware of him in a different way. Seven years of confinement had begun a deterioration of feelings, taste and other physical qualities in the man. I understood this only too well but still was not able to imagine what it must be like never to see beyond the confines of a giant, gray wall. No opportunity to see early morning dew or the orange moon at night as it rises over tree tops. Behind prison walls one is blind to the world on the other side. To know even the changes of season or see the new, green shoots of spring vegetation are not possible. For Soul and others, too, it had been like seven years submerged in a submarine.

The 12 soaked up the first week of teaching. Doug Coe and John Staggers reported difficulty keeping up with their eagerness to learn.

Despite limited educational backgrounds, they studied Scripture relentlessly and their thirst for more seemed unquenchable.

Their spirit was contagious. Fred Denne, a Pan-Am pilot and one of those who was driving inmates to Washington, decided to stay the whole two weeks, moving into a basement room. "Can't think of any way I'd rather spend my vacation," he explained.

Near the end of the first week. I asked Bill Simmer at the Mission how the inmates were behaving. "Very well," he replied. The only rule they have broken is to stay up after lights out—praying and singing."

On Saturday afternoon we had a wild softball game between the "straights" and the "cons." I played third base on the prisoners' team and we scored 10 runs the last inning to win 17–16. There was something symbolic in that victory.

The week's schedule had been grueling. Fred announced that Sunday after church would be free time. The inmates could decide what they wanted: rest, sightseeing, whatever, and we would arrange it.

Soul emerged from their huddle. "We'd like to visit the Arlington County Jail and witness to the men."

And so, the convicts chose for their first afternoon of free time to go back to jail. They moved easily from cell to cell; there was instant rapport with those inside. As in every jail, the population ranged from vagrants and drunks to murderers and rapists. Then Soul asked to go into the maximum security segregation unit. The officials were at first reluctant, but Bill Simmer, who ministered regularly in the jail, was persuasive.

Three men—Soul, Simmer and a deputy sheriff—walked down the long, barred passageway, through an electrically locking steel door, past two policemen and to the "tank." They were met with jeers and taunts. Since most of those behind the thick iron bars were black, the sight of Soul, dressed in a suit and accompanied by two whites, one a deputy sheriff, started an uproar.

"Sell out to whitey . . . honkey . . . traitor," and cruder abuse, was heaped on Soul, who stared back at them impassively. Soul's bulging arms were folded and his feet spread apart, as if to buttress his huge body. When the jailer began to unlock the entrance to the tank itself, and it was apparent that Soul was going inside, the shouts stopped.

The others waited outside while Soul sat in a far corner of the cell talking to a small group of subdued inmates. A half-hour passed.

Then, muffled sobs could be heard and minutes later Soul walked back to the door, his giant arms around the shoulders of two men. Both were in tears. "These are two new brothers," he grinned.

Throughout the first week we had held our breath for fear a court order from our neighbors might stop our program. Nothing happened. Then came a crucial event. We invited all the neighbors to come to a luncheon at Fellowship House. The prisoners attended in regular street clothes, some of which we loaned them.

Such luncheons are common at Fellowship House. One day the wives of congressmen will be there after a Bible study. On another occasion it will be a gathering of judges or American Indians or congressmen or foreign ambassadors or businessmen or pastors.

At this luncheon we interspersed the prisoners among those who were there from other Bible study groups. Then we introduced the neighbors. When I asked some of them to identify the prisoners among the other guests, it was amusing to watch the bewildered expressions, the false starts, the faltering, "Let's see, that one . . . no, over there, perhaps."

Nine out of 10 made the wrong identification. I later told audiences only half jokingly that they had picked congressmen. When the neighbors began mingling freely with the prisoners, finding mutual interests, the point was made, once and for all. No further complaints have been heard from Tommy Corcoran or other neighbors.

Similar episodes have provided moments of comic relief.

Once a man walked into our study room at Fellowship House, stopped and surveyed the inmates sitting in a circle with their Bibles open. Then he turned to leave, stopping at the door to apologize for the interruption. "Sorry, I was looking for the prisoners."

On another occasion a class attended the Fourth Presbyterian Church, pastored by our gifted associate and friend, Dick Halverson. The sanctuary was crowded this morning when our inmates arrived, so they dispersed and found seats where they could. Tony Bucaloy, a Filipino who had spent 20 years in Leavenworth Penitentiary, sat next to a distinguished older woman with a fur stole draped around her shoulders. Tony (who two years later was to join our work) has a winsome personality; while they waited for the service to begin, Tony struck up a warm conversation with the woman.

Before the sermon, Dick Halverson announced that there were 12 disciples from federal prisons in the audience and asked that they rise and be welcomed. As Tony started to stand up, the older woman pulled on his arm, "No, no, young man. He wants the convicts to stand up."

Such incidents were always good for a laugh, but the point was obvious. Too many people think of all prisoners as murderers, rapists and child molesters who probably carry some communicable disease. Some are dangerous and need to be kept behind bars, but more than two-thirds have been imprisoned for nonviolent offenses. Fear and ignorance blinds people from seeing most inmates as individuals just like your friends and neighbors next door.

During the second week, Senator Lawton Chiles of Florida invited us to bring the inmates to his office. Harold Hughes accompanied them. I am sure it was the first time that 12 convicts ever gathered in the office of a U.S. senator.

Shortly after the group was settled into black leather chairs and sofas around Senator Chiles' desk, another senator walked in.

"Didn't mean to barge in, Lawton," the second senator said. "I just wanted to ask you about a vote today."

Senator Chiles urged his colleague to join him and "some Christian friends." The senator did.

Soon the inmates were sharing stories of their experiences in prison. Senator Chiles then told of his own struggles as a Christian. Meanwhile the senator who had walked unknowingly into the circle was stunned when he discovered who the "Christian friends" surrounding him really were.

After lunch and a visit to the State Department, the prisoners divided into two groups to tour several government buildings. At this point the mix-up took place. Two of the inmates who had been riding in the van with Fred Rhodes told him they would return to the Mission in the other vehicle. Fred arrived back at the Mission about 4 P.M., the other driver shortly thereafter. The two prisoners were not with him!

Fred sought me out, panic on his face. What we had most feared seemed upon us. Two missing men. Was it a clever escape plan? A misunderstanding? The only thing to do for now was wait. If the men had gotten separated, they had our address and telephone number. We would give them until dinner. If they didn't call or show by then, there was nothing else to do but make that call to the Bureau of Prisons we had fervently hoped would never have to be made.

Five o'clock came. It was free time, but all of us, including the prisoners, were moving about restlessly. Had we blown it? Been too trustful and not realistic? If we had to put through that call to Norman Carlson, the aura of trust in the trainees would be shattered. Months of work, hopes, prayers, plans—all down the tube. My heart was sinking down, down, down.

At 5:45 P.M. a cab pulled up in front of the Mission. The two missing prisoners climbed out, paid the fare and walked sheepishly inside. They had gotten lost, wandered about for an hour looking for us, then taken a cab. "Sorry if we caused you any uneasiness," one said ruefully.

Uneasiness! I laughed. I wanted both to hug them and kick them in their butts. But so far our trust in these 12 had been justified.

The prisoners' visit to Senator Chiles' office bore fruit in an unexpected way. A week or so later I was speaking at a prayer breakfast in another state when I met the same senator who had joined the prisoners in Senator Chiles' office, a man who attended prayer breakfasts but had never made a profession of faith.

"I must tell you a brief story," he said as he sat down beside me. "Several days ago I walked into Senator Chiles' office and found 12 people sitting there. I joined them."

He went on to recount the story of how startled he had been to learn they were convicts and how deeply moved he had been by the quality of their faith.

"That night I went home and told my wife about these prisoners. I told her that we needed what those inmates had. So the two of us prayed together that Jesus Christ would come into our lives as He had in theirs."

How often God chooses the powerless to touch the mighty.

Saturday, November 15, 1975, was graduation night for the first prisoner class. The service of dedication, the awarding of certificates, then the communion took place in the second floor living room of Fellowship House. Most of the wives and husbands of the prisoners were on hand.

It's possible to crowd 100 chairs into this room; by squeezing we can seat 125. When more than 200 arrived, people were sitting in adjoining rooms and on the floor. Although no attempt was made to publicize the seminar (we had learned our lesson from the Corcoran episode), word had spread. When the service started about 8 P.M., an atmosphere of live expectancy permeated the room.

There were short talks from the staff, but the real impact came from comments by the prisoners themselves. They were summed up in the moving statement by Pete: "I've learned a lot these two weeks about prayer, fellowship and what a disciple of Jesus is supposed to be. I feel clean inside, as though a lot of dirt has been drained out of my system. For the first time in years I believe I can give love to others and receive it."

Then the communion service began: "At the last supper Jesus sat down with His disciples, knowing all that lay ahead for Him. He took a loaf of bread, looked at the faces around the table, then broke it. 'This represents my body,' He said, 'broken for you. Eat it in remembrance of me.'"

Each of the prisoners sat there motionless, eyes intent on the speaker, holding in their hands pieces of broken bread. They understood brokenness; now they could understand how their broken lives could be mended.

The next day as they departed, one prisoner summed it up perfectly. "I do not go back as a prisoner but as a disciple on a commission for Jesus Christ."

Evangelism is one beggar telling another beggar where he found bread.

D. T. NILES

Evangelism is the spontaneous overflow of a glad and free heart in Jesus Christ.

ROBERT BOYD MUNGER

6. Breaking the Good News

Patty was troubled and it came out one morning at breakfast. "You aren't thinking of becoming an evangelist, are you, Chuck?"

I laughed. "You can't be serious."

"Then why these speaking trips?"

When I explained that I had agreed to make a few speeches for the Fellowship and for certain friends, she wasn't satisfied. "It isn't just the speeches, Chuck. I know you. There's something burning inside of you when you talk about the Lord."

It was true. As a new believer, perhaps my zealousness was showing. The urge to witness, to give testimony, or whatever phrase you want to use, was hard to resist. And even though some of these encounters were bruising—like with Jim Fuller—I yearned for the best way to tell people about the truth of the gospel.

Then came an experience at a large community church in a midwestern city. Pressure from a friend had led me to accept the invitation to speak there. Since it was to be a citywide rally, the fee was sizable; it would cover a good portion of the expenses for the first prisoner seminar.

Since Eastside Community Church was the largest church in town, its pastor had assumed the leadership of the rally. I was to give the closing talk on the final night.

When I finished my testimony, the pastor grabbed the mike and asked the thousands in the hall to bow in prayer. Lights were dimmed, the choir began singing "Just As I Am," and the pastor called those forward "who would this day register their decision for Jesus Christ." I had taken part in altar calls before and often felt a powerful moving of God's Spirit. I'd seen Billy Graham do it masterfully.

People began to stream forward, slowly at first then in a steady procession. Some came in tears—others with that unmistakable glow on their faces. There were more than 50 of them. I tried to keep my eyes down and not count. But it was joyous knowing how God was using the occasion.

The pastor told the choir to continue, then his appeals became more fervent. He prayed the sinner's prayer again. The fifth chorus of "Just As I Am" began. Two more walked forward. *It's over now,* I thought.

"This is your day," the pastor roared into the mike with a fresh surge of enthusiasm. "Come now, receive Christ and you can also enroll in the Eastside Community Church." The music kept going.

The sight of counselors preparing to hand out church registration cards to those in front appalled me.

All at once I felt a quenching of the Spirit. The "Just As I Am" continued. The words which had always warmed my heart now seemed stripped of meaning. The music sounded like the tinny tunes endlessly replayed at small-town carnivals. The pastor's voice reminded me of a barker, luring the unsuspecting into the fat lady's tent. "This isn't evangelism, it's tyranny," I muttered under my breath.

"I know there are more of you who need to come—there, over on the right, the man in the light blue suit, come on now." He began pointing to individuals, some of whom stared back sheepishly and then obviously intimidated, moved slowly toward the front.

"Oh, God, what am I doing here?" I asked, my head bowed more in sorrow and shame than in reverence. The Almighty, I was sure, had fled the hall. Angry thoughts flooded my mind: man's manipulation . . . using God . . . using people . . . using me!

Then the pastor raised his arms high, his jacket flung open, his head back and eyes staring straight up: "Praise the Lord! There are 20 more here. I know it! The Lord just told me."

The music droned on; people were escaping by the side and near exits. I would have joined them if I could.

"The speech tour is over, caput, finished!" I shouted at Fred Rhodes afterwards. "Cancel whatever else we have." I was completely disillusioned with the evangelical circuit.

A Christian for just over two years, I began going through my own "wilderness" of sorts; something which happens to every new believer. The saints have been through it too, I learned. Paul spent three years in the Arabian desert and then (which most people forget) 10 more years in Tarsus waiting to be called into service. John Wesley struggled for more than a decade with doubts; even while chaplain at the colony in Savannah, he questioned whether he had found a true relationship with the Lord. Only when he was back in England did he experience the "strange warming of his heart" that convinced him he was chosen by God. Martin Luther spent years in a monastery, desperately trying to work within the church; that long period of anguish prepared him to become a leader of the Reformation.

For me there had been almost a year of quiet coaching by Doug Coe, Harold Hughes and my prayer group, then seven months in prison, then another period of months writing and studying with Fred. Despite this and despite many years in politics, I was still a babe and not prepared for the disillusioning experiences that can come from fellow Christians.

The lesson from these experiences was clear: Follow Christ, not the things people do in His name. Human beings will always let you down, Jesus never does.

I was finding this world to be a spiritual battleground. Just as a new army recruit is given basic training before being sent to the front lines, so too the new believer needs to be equipped for spiritual battle. Satan likes nothing better, I am convinced, than to prick the balloon of the dreamy-eyed new believer, even as the choruses of "Just As I Am" are still ringing in his ears.

What I needed was more time to understand what God was doing in my life, more time to study, to learn, to pray, to experience what a personal relationship with Christ means and what it calls us to do.

Questions about how to make an effective witness to others continued to nag at me. Was the arm-twisting technique valid?

"The Bible clearly shows us that Christ's disciples are to be bold in their approach," said one young man named Jeff who met me at the airport whenever I visited his city.

I had been walking with Jeff on a downtown street one day when a car pulled to the curb to ask directions. Jeff approached the driver's open window, and I watched as he gestured and pointed, obviously describing the turns ahead. The driver was smiling, nodding and apparently answering questions. Quickly my friend slipped his hand into his left coat pocket and pulled out a tract. I moved over more closely to observe. Gently but firmly my friend was leading the driver through the steps to conversion.

Embarrassed I backed away. A minute later Jeff wearing a broad grin, rejoined me. "That's another one," he chortled. "The angels are rejoicing."

When I ran into Jeff again some months later, he was still at it. We were leaving an office on the 18th floor of a new office building. Jeff spotted a likely prospect, a plumpish, middle-aged woman standing alone in a corner of the elevator. He smiled; she returned it. Then he began, "Do you know where you are going if you die today?"

There was a nervous laugh and the woman looked away. Jeff was not deterred. Next came three easy, neatly packaged steps to salvation.

The elevator stopped at 16, then 15, then 12; people got on, some got off. My friend was oblivious to anyone other than his prey. The elevator was now crowded but he kept pressing; the woman, red-faced, was shrinking into the corner and staring upwards. By the sixth floor she was clutching her purse against her breast, ready, I imagined, to swing it in self-defense. As the elevator emptied out, she brushed by Jeff, shrugged her shoulders defiantly and strode away.

Jeff, who has obviously brought many to God through his boldness, shrugged this off as one miss amid many hits. I couldn't help wondering if Jeff's aggressiveness didn't drive away as many as it brought to the Lord.

Yet the Scripture tells us never to "be ashamed of the testimony of our Lord" (2 Timothy 1:8). The book of Acts is a thrilling adventure story of a few apostles courageously proclaiming their faith, undaunted by threats of reprisal, prison and torture. Stephen was stoned to death for his eloquent defense of his faith. Peter and John defied the Sanhedrin: "We cannot stop speaking what we have seen and heard." When Paul's very life was at stake in Jerusalem, he continued his astonishing claim that Jesus is Lord, risen from the dead. The apostles must have appeared as mad to their fellow citizens as Jeff did to the lady in the elevator.

As I pondered the subject of boldness, I remembered the first day I walked into the executive suite of Tom Phillips in 1973. I had not seen him in four years. Within minutes, it was obvious he was a changed person—kind, compassionate, caring about me. It seemed incongruous somehow: this self-made, hard-driving young man had catapulted in a few short years from a middle-echelon engineer to president of Raytheon, one of the largest corporations in America. Yet, he was gentle in his demeanor.

When I pressed him about what had happened he replied, "I have accepted Jesus Christ and committed my life to Him." It was said as matter-of-factly as he might have described the plate of ham and eggs he had eaten for breakfast. I was stunned at the strange sounding words which I had never heard before.

That bold witness led me to make a similar decision which radically transformed my life back in 1973 and when publicized startled many people in Washington who had singled me out as the arch villain of the exploding Watergate scandal. Headlines circled the globe. Many were affected, as I know from their letters. My conversion later was used to touch the lives of thousands of others through the book I wrote. I wonder if any of this would have happened without Tom's straightforward statement of his own commitment.

Tom told me years later that he prayed the night before our scheduled meeting. The answer he seemed to get was: "Tell Chuck Colson about Me; he needs a friend." This was not easy for Tom Phillips. His natural reserve rebelled against any outward show of religiosity. He knew nothing of the inner hollowness in my own life that I had experienced since election night, 1972. I had disguised my torment well.

Tom carefully rehearsed what he would say. But the next day when I walked into his office, seemingly proud and confident, he suddenly felt timid, fearing I might think him some sort of religious fanatic. He took several deep breaths and found an opportunity to make his statement of faith. When I failed to respond positively he was dismayed, convinced he had failed.

To this day, I wonder what might have happened if Phillips at that critical moment had flinched and ignored what seemed to be God's clear call. Neither of us in our wildest fantasies could have imagined all that would follow from that one moment in the spring of 1973.

Tom's boldness to me went against his low-keyed nature. Yet it was so obviously right.

Then I asked myself why Tom's boldness seemed so appropriate to me and Jeff's so offensive. This led me to ponder the power and authority of the Holy Spirit. Evangelism means the preaching or spreading of the good news—that Christ came among us to redeem sinful men and women. We Christians accept that staggering statement because we believe Jesus is who He says He is. The words came to us from God through Jesus. Only under the power of God's own Spirit can such an extraordinary statement be made with believability.

Thus the same words which sound hollow or repugnant coming from one man's mouth will ring with sincerity and truth from another. Jeff's approach was contrived, possibly the result of a human desire to "run up the score," like someone wanting to better his golf handicap. It was no different from the pastor who wanted to swell his church membership so that he could have the biggest church in town.

Tom, on the other hand, wrestled with God and himself. When he knew there was an authentic working of the Spirit through him, he opened himself and spoke with authority and power.

Doug and others in the Fellowship believe in "living out" the model of the Christ-centered life, consciously avoiding evangelical clichés and the language and techniques which, though meaningful to some believers, can be offensive to nonbelievers who view Christians as members of an exclusive club. "If you live your life as a follower of Christ, He will draw others to you," Doug would often advise.

As I thought more about it, Tom Phillips' words got my attention. But it had been the model of Tom's life, his bearing, his compassion which had drawn me to him. He had something I knew I needed and wanted, something I could not resist and had to learn more about.

I was discovering the truth of this in my own family. Patty, though frightened at first by the suddenness of my experience and fearful that her own Catholicism would be threatened, was growing steadily. In her third year of attending a community Bible study program, she was at last comfortable among most believers except for those well-meaning but overly zealous Christians who would accost her at public events. "And when did you accept Christ, Mrs. Colson?" they would ask, an expectant breathlessness in their voices.

Patty would freeze and later vent her frustration on me. "But I don't have a testimony," she would protest. "I've always believed and I'm still learning." There were times when Patty refused to go to public events for fear she'd be put on the spot or called on to speak.

Through all the harassments Patty and I were drawing closer together in our beliefs: simply to live day-to-day the life Jesus calls us to, realizing His healing presence in the difficult moments every couple encounters. But our children were another story. Emily showed signs of inching toward a personal faith, Chris seemed interested, while Wendell was thoroughly saturated in the humanist philosophy.

During Christmas vacation of Wendell's senior year, we spent three evenings in friendly but spirited debate. The last night we got to the heart of the issue: Who is Jesus Christ?

"Okay, Son," I pressed, "there is much historical evidence about the life of Christ. Look at the miracles He performed. Men couldn't do that."

Wendell leaned forward across the kitchen table. "There were lots of magicians in those days; Jesus was obviously a good one."

"But what about the resurrection? Five hundred eye witnesses saw the risen Christ. All of the later evidence, like the shroud, support the historical accounts surrounding the life of Christ. His life and resurrection are facts of human history that many have tried to disprove but haven't succeeded."

We talked on and on until Wendell finally sighed and leaned back in his chair, a faint smile spread across his face. "Okay, Dad," he said. "I can't buy it all, but I have to admit one thing: the change in you is real. I mean, Jesus must be real because you and your other friends are different."

It was a big concession for Wendell. He was watching, I knew, suspiciously looking for the slightest sign of hypocrisy or actions which were contrary to what we professed to believe. A basic truth had emerged: the lives we live are incomparably more important than the words we speak.

My decision to end all speaking engagements was made just before the first class of prisoners arrived in Washington on November 2. In the middle of the second week of sessions, I was in a class with the 12 inmates when one of the secretaries at Fellowship House tiptoed into the room to hand me a note. It read, "Call Doug Coe. Emergency."

I reached Doug in Oregon. "Chuck, we need you out here as soon as possible," he said. "Harold has had to cancel his speaking dates here. His daughter, Carol, is very ill. Will you come out and fill in for him?"

"I heard about Carol, Doug. We're praying for her. But I can't leave here now. The prisoners are more important. Besides, Doug, you know I'm off the speaking business."

Doug persisted, explaining the importance of two governors' prayer breakfasts coming up and the agony Harold was going through with Carol who had suffered through nine operations in 10 years as she battled cancer.

My resistance subsided. Harold had certainly made countless sacrifices for me. "Okay, Brother," I replied. "Somehow I'll be there tomorrow."

As I hung up the phone, my mind was whirling. Could I face the crowds again? The disillusioning altar call in the midwestern church was still fresh in my memory. Meanwhile I would have to say goodby to the prisoners, rush home to pack, then catch an all night, coast-to-coast flight to Portland.

When I announced to the prisoners that I would have to miss the next several days with them, I watched their faces reflect what I was feeling inside. Then I told them of my own misgivings about giving my testimony to audiences.

One of the inmates, Chris Meece—a bright-faced young man—stood up. "Brother Chuck is going to need our prayers. C'mon guys and gals." In those next moments I found myself seated and surrounded by 12 convicts, each with his or her hands on my shoulders. There was such a simple eloquence in the prayers that I experienced a surging of the Spirit and a new assurance about going back to public speaking.

I needed it during the busy five days which followed in Oregon. I would need it a few weeks later as well.

Until now I had shared my conversion experience mostly with believers who, while not always friendly, had been open. I was not prepared for the wild evening at George Washington University, where the student body is one half Jewish and mostly liberal. For students living there in the nation's capital and reading the *Washington Post,* memories of Watergate and Vietnam were like continuing, festering sores.

I had been moved by an appealing letter from a young Methodist minister, Dave Schneier, who, with his wife Leslie, had turned an old Victorian townhouse next to the George Washington campus into a Christian student center. They urged me to come and told me it would be an informal time with a small band of struggling believers at a tiny and embattled Christian beachhead.

When Fred and I arrived at the Schneier's home around 7 P.M.,

Dave and Leslie, a bright, attractive young couple, stunned us with the announcement that as many as 800 students might attend. As word had spread of my visit, the demand for tickets had grown; the Schneiers kept changing to larger halls. Now they had booked the biggest one on campus.

I took a few deep breaths and started mentally constructing a speech about prisons that I hoped would have universal appeal, especially to cynical, nonbelieving students.

Dave and Leslie appeared increasingly nervous about the evening as we talked. "This can be an . . . uh . . . well, a tough crowd," Leslie said with a tense half-smile. When we prayed together Leslie several times asked for the Lord's protection. Dave, a converted Jew himself, prayed especially for the large body of Jewish students they expected.

The brisk fall air was invigorating as we walked the short distance across the campus to the student center. Along the way were several small clusters of gawking students, but no one smiled or even nodded to us.

The hall was jammed beyond capacity with people standing in the back and seated on steps; I looked up at the packed balcony and saw a colorful pattern of arms and legs draped over the railings. When we entered, running conversations stopped; a uniformed policeman guided us by the students seated on the steps and led us into the hall. The hostile electricity in the air started my adrenalin surging.

"There must be *some* Christians here, Fred," I whispered as we made our way to the podium.

"I'm sure of it," he replied. "I saw two people smile."

Dave Schneier opened the meeting with a few brief statements, and then turned to Fred who was to introduce me. The ashen-faced Schneier seemed to be dropping a white-hot coal into Fred's lap.

Fred Rhodes is a skilled speaker and raconteur, always ready with timely jokes that start most audiences roaring. But not this one. Fred's voice was quivering, and I detected a tremble in his hands. He tried, but the crowd sat, steely-eyed, like a giant cat stalking its prey.

When I approached the rostrum, I noticed open floor space immediately in front of the platform. In an attempt to snap the tension I invited those standing in the back to move down front. "There's room here to sit down," I said with a smile. "And I promise not to preach to you."

That did it. A bearded young man in a red woolen shirt started down the center aisle, shouting, "You've preached at us enough, Colson, from behind the safety of those iron gates at the White House." He was shaking his fist furiously while a swelling chorus of "Right on, right on" came from the audience.

Another young man rose, his face flushed with anger and called out, "You belong back in jail."

There was applause, laughter and then a rising crescendo of shouts and jeers. Some were yelling, "Let him speak!" Others were chanting obscenities.

My heart was pounding. There was only one campus policeman in the hall. I had spoken in front of hostile political audiences before, but this was the first time I had had the palpable feeling of near-exploding violence in an audience.

I grabbed the mike close and heard myself say, "I think we should begin this meeting with prayer."

There were audible, sucking-in gasps of surprise. Angry voices became mutters. The lad in the red shirt waved his fists several times, then abruptly sat down. Within seconds the hall was absolutely quiet.

With closed eyes I asked the Lord to calm us. Though I knew it might be an offense to many in the crowd, I ended the prayer, "in the name of Jesus Christ."

Then I opened my eyes; before me was a subdued crowd. The huge lump in my throat began to dissolve and I could feel blood again flowing through my legs which had been like limp spaghetti. In an instant I changed my topic from prisons to how Jesus Christ had come into my life. I confessed my arrogance and pride and wrongdoing and told how the Lord had guided me through a painful prison experience. No one walked out, nobody interrupted, though I talked for 45 minutes. There was even some applause at the end.

Then came the questions. Students lined up, eager for their turns at mikes placed in the aisles. I braced myself for the onslaught.

"Do you think you've been punished enough?"

"I don't know. All of us are sinners. We can be thankful God is merciful or we wouldn't have a chance."

"I don't think you have been punished much," said another.

"I've spent seven months in prison, my Dad died, I've been disbarred. Right now I'm an unemployed ex-con."

"But you still live in a nice home."

I fought back the anger. "I don't think my wife and family should suffer any more."

"John Dean gets five thousand dollars when he speaks. How much are you getting for tonight?" The electricity was surging again, the hall was hushed.

"Not a cent. I'm here for free. When I do get paid, the money goes to support our work in the prisons."

"Do you believe that only Christians go to heaven?"

"Yes."

"What about Jews?" The questioner was speaking for much of the audience on that one.

"Everyone must seek God in his or her own way. I do not judge others and I respect others' beliefs, but I know what is truth for me. I can't compromise what Jesus says and I won't because I believe it."

I thought that answer might produce anger, but it didn't. The questions continued.

"Henry Kissinger has been very critical of Richard Nixon. Do you agree with what he said?"

Before answering, I glanced at Fred Rhodes who was grimacing at the question and looking around the room, I assumed, for the nearest exit. Then for the first time I saw policemen in every doorway; they must have been called after the initial outburst. Any Nixon question was tough before this crowd. *I can duck it,* I thought. *Otherwise their fury might break loose again.*

"Well," I began slowly, "we all know Mr. Nixon's negative qualities. He's been dissected in the press like no one in history. I could tell you his good points, but I don't believe I could persuade you to accept them." Deep breath. "But what it comes down to is, no, I don't go along with Henry Kissinger's comments. Mr. Nixon is my friend. And I don't turn my back on my friends."

The final sentence came out with a more defiant tone than I intended. In that instant, I thought, the roof would fall in. In a way, it did. But not as I expected. There was a moment of silence, then a thunderous ovation, some students even standing. I stood there speechless.

The chemistry of the audience suddenly changed. The tension was gone; also, most of the hostility. Affirming loyalty to a friend, even though it was someone they despised, to my astonishment had struck a responsive chord in these people. Vietnam and Watergate had disillusioned millions of the young, but they were still holding on to some values, one of which was friendship.

The question period ended and I invited any students who wanted to talk seriously about Jesus Christ to come back with us to the Schneiers' home. Surrounded by police, we made our way through the crowd; some students asked for autographs, others had serious questions. Each time I stopped, a worried officer would pull on my arm. He couldn't sense, I suppose, that the danger was over.

The young man in the red shirt was waiting at the outer door. I tensed as he thrust through the crowd toward me. "Mr. Colson," he began. "I want to say something to you. I was at the courthouse when you were sentenced. I stood in line to get in. I wanted to see you put away for life."

"I'm sorry you were disappointed," I said.

He reached for my arm. "No, you don't understand. I want to apologize." His face was no longer angry; his eyes were fixed on mine. "Please forgive me."

Startled, I reached out for his hand. "Of course. Of course. Come join us now." I lost his grip; other faces were swirling past as the police pulled us through the crowd.

It was fortunate that the Schneiers' new home was only sparsely furnished because the young people kept coming, about 100 in all. The living room, hall, kitchen and front steps were wall to wall with blue-jeaned bodies.

I answered serious questions and we sang a few songs. As we were winding up, Dave asked me to close in prayer.

I did and in that moment of quiet that always follows a heartfelt "amen," I heard a sobbing voice from a far corner of the living room.

"God, take over my life. I want You. I want to be like these people. God, please take me."

It was the young heckler in the red shirt.

> *To care means first of all to empty our own cup
> and to allow the other to come close to us . . . to
> take away the many barriers which prevent us from
> entering into communion with the other. When we
> dare to care, then we discover that nothing human
> is foreign to us, but that all the hatred and love,
> cruelty and compassion, fear and joy can be found
> in our own hearts . . . we can participate in the
> care of God who came, not to the powerful but power-
> less, not to be different but the same, not to take
> our pain away but to share it. Through this participa-
> tion we can open our hearts to each other and form
> a new community.*
>
> HENRI J. M. NOUWEN

7. Disharmony

Early in 1976 we received encouraging news from our friends in Minneapolis. After digging through the newspaper morgue and court records, Kirk Schenk's story was checking out; it did appear that this young prisoner, whom we had met in Stillwater, was being penalized for his refusal to testify for the prosecution. The state attorney general's office was defensive. Hardly anyone would talk about the case.

Counsel was hired for him. I enlisted Harold Hughes' help and we prepared for an all-out assault on the governor's office, if necessary. Maybe we couldn't abolish the inhumanity of the whole prison, but with God's help we were determined to get one man out.

That next week came a long-awaited call from another inmate, for whose release we had worked months. Paul Kramer would soon be freed. We had offered to provide a halfway house in Washington for the last three months of Paul's sentence. Surprisingly—the first break Paul had gotten—it was approved. "I'll come directly from prison to Washington," he told me during a late night phone call.

"Great news!" I exclaimed. "Just write and let us know your arrival time."

We had also heard from Lee Corbin, Paul's and my close friend at Maxwell, who had now been released from prison. Suspecting that he was jobless, I had offered him money. He declined saying he had taken a series of part-time jobs. He called several more times to say he was okay. I took him at his word. I hadn't yet learned to see through Lee's surface statements.

When Paul learned the exact date of his own release, he wrote us a letter saying he would come by bus, a 24-hour trip from Montgomery, Alabama. On a cold, windy, Saturday afternoon he arrived at the Washington terminal and bounced down the steps of the bus carrying a small duffel bag with all of his worldly possessions. Paul looked anxiously in all directions for Patty or me. There was no sign of either of us. As he later told us, it was a complete letdown. He had $25 to his name and didn't know anyone in Washington except us.

The Washington bus station is in an old building in the heart of a deteriorating, downtown neighborhood. Inside, Paul saw a few drunks stretched out on wooden benches. The scuffed tile floor was littered with candy wrappers and cigarette butts, and the pungent odors from the heavy toilet disinfectants reminded Paul of the building he had lived in for the past two years. There were no friendly faces to greet him, only stares from people huddled by the doorways to avoid the wintry blasts outside.

At that moment, Paul's letter telling us that he would be arriving a week earlier than we had expected was buried in a stack of unopened mail in my basement. Patty and I were out of town.

Paul dialed our home number. No answer. He called Fellowship House. No one there knew anything about his arrival. Then he remembered from a letter I had written him that the first group of prisoners stayed in nearby Arlington at the Good News Mission. Paul flagged a cab, stowed his bag inside, and gave the driver the address of the Mission he found in my letter.

Most prisoners spend years dreaming and building up inflated expectations of what the world will be like when they are released. The cold reception most receive when freed is the kind of rejection which triggers in many the very flaw which sent them to prison in the first place.

Fortunately, Bill Simmer, the Mission director, greeted Paul warmly. A bed was found for him. Two days later we returned to the city.

We had a joyous reunion, explanations were given and Patty and I took Paul to our favorite Chinese restaurant. There we pushed at him successive courses of Peking duck, shrimp, sweet and sour pork, chicken with almonds. In spite of our desire to make Paul feel at home, he may have viewed it more as an assault than a banquet.

My own expectations were inflated too. I thought Paul, free after two years behind bars, would be jubilant; but for most of the meal he was sullen, his large brown eyes listless and his athletic body sapped of vitality. Prison psychiatrists say that men are never the same after confinement; the toll it had taken on this young man was painfully apparent. I should have remembered how debilitated I was after only seven months; but a year of freedom had begun to heal the wounds and dim the memories.

"What kind of work will I be doing?" he asked.

"Another group of disciples will be coming in a few weeks. You'll be in charge." The first seminar had gone so well we had immediately begun plans for a second.

"And then what?" he pressed.

I knew what Paul was after; he wanted to know where my heart was. Was this short-term or for real? He had been betrayed many times: his parents had divorced, his own marriage had failed, friends had deserted him when he went to prison. Paul now hesitated to throw his life into this new enterprise of mine, only to have it, in turn, pulled out from under him.

My generalities didn't satisfy Paul. We'd known each other too well in prison; his expression became penetrating every time I was vague. But I couldn't explain Patty's reservations, my indecision and the nagging question which transcended all else: What does God really want from my life?

We agreed that Paul would remain housed at the Good News Mission until his sentence was over and he could either move into Fellowship House or a separate apartment. His work would be divided between the Mission and our growing prison work.

Meanwhile I was troubled about my relationship with John Staggers. Had I been arrogant in describing my vision of prison seminars as on a national level while his work was local? Yes, I probably had. John had given up his post as a high official in the District of Columbia government to give most of his time to the Lorton prison ministry. It had begun with John traveling the twenty miles to Lorton every week to get to know the men, 97 percent of whom are also black. One by one he talked to inmates about Jesus. After a few months, a small fellowship group began meeting regularly.

Under Staggers' dedication the group began to expand. Conditions began to improve inside; stabbings and beatings became less frequent.

It was a logical move to enlist John's regular help with our prisoner classes. His work with the first group had gone so well I assumed any differences we had were resolved. When I next saw John at Fellowship House I asked him to keep the last weeks of February clear on his calendar. John didn't smile.

"What's wrong, Brother?" I asked.

"Don't you think we should plan it together?" he replied.

"Why, sure . . . if you want . . ."

"Well, man, I sure do," he said somberly.

I had become the old Chuck Colson, I realized sadly, the high-handed executive, making decisions, issuing orders, often insensitive to others.

We met one afternoon at Fellowship House. Harold, Fred and Doug joined us. I went through our plans for the second group of inmates then being selected. John was quiet. Fred asked John if he'd take charge of the teaching. John hedged.

Doug kept pressing. "What's wrong, Brother?"

John was resistant. "You guys bring me in and want me to do my thing, but I don't have any say in what we are trying to accomplish." It was a fair point. "The one group was okay," he continued. "I went along. But, man, I don't think this is going to work if you want to keep doing it month after month."

I started to argue. John just shook his head, his eyes fixed on the floor as if he'd already passed final judgment. "I been beating myself silly for two years, racing back and forth to Lorton. It's a little deal. Now, Chuck, you come in here with a big deal, and you're going to take over the whole country."

"This isn't my program, John," I replied. "It's for the Fellowship. I'm willing for you to take it over."

Harold raised his hand. "Hold it, hold it. We're in this to follow God's will, not to prove ourselves," he boomed. Conversation stopped.

I broke the silence. "I'm sorry, John."

"I don't know. I don't think it will work," he shook his head.

"We can't go any further until we're of one mind," Doug argued. "The prime purpose of the Fellowship is to bring people together around Christ."

Harold agreed. "This must be resolved before we can do anything more." We decided to continue with the second class but not plan any further classes until there was agreement among us.

In an effort to bring us closer together, John asked me to give a talk to the prisoners at Lorton. The occasion was the first prayer breakfast, sponsored by the core of new Christians inside. Officials from the District of Columbia government would be there, a hundred or more community volunteers and as many of the 2,000 inmates as the Christian prisoners inside could entice to come.

The Lorton State Penitentiary is located in the rolling Virginia countryside, surrounded by high barbed wire. Prisoners are under the constant surveillance of guards in towers, each of them bristling with weapons. Shotgun-armed police patrol the perimeters.

Despite the rigid security there have been enough escapes to make Lorton an unwanted federal intrusion into the sleepy, rural countryside. Almost every year bills are passed in the Virginia legislature to close down Lorton. It hasn't happened because there is no other place close to the nation's capital to put it.

As with all maximum security prisons, the checking-in process at Lorton is rigorous. Visitors must have identifications, check their valuables, pass through a metal detection device, have their hands stamped with ultraviolet dye and then be physically searched. The guards aren't gentle about it.

Once inside the grounds, the deadly depression hits like a blast of hot air from an open furnace: the empty stares, men clustered together in the shadows of the drab buildings, dirt everywhere. There is a grayness to it all, punctuated only by the occasional splash of color from a bright handkerchief around an inmate's neck or the garish stocking hats so popular in many prisons—the only symbol of separate identity men are allowed. The maximum security cellblock buildings are ringed by rows of one-story, brick dormitories. More than half of the windows had been broken, grim symbols of the violence rampant inside.

Dormitory living can be a special horror in tough prisons like Lorton. Introduced as a supposed reform in the 1930s the dormitories were in reality an economy measure. Most are now dark pits where men have neither safety nor privacy.

The prayer breakfast was held in Lorton Chapel, a large room with a beautiful, eight-foot-high wooden cross and a remarkable lifelike statue of Christ the inmates had carved. Compared with the deadness in the prison as a whole, there was almost a festive atmosphere in this packed room. Along the back wall were rows of inmates in white robes. "They're Muslims," John Staggers told me as we worked our way through the crowd.

The warden, who appeared nervous over the size of the gathering, introduced me. When I stood up to speak, I realized the contrasts. I was white; every inmate in the chapel was black. I had worked at the Nixon White House; they were from the streets of Washington's ghettos.

Fred Rhodes had taken a seat in front of the speaker's rostrum, as he always did when I spoke. This was by design so he could flash me signs and signals.

Groping for common ground, I began by sharing some of my own experiences in prison, trusting the Holy Spirit to guide me. Then I told the story of the young black I'd met at Maxwell who didn't know why he had been sentenced, or for how long.

"As I looked into this black boy's eyes," I said earnestly, "I realized how the system penalized those without education or money. This boy and I became good friends."

In front of me I saw Fred wince, like a sharp pain had jabbed his side. *What's wrong?* I wondered. I kept on.

It was not until after the speech, when John, Fred and I were walking through the mess hall, being greeted warmly by the inmates, that I learned what I had done.

"You call a black in here 'boy' and he will slit your throat." John shook his head, amazed at my naïveté. I was incredulous, too, that I'd lived in a prison where half the inmates were black and had either forgotten or never understood this sensitivity.

"Not just once, but 11 times you did it," Fred chimed in. "I was looking for the exits."

"The Holy Spirit must have blotted it out. It was no offense to them. Amazing. Amazing." John was still shaking his head.

We had been spared, but I was furious at myself for weeks thereafter. How could I be so insensitive, so blind to the obvious? My poor relationship with John Staggers and my clumsy efforts at Lorton made me realize how little honest effort I'd made to understand black attitudes and concerns. Half the nation's prison population is nonwhite.

"You know, Fred," I mused later that day, "maybe I'm just not cut out for this work. I've sure got a lot to learn."

The second class of prisoners, 14 in all, 12 men and two women, again about evenly divided between blacks and whites, arrived on Sunday, February 15, 1976. Fred Rhodes and Paul Kramer handled all of the logistics. It was Paul's baptism; technically he was still a prisoner himself, only four weeks out of Maxwell and under parole supervision while he lived in the Good News Mission.

In the evening, Paul gathered the new class together in the second floor classroom at the mission so that Harold and I could meet them, lay down the rules and give them a challenge. My eyes darted around the long rectangular table as Harold and I were ushered in; every eye met mine. The inmates were as curious about us as we were about them.

Halfway down the table to my right, my eyes stopped. I couldn't believe what I saw. I looked over at Harold; he was staring as well, jaw down, mouth open. One of the two women prisoners, strikingly attractive, was wearing a filmy, see-through blouse and no bra! She was smiling at us, then she tossed her head back, flipping a shock of long blond hair out of her eyes.

Harold nudged me under the table. "Am I seeing things?" he whispered.

"I'm afraid not," I answered. "I have on my new glasses."

Most of the men seemed uncomfortable, self-consciously avoiding any stares in her direction. Men in prison have plenty of difficulty restraining their normal sex drive. This group would have temptations enough just being out of prison for two weeks without having to cope with a seductress in their midst.

After our closing prayer, Harold stood and motioned me toward the door to the adjoining room. I nodded to Fred, Paul and Molly Kay Moerschbacher, a Fellowship staffer who had stayed with the two girls in the first class and then volunteered for the same assignment with this one. Harold was almost shaking with anger.

"How did she get in here? What is her name and what is she in for? Prostitution?" I was certain his thundering voice could be heard three rooms away.

Paul explained that these 14 had been first selected by our friends in each community, then the prison chaplain had approved them. I reminded Harold that we never looked at anyone's file; if God could forgive—and forget—we weren't going snooping into their past. "These disciples are always impressed that we take them as they are," I said.

"Well, we aren't taking her as she is," he growled. He wheeled around to Molly Kay. "Get a bra on her. Tonight!" Before a startled Molly Kay could reply, Harold added, "and a wool shirt and dungarees—loose ones too."

Her name was Jennifer, we learned. She had been an alternate selection at Lexington Prison. When the inmate our representatives wanted was turned down, the chaplain insisted we take Jennifer who, it turned out, was his clerk.

We soon learned more about Jennifer. She was a world traveler, fashion model and had been well educated. She had been arrested for being part of a narcotics conspiracy, led by the man she was living with. We were to discover, through some uncomfortable moments, that Jennifer was a poor choice indeed.

There was one bright spot the first night. John Staggers arrived near the end of the meeting, accompanied by several friends from a black church. Their singing and prayers lifted everyone's spirits. For the next two weeks John threw himself into his teaching assignment with gusto. He is a magnificent leader and the inmates loved him.

We soon discovered that this group fell far short of the commitment of the first 12. Jennifer was not the only discordant note. One of the men was often absent from the group and his dilated eyes made us suspect that he was using some form of narcotics. Paul confronted him, and he admitted it. We offered him a second chance which he took, and in the succeeding days straightened out, becoming one of the most studious members of the class.

Unlike the first group, there were numerous rule violations. By the end of the first week Paul was nearly exhausted from long counseling sessions with prisoners. The study sessions also were listless, progress slow. Something was missing.

The chief problem continued to be Jennifer. I sat in on one of Fred's meetings with her, a study in contrasts: Fred, the elder church statesman, serious and fatherly; Jennifer, the shapely blonde, young, coquettish, and flip. It was difficult for Fred to find a comfortable starting point, and Jennifer enjoyed making him work at it. Finally he cleared his throat a few times and began gingerly.

"You know, young lady, without realizing it, of course, you may be . . . well, let's say tempting some of these men. I mean . . . it could trigger an incident."

"I can take care of myself," she replied.

"What would you do if one of the prisoners forced himself on you?" She shrugged. "If I liked him, it would be fun."

"And if you didn't?"

"I've dealt with difficult types before without causing any trouble.

You see, I believe God gave us the good things of life for enjoyment, that it is unhealthy to cover ourselves up with a lot of unnecessary clothing and suppress our natural desires."

Shaking his head at her answer, Fred changed direction. "What do you think the purpose of this seminar is, Jennifer?"

"To study the Bible, to learn about fellowship."

"You will find that the Bible is quite specific about sexual behavior. In the Old Testament God gave us the Ten Commandments. Fornication and adultery are sins, Jennifer. We are also told that fornicators will not be able to enter the kingdom of Heaven and that it is wrong to place temptation before another person."

Jennifer tossed her head. "I think those laws were for people two thousand years ago. Life today is different; times have changed; we are more enlightened today about body hygiene and sex."

Fred was becoming insistent now. "No, I'm sorry but that's not the truth. God's laws are unchanged. He wants us to live moral lives. Times change but not God. The first duty of a disciple of Christ is obedience—unqualified and without reservation. We must live under His authority and under the authority of the Bible. He loves you, Jennifer. He is patient and forgiving. But I can assure you that He does not approve of your life style."

For a moment there was a crack in Jennifer's outer appearance, a tremor of wistful longing that came and left. Then she resumed her cool, stubborn line. "I think we have been freed from the superstitions of the past."

"I hope you'll think differently after the seminar. Meanwhile we expect you to adhere to the rules. If there are any incidents with the other prisoners, you will be returned to prison at once. Do you understand, Jennifer?"

She nodded with just a flicker of defiance on her face.

Two factors saved us from an incident with Jennifer. One was prayer; the other was the presence of the second woman in the class—Jackie Butner. Jackie was a young, soft-spoken southerner in her 20s who had been an officer in a bank. She became angry because her male counterparts were being paid more for the same work and so to even the score engaged in some "creative accounting," as she described it.

Jackie's commitment to the Lord had deepened in prison. Aware of the danger Jennifer posed to the group, Jackie kept close to her for the two-week period, day and night. Jackie and Molly Kay, in fact, chose the clothes Jennifer would wear, although sometimes, they told us, getting them on her was like corralling a wild horse.

At the graduation service, it was Jackie's eloquent statement of faith that touched hearts most deeply. Something told me we'd be seeing more of Jackie Butner.

When the 14 inmates were returned safely to their prisons, we breathed deep sighs of relief. God had spared us from an incident that might have undercut the whole program. During our post-mortem we realized we hadn't deserved to be protected: I had not given sufficient attention to the selection; there hadn't been enough depth and thought given the teaching; changes were needed. For one, we knew we should obtain an outside teacher. And no more coed classes; in the future we would periodically have a separate group of women inmates.

Most significant was the dampening of the Holy Spirit through our disunity. Of all of the Apostle Paul's exhortations to the turbulent first-century churches, none is delivered more often or with more passion than the plea to be of "one mind and one heart." Before His ascension, Jesus commanded His disciples to go to Jerusalem and wait. Fearful, guilt-ridden, bewildered, they obeyed and for 10 days *all with one mind* devoted themselves to prayer (Acts 1:14). It was then that the Holy Spirit came upon them, producing the most powerful spiritual explosion in the church's history and welding them together in a loving, united fellowship.

I hoped that the disappointing results of the second class were because of our disunity, not something much deeper. We would soon find out.

Attempt something so impossible that unless God is in it, it is doomed to failure.

JOHN HAGGAI

8. Learning to Trust God

At 5:30 A.M. on February 18, 1976, Fred and I walked out of the hotel. In the early morning darkness, the Manhattan streets were nearly empty. It was publication day for *Born Again,* and the NBC "Today" show had invited me for an interview.

A short, brisk walk in the chilled air got us to the Rockefeller Center studios well before the show's 7 A.M. starting time. I wanted a brief talk with Barbara Walters, the program's hostess, before she questioned me on camera. She had grilled me hard the six previous times I had appeared on her show. Incisive and professional, Barbara Walters always probed for embarrassing disclosures and undiscovered news. But she could also show uncommon compassion as she did on the air the morning I was to enter prison. This day I had a special request.

As we waited in the anteroom, Fred handed me an article he had clipped from the current issue of *Christianity Today* about George Whitefield. It described how the stirring preaching of this evangelist had set the colonies on fire in the 18th century. I looked through it quickly.

"Do you suppose Barbara has read your book?" Fred asked, as I was reading the Whitefield clipping.

"Absolutely. This woman does her homework."

Barbara, wearing a huge plastic bib to keep make-up off her dress and rubbing sleep from her eyes, stepped out of her dressing room to greet us. "I've got a whole list of questions here," she announced.

"Wait a minute, Barbara," I interrupted. "You said we have 14 minutes. Why don't you use seven minutes to ask about Nixon and politics and then give me seven minutes to talk about my subject."

Barbara was suddenly wide awake, a flash of anger in her expression. "You know we don't rehearse these shows."

"Of course not, but it will be simpler if we agree in advance. Otherwise I'll find a way to bring our discussion around to my faith."

Barbara stared at me impassively for a moment, shook her head and then broke out in a grin.

She must have taken me seriously: after firing a string of political hardballs at me for the first seven minutes, she sat back in her chair, smiled, and seemed to relax, "Tell us, Mr. Colson, about your experience with Jesus Christ."

Fred told me later that the cameramen cast curious glances at one another; a man running a monitor looked up in surprise and a hiss of whispers went through the control room. Barbara, it was said, seldom used the Lord's name over the air.

The item Fred had given me about Whitefield provided the perfect lead. I referred to the "great awakening" of 1740 and suggested that the only real hope for today's civilization was a similar revival. Then I told how my own awakening had completely changed the direction of my life.

Meanwhile my publisher was jubilant. The first printing of 40,000 copies of *Born Again* were sold out by publication day, tens of thousands were on order.

Writing this book had dominated most of my time and energies during 1975. As work on the manuscript progressed, my editor, Leonard LeSourd, and his wife, Catherine Marshall LeSourd, spent many hours with Patty and me attempting to pick a title. Catherine had been through this 15 times with her own books. "The right title can catch people's imagination, Chuck," she stressed. "We need to pray that God will give it to us."

But I soon became frustrated as I collected hundreds of suggestions, making long lists on yellow pads from which we eliminated, added, reflected and tried again. Up against the printer's deadline we had narrowed it down to three. Then I finally chose "A Mountain Yet to Climb." But there was no inner assurance that this was the right title.

Two days later, as I sometimes do, I accompanied Patty to mass in her parish church. We took our place in the pew and Patty reached down for the people's mass book. She flipped it open and while turning the pages to find the hymn listed in the bulletin, suddenly stopped and stared. Then she showed the book to me, pointing. At the top of the page was the title "Born Again." Patty nudged me and whispered, "That's you. That's your book."

Startled, I stared at the two words. I'd read them in the book of John, but had never used them in conversation or writing. Could God have pointed us to that page?

The minute we got home I called Len. "Not bad," he reflected. "Over your name it might be provocative. But it is a very overworked Protestant cliché."

"It came from the Catholic hymnbook, Len." I suppose it sounded smug. There followed a long silence.

"Let's try it out on others." he said softly.

The reaction was cool. Harold and Doug thought it sounded trite. The publishers thought it was too religious. But as the days passed, my own convictions deepened and support for it grew.

The fourth and final draft had been finished in October, only eight months after my release from prison. Publication was set for February 1976. After copies had been circulated to the *Reader's Digest*, book clubs and major secular magazines in November, we waited hopefully.

The first outside response to *Born Again* came in late December: a flat, unanimous rejection! The manuscript was bounced back quickly from each of the dozen or so secular magazines and book clubs we contacted. We fought against discouragement and prayed, relinquishing our personal desires for the book and asking the Lord to use it.

Soon things began to happen. Jack Anderson was taken with the manuscript and ran an item in his column on it. Then another. Ten days later Anderson featured the book a third time. *Time* quoted several paragraphs on Richard Nixon from the book. Then came another surprise. Christian publications began showing sharp interest. By publication day in late February, orders for the book were snowballing.

After the "Today" show Fred and I drove to Philadelphia for the next interview with Mike Douglas. The drive gave us some time for reflection. "That clipping on Whitefield was helpful, Fred," I mused, "not only on the air, but it also showed me how much I need to learn about the Christian faith.

"There's something else," I continued. "I need to be accountable. All these interviews and attention can puff a guy up. I need the protection of someone with me on these trips who can correct me if I get off base."

Fred hadn't said it, but I knew this was worrying him too. The obvious temptations were less of a problem to me than the more insidious and unseen enemies—ego, pride, vanity. Furthermore, I was learning that my nature followed a certain pattern: a period of intense spiritual enthusiasm, then a flagging of zeal, soon followed by a resurgence of faith, then another falling away, and so on. We humans obviously have a problem maintaining a steady level of spiritual fidelity. One solution: the continual checking and encouraging of a trusted Christian friend.

"And so, Fred, I'm going to make a commitment. If you don't think I should do something, say so and I won't. And vice versa. We'll check and correct each other. Agreed?"

"It's a big responsibility," said Fred, staring out the window at the billboards speeding past, and rows of grey, soot-stained buildings in the distance, "If that's what you want, I'm with you."

For Fred, now 62, joining with me meant a big sacrifice. After his many pressured years in high government office, Fred and his wife, Winona, had looked forward to a quiet homelife and leisurely travel. If Fred was to be the one to hold me in line, he would have to make every trip, and the publisher had lined up a man-killing schedule: 20 cities and almost 200 radio and television interviews in the next two months.

As we were ushered backstage for the interview with Mike Douglas, I noticed a young man writing sentences with a large black crayon on big white posters. The producer explained that Mike doesn't like to ad lib; every question is prepared and written out on cards, held just off stage but in Mike's line of sight so he sees them as he looks at his guest.

Everything about the program was handled with precision: we were escorted to a waiting room which had my name on the door; another member of the staff promptly served lunch; someone else announced the exact minutes still to go before air time. Everyone was carrying sheets of typed instructions which had been carefully thought through to the most minute detail.

The purpose in being here is not just to launch a book, I thought, *but to tell about the Power who can change lives.* Tough to do if the script was already written. What's more, I had been told that Mike Douglas, although a man of faith, did not like to discuss religion on his program.

My discomfort increased when I saw that I was to join two other guests, Barry Newman and Anne Meara; they would not let the conversation remain serious very long. The obstacles seemed overwhelming as the overhead lights flooded the set brighter than day, and the little red warning lights on the top of the cameras flashed. We were on the air telecasting a show millions would see.

Mike greeted me warmly on the air. I glanced to the side; the giant cue card was there just as the producer said it would be with a sledge-hammer question I'd been asked dozens of times. "How could you men in the White House have done such horrible things?"

After the introductions Mike glanced quickly at the cue card. There was an awkward silence as his smile turned to a frown. Something made him change his mind and reject the cue card.

"Tell me, Mr. Colson," he began, "as a man who has had all of the real power in the world, how can you now be off in this unreal world, I mean with all this spiritual business?"

A perfect opening! "Mike," I replied, "the only reality for me is in Jesus Christ . . ."

Anne and Barry shifted uncomfortably, but Mike stared at me attentively as I briefly told my story. It produced several questions about the meaning of being born again with the other guests joining in. Mike never went back to his cue cards.

Following my interviews with Barbara Walters and Mike Douglas came a fascinating turn of events. One enterprising reporter, having seen the book title several times on television and in the newspapers, sought out the bevy of presidential candidates trudging through the snows of New Hampshire in the country's first primary.

"Are you born again?" he asked Ronald Reagan, who looked startled, said nothing and walked on.

Jimmy Carter, then the obscure former governor of Georgia, was approached. "Yes, I am born again," he replied. A few weeks later Carter won a surprising victory in that primary and overnight became big, national news; so did his strange sounding answer about being "born again."

Soon every political columnist was trying to explain what the two words meant. They were bannered across news magazine covers; there were television specials. Within a few months it became the most fashionable, popular, new catch phrase of 1976.

Wherever Fred and I traveled, we encountered people who expressed common concerns and needs. The most widespread seemed to be wives troubled about their unbelieving husbands.

"My husband isn't saved. Pray for him. Sign this book to him—maybe this will do it."

Once in a while there was a hint of conspiracy in their approach. Like the brawny woman who gave me a knowing wink and whispered hoarsely, "We'll get him yet, Mr. Colson. You and I and the Lord." I shuddered to think what her husband's home life must be like, imagining him gamely trying to avoid the myriad traps she set for him.

For most who appeared so deeply troubled, some nearly in tears, I felt tremendous sympathy. "Relax and let the Lord do it," I would answer, but it sounded cavalier.

Often I reminded them of the story of the Philippian jailor (Acts 16, RSV). After the midnight earthquake when God freed Paul and Silas from jail, the astonished jailor asked, "Sir, what must I do to be saved?"

"Believe in the Lord Jesus," they said, "and you will be saved, *you and your household.*" That is the promise.

Much of the time these women were reflecting cultural pressures, I suspected. Surely they wanted their husbands to become believers so that they could share the Christian life together. But deep down there was something else. What did the gals at the Tuesday Bible study think of poor Millie who had to live in a pagan household? And poor Millie couldn't be much of a soul-saver if she couldn't even reach her own husband.

More often than not, the family tensions created by the over-eager Christian spouse probably drove the so-called "unsaved" mate in precisely the opposite direction. I know of many such cases, even some where the couples have tragically separated, others who have stayed together but live in their own hell. How could I get across the idea that it is God who regenerates and makes faith possible—that conversion is not the work of man? Bludgeoning a wife or husband into mouthing what we evangelicals regard as the magic words accomplishes nothing unless the Lord makes the real transformation occur in the heart.

I was learning how important it is to be sensitive to the feelings of others through my own experience with Patty. As a lifelong Roman Catholic, Patty was comfortable with the formal liturgy of her church and understandably unsettled to be in a friend's living room when everyone got on their knees and began praying aloud. Terms like "accept Christ" and "sister in the Lord" used in such unabashed fashion sounded foreign and threatening. Friends warned her that evangelicals would try to pry her away from her church.

"I have always believed in Christ," she told me one night, "ever since I was a little girl. The communion has always had great meaning for me. But your friends make it sound as if everything has to be dramatic and sudden."

Patty began attending a Bible study at Washington's Fourth Presbyterian Church where the gifted preacher, Dick Halverson, is pastor. Soon she had recruited several women from her own Roman Catholic parish in McLean to attend. Without pressure, Patty was finding her own way into an ever deeper relationship with the Lord. It has grown and continues today. Christ is the center of our lives and marriage. I don't know what would have happened had I pushed Patty to meet my timetable.

From many encounters while autographing books I was discovering that evangelicals expect everyone to fit the same mold. Our culture, as distinguished from our theology, puts a premium on three things: (1) knowing the exact moment a person is born again, (2) the emotional feelings that occur (3) and the language used. This approach creates dangerous distortions.

As to the first, many simply cannot pinpoint the precise moment in time. For some it is like riding on a train crossing state borders; since the trees and plants look alike, say in both North and South Carolina, only when one sees a sign does he realize he has crossed that line. But the objective fact is that the line was crossed.

Second, the emphasis on feelings can be misleading. After his profession of faith, evangelist Dwight Moody was asked by his pastor, "What has Christ done for you which entitles Him to your love?"

"I don't know," Moody replied with obvious diffidence. "I think

Christ has done many things for us. But I don't think of anything particular right now." Hardly the exuberant response evangelicals expect.

Billy Graham says he felt no emotion after his decision for Christ. Surely no one would doubt that these two, perhaps the greatest modern-day evangelists, were indeed born again.

A man in a solitary cell in a southern prison pleaded with me. "I want to be born again, Mr. Colson. Why can't I?"

"You can be," I assured him and took him through several Scripture verses.

"But I've done that a dozen times," he protested. "It hasn't taken."

"What do you expect?" I asked.

"Well, something dramatic like happens in every book I've read, including yours." I apologized for the impression given by my book and explained that one can be born again in a moment of quiet decision as God's grace becomes real within the person. The man's countenance brightened as if a heavy yoke had been lifted from him. He is now active in a prison chapel program.

The third misconception involves *the language used.* One woman told me that her husband "was a Christian, I guess, but not the way we know it. I mean, not really born again."

She went on to explain that her husband had always been a church-goer, that he was a believer but hadn't had a "real experience." What she meant was that he wasn't outgoing enough, didn't use the evangelical "in-language" or allow bumper stickers on the family car.

What I wanted to say to her, but didn't, was that her husband's faith might have more depth and substance to it than her own.

One autograph party tested my faith in a very physical way. I was alone—a mistake. Paul Kramer had traveled with me to Atlanta to give Fred a break, but Paul was visiting family.

I was seated at a small table in the back of the bookstore; the line was nearly at its end. A lovely, gray-haired lady clutched her book, smiled appreciatively and stepped to the side.

Before me was a gaunt, ashen-faced young man dressed in a surplus army field jacket, his hair stringy and tied in the back. For several seconds he said nothing, nor did he reach for a book.

"I've been trying to decide if I'm going to kill you tonight," he said coolly. He was staring straight at me, but his eyes, which were dilated, had difficulty focusing on mine. His voice was flint-hard, however, and one hand was hidden menacingly inside his jacket pocket.

A young salesgirl standing behind me let out a shrill gasp. "I'll get the police," she said in a pitch two octaves higher than normal. I grabbed her arm and told her not to move.

Did he have a gun in his pocket? I stared at the young man, wondering whether to try to talk to him or pray. I did both.

"If you kill me, I'll be okay because I know where I am going." I hoped he didn't hear my heart pounding.

"What do you mean?"

"I mean that when I die I'll be with Jesus Christ."

"That's what I hate. You think you know all the answers. You guys are trying to destroy me and people like me."

I stared back, saying nothing. The young man's angular face was filled with hate and anger, but it was also pathetic. He was finding no peace from drugs and now no comfort from my reaction. *What hope does he have?* I wondered. *How desperate his world must seem.* I wondered if he would lash out with a knife. He could have either a gun or a knife in the pocket of his field jacket. *Lord, calm him,* I prayed.

The decision was made and his facial muscles began to relax. "I'm not going to kill you now. Perhaps some other time. You ought to thank me."

"I do—thanks."

With that he slowly backed away, never taking his eyes off me, retreating out the exit door.

"Can I get the police now?" the salesgirl's lips were colorless.

"No. We're okay now. Just hand me another book." Her hands were shaking so badly she dropped it.

Had it been a serious threat? Or did he just want to scare me? I couldn't tell. But I do know something that moved me deeply: the awareness of the Comforter's presence at a time of crisis.

On the tour, we discovered how God sometimes uses seemingly insignificant events to trigger major happenings in our lives. One day in Nashville a man grinned and thrust a book into my hands. "Saw you on the 'Today' show. Read this. It will make you think." It was a copy of *George Whitefield and the Great Awakening* by British biographer, John Pollock.

On the flight back to Washington I opened the book. Quickly I was enthralled. Whitefield, young and brash, preached up and down the colonies. Banned from the church because, among other things, he practiced the "heresy" of extemporaneous prayer, and constantly demanded that people experience a new birth, Whitefield took to the open fields. As tens of thousands flocked to hear him, a great revival swept through the colonies, changing the course of American history.

The Whitefield book led me to one on John Wesley, which proved just as thrilling. Later came books on Luther, Calvin and the Reformation; and Malcolm Muggeridge's magnificent *Third Testament,* the stories of six great men of God from Augustine to Bonhoeffer.

A pattern was emerging from my reading: the great reforms of history, I could see, came about not so much because of political institutions but as a result of God's power flowing through righteous and obedient people. Not only was my reading giving me a fresh perspective on history, it was stirring a deep hungering for more knowledge about the way God works in the world. The result was a course of self-teaching, which included Bible study with Doug and Harold, a long list of good Christian books, and whatever occasional seminars I could cram in.

A tough assignment I had been putting off for months was a visit to the Sandstone Federal Penitentiary near Minneapolis, Minnesota. We had no volunteers covering this prison and we wanted to bring some inmates out to future Washington classes.

Since Doug Coe also had been urging me to visit the Minneapolis–St. Paul area to encourage the many small groups of Christians meeting there, I accepted an offer of several Minneapolis businessmen who said they would raise $5,000 for our prison work if I would make a series of local appearances.

It turned out to be a blitz of the Twin Cities and environs for two and a half days, covering schools, service clubs, business groups and churches. My hosts arranged to leave the last afternoon free for me to fly by private plane to Sandstone, which is 90 miles north of Minneapolis.

Located in open farm country, Sandstone is among the most isolated prisons in the federal system. We had received reports about poor morale there, with men contracting "arctic fever" because icy winds and drifting snow kept them confined indoors from October to April.

On the way to the airport, Bob Glockner, the man who had put the grueling schedule together, was downcast. "I'm not sure how it happened," he began, "but we've only raised $3,400. We did our best. I'm really sorry."

I couldn't tell Bob how much we had counted on the funds. Nor had I ever worked so hard during any three-day period. "Bob, I know you were faithful and I hope I was. We'll trust the Lord to provide."

Bob nodded. He had been in Christian work for years. I sensed what he was thinking about me: *Chuck's a new Christian and naïve. I hope he doesn't become disillusioned.*

I meant every word of it; I felt a surety. Besides there were more important things to worry about, like the ominous gray sky overhead. I had been uneasy about flying in small planes ever since I nearly crashed in a small military aircraft while in the marines.

At the airport I met Dave Rolschau, a 40-year-old businessman, who was walking around his single-engine Bonanza, intently checking the ailerons and landing gear. The strong wind made my eyes water as Dave and I stepped onto the wing and into the cockpit. Broad-shouldered and sturdy, Dave Rolschau is one of the most engaging men I've met anywhere, but at that moment I was more interested in his flying skills than his personality.

"Are you sure we're okay to fly today, Dave?" I asked, expecting quick reassurance.

"You never know around here," he answered soberly his eyes darting from gauge to gauge. "But I think so. Tough wind, though."

Dave then snapped on his earphones, revved up the engine and began taxiing toward the runway.

Buffeted by wind gusts, the little plane literally bounced into the air, banked sharply and headed due north into the darkening sky.

Dave sensed my nervousness: "Don't you trust the Lord?"

"Sure," I replied, "but I don't like to put Him to more work than necessary." I made a mental note to study up on the difference between trusting and testing God—if I ever got back from this flight.

The countryside north of Minneapolis is dotted with thousands of picturesque lakes, but on this day it was only a vast expanse of white from an early spring snow. Tiny spirals of smoke came from scattered farmhouses. During the flight, I talked about our vision to go into prisons. Dave said very little; for him, as for so many people, it was like describing life on another planet.

"We've got to bring something to those men," he finally said. Rolschau was a new Christian whose encounter with Christ had so penetrated the core of his soul that at the mere mention of Jesus, tears would well up in his eyes. He agreed to start visiting if we got an open-door reception.

"There it is," Dave exclaimed pointing through the window at what looked like a toy fortress perched on a giant blanket. We banked, turned toward it and began descending rapidly. When we were about 500 feet overhead, Dave suddenly gunned the engine and turned the little Bonanza on its side. I clutched frantically for the bottom of my seat, thinking my friend was reliving his glory days as a fighter pilot.

"Sorry," he explained, "I told the chaplain I'd buzz the prison so he would know when to drive out to the airport to meet us."

The prison beneath us appeared absolutely deserted—not a single person in sight. Walled-in by cream-colored buildings on all four sides leaving an open compound in the center, it looked like a French Foreign Legion post right out of the movie, *Beau Geste.*

The airport was a rectangular runway strip cut out of the trees, identifiable only by a single pole with a tattered windsock flapping noisily. We landed smoothly and minutes later the chaplain arrived to drive us back to the prison.

The chaplain was middle-aged, bearded and nervous about our visit. We asked him if we could meet with the Christian inmates. He looked puzzled, then ran his fingers through his beard. "We'll get some of the men who come to chapel on Sunday," he replied.

My questions about Bible studies or fellowship groups were met by uncomfortable pauses. We rode on in silence.

Most career chaplains, I was discovering, are good churchmen who go into prison work out of compassion for the imprisoned, only to have their initial zeal beaten down by the constraints of the system. Some become embittered, others tire of the lonely struggle and resign, while a few become legendary figures. There is a small minority who settle comfortably into the routine and unconsciously become as institutionalized as the guards and long-term inmates. The one paralyzing obstacle to any creativity is the day-in, day-out depression of existence behind the walls.

We arrived as the guards were conducting a late afternoon count in the dormitories and cell areas. Each cell block is locked off and the men are required to be at their bunks as the guards physically count them. The total is then reported back to central control. There is such a high probability of human error that the count often has to be repeated. For the men the counts—sometimes up to eight a day—become as nerve-grating as a dripping faucet.

Dave and I asked to be taken through each housing unit and to the mess hall. That way the inmates would see us, and we hoped the Christians would identify themselves. Somewhere in here we hoped to find two men for our next Washington class.

In the first dormitory, the men were jammed into the hallway waiting for their turn in the mess hall. A few inmates nodded as we passed. One man shouted, "Hey, are you Colson?" A hush fell over the crowd.

"Yeah," I replied, "how are you doing?" The answer came with a few choice expletives.

Then the inmate, now grinning broadly, asked in a loud voice, "You coming back in? I thought you was sprung last year." Laughter rippled through the crowded hall.

"I'm back but not to do time. Maybe to start a Bible study though," I replied. The laughter started again, this time derisively.

Dave and I stood there while the men filed out. *Surely one Christian will come over to us,* I thought. But no one did.

We moved into the next dormitory. Bunks were double-decked, each covered with a drab army surplus blanket. The uniforms were the same olive color as were the nearly threadbare field jackets, the only protection the men had against the cold outside. Blankets hung over the frosted windows shut out the light, if not all the cold, and gave the smoke-filled room, illuminated only by a half dozen 100-watt bulbs hanging from the ceiling, an eerie, greenish-gray tone. The stale air was steamy from the open shower room.

"This must be what hell is like," Dave whispered.

"It's like all the others," I sighed.

We passed from bunk to bunk. A few men talked to us; others rolled over to signify their annoyance at unwanted visitors. One old man asked why we were there.

"We care about you men, that's why," I replied.

"From Washington, are you?"

"That's right."

"You're government inspectors," he said, pleased that we hadn't put one over on him.

"No, no," I insisted.

"I got nothin' to say," he continued, grinning.

We looked for Bibles in lockers which would be a sure clue. There were none.

In the third dormitory, an honor unit recently renovated, was a young man who eagerly began talking. Dave was impressed. He was only recently sentenced and had been a radio announcer, he explained. And yes, he was "born again." As he talked I sensed something wrong and then noticed one older black inmate walk away, shaking his head.

"Sorry, Dave, he's not our man," I said as we walked outside. "Something fishy about him. No new prisoner gets into the honor unit. If he does, he's suspect and resented. Besides he'd say anything he thought we wanted to hear." Rolschau's education was starting.

Two hours later we had completed the tour without meeting one man who we felt was a committed believer, certainly no one who could be our leader inside. Driving to the airport strip I suggested to Chaplain Nissen that Dave start visiting the men regularly. He smiled and said, "That would be fine—if you want to." His tone indicated he had had such offers before and nothing had come of them.

As we were taxiing out to the end of the strip, daylight fading fast and the sky more threatening than ever, the absurdity of it all struck me: we were miles from anywhere, fastened into a little green and white airplane about to take off into a cold, bleak Minnesota sky. I was exhausted and hoarse from three days of steady speaking. We were short of the funds we needed in Washington. My vision about the prisons had caused divisions among my closest friends. Nor was I lighting any fires in the prisons. I had muffed it at Lorton, and here at Sandstone, which houses 500 inmates, we hadn't found a single Christian. The chaplain, I believed, was happy to see us go.

I looked over at Dave who was leaning forward, straining to see the runway through the fogged up windows. "Dave, can we stop and pray?" I asked. He looked surprised, then cut down the engine to a low purr.

"Lord," I began, "we may be a couple of fools, but we claim this place for you. It's impossible, I know, so if You want us here, You'll have to do it. Show us how, Lord . . . and whatever happens, thanks for Dave, a beautiful brother."

> *It must be acknowledged that the penitentiary system in America is severe. While society in the United States gives the example of the most extended liberty, the prisons of the same country offer the spectacle of the most complete despotism.*
>
> ALEXIS DE TOCQUEVILLE

9. "Right On"

The back-breaking tour for *Born Again* wound up in California. In one situation there, Fred and I demonstrated good teamwork. But not in another.

Having arrived late at the hotel one night, we went to the coffee shop for a snack. The room had a Spanish motif: red tile on the floor, wrought iron tables and chairs, pictures of bull fighters on the walls. It was less than half filled. A waitress in a pink uniform sidled up to us with an order pad.

"Two cheese omelettes, one milk, one iced tea," Fred told her.

The waitress reminded us of a young Eve Arden, blondish hair, raw-boned, pleasant-faced. She took our order briskly, then marched toward the kitchen.

Fred and I reviewed the next day's schedule for a few minutes. Then I suggested that Fred ask the Lord's blessing on the food that would shortly be served. We bowed our heads. As blessings go it was a fairly long one. When we raised our heads, the waitress was standing nearby, omelettes in her hands.

"Hey, were you guys praying?" She seemed surprised and spoke so loud that everyone in the small room turned to look.

"Yes, we were."

"Hey, that's neat. I've never seen anybody do that in here before. Are you preachers?"

"No, not really. But we work in the same business."

That stopped her for only a few seconds. She was full of questions and asked them with such naïve spontaneity that we quickly warmed to her. "I'm a Christian," she said. "At least I was once."

"What happened?"

As she stood there a sad nostalgic expression crossed her face. "I accepted Jesus as my Savior at a rally when I was a teenager. Then I went to live in Hawaii. Well, I just lost interest, I guess. Forgot about it."

"I don't think you lost it," I said gently. "You just put it aside for a while."

She was thoughtful. "It's funny, but the moment I saw you guys praying I felt excited all over again."

"Once you accept the Lord, He becomes a part of your life," said Fred. "You can try to turn away from Him or shut Him out or do things you know He won't like, but He's still there. He loves you and, like the prodigal son, will take you back."

"You know, I think you're right," she said with quickening excitement. "Funny, a girl friend has been trying to get me to join her Bible study."

She left to wait on other tables. When we were finished, she returned with our check, smiling. "Thank you. I mean it: thank you."

The next day, hoping to find the same waitress, Fred and I returned to the coffee shop for lunch. She appeared through the swinging doors to the kitchen, carrying a loaded tray. "Hey, you guys," she gave us a big grin and came right to our table. Holding the tray on one shoulder while her hungry customers nearby fidgeted anxiously, she proudly told us that she had called her friend and the next day she was joining a Bible class. "And I'm going to find a church, too. I've come back. Thanks, guys."

Until that night, I had felt awkward at times praying over meals in crowded restaurants. Never again.

The next day Patty and Fred's wife, Winona, joined us in California. While there, Patty and I decided to call several friends, including some of my erstwhile White House colleagues. Healing wounds which Watergate had opened was a special burden to me; if I believed what I preached, I had to make the extra effort.

The Deans—John and Mo—were the first we called. John and I had been enemies, representing two opposing camps. He aimed the battering ram against the White House gates while I stood on the battlements to repel the assault. But we were cellmates after that and prison breeds its own forlorn camaraderie. It was a time of reconciliation.

Patty and I had taken the Deans to dinner in Washington several months before. Now that we were in their territory, the Deans invited us for dinner—a quiet evening alone in their home.

The next morning when I told Fred about the invitation from the Deans, he looked troubled. "I don't like it. I don't feel right about it."

Surprised, I searched his face. "Fred, I see it as an opportunity. John was a Bible student once and studied for the ministry. Mo admitted in Washington she was searching for meaning in her life. I think they're reaching out."

Fred kept shaking his head. "You told me to be honest with you. I don't feel right about this. You and John are still on opposite sides. Your book is now getting a lot of attention; John's isn't out yet. Who knows what trap might be set for you there?"

I recalled my vow not to go against Fred's advice, but this didn't seem to be a spiritual issue. Nor did his advice make any sense to me. I agreed to think about it, but later that morning as we were riding in the car together, I told him of my decision to go to the Deans. Fred did not protest.

Around 7 P.M. that Friday our rented Chevy climbed up narrow serpentine roads to one of the mountaintops above Beverly Hills. The final turn led into a cul-de-sac and a breathtaking panorama of the canyon below: millions of flickering lights in a sea of black. John, whose celebrated testimony earned him the enduring enmity of die-hard Nixon supporters, had gone to elaborate lengths for security. We spoke to a remote-controlled box; iron gates then slowly swung to the side, opening the way up a steep concrete driveway to the Dean's house which was perched on the edge of a cliff, with a swimming pool precariously cantilevered over the precipice.

John came outside to meet us as we parked on a slope. "Put your emergency brake on," he laughed. "We lost a Volkswagen bus over the edge last year."

"I brought my oxygen," I quipped back.

The Deans greeted us warmly and escorted us into an elegantly furnished living room which looked out over the spectacular view below. A glowing fire dispelled the California spring chill.

John introduced us to a last-minute guest. "This is Taylor Branch, my editor. We've asked him to join us. Hope you don't mind."

Branch was a bright-faced young man in his late 20s. A writer from the east, he was staying with the Deans to help John through the final draft of *Blind Ambition.*

"Of course not," I replied, gripping Branch's hand. John walked to his bar in the corner of the big room. "Scotch for everyone?" he asked. I nodded. Many times in pre-Watergate days John and Mo had been in our house and we in theirs. He knew that I always used to enjoy cocktails before dinner. This night was no different to John. I gave it not a passing thought.

Taylor Branch, it turned out, was a Watergate buff and a political activist with a strong leftward bent. As John and I began reminiscing about our White House and prison experiences, he seemed enthralled at the firsthand accounts of events which had made so much world news. The knowledge that at 7:30 the next morning I would have to be in a Hollywood television studio caused me to nurse my one drink.

During the Watergate testimony Mo Dean's strikingly beautiful face became familiar to millions of Americans. Now living in the center of Hollywood glamour, it would be hard to imagine her slaving over a hot stove. Yet she prepared us a sumptuous meal—beef Wellington, fresh vegetables, roasted potatoes, topped off with homemade popovers served piping hot. As Mo cast aside her apron and sat down, John looked at me with a quizzical smile, hesitated an instant and then asked if I would say the blessing.

Patty has an irrepressible wit, her Irish heritage. Seeing the steam rising from the serving dishes and remembering some of my lengthy prayers, she couldn't hold it back: "Sure hope the dinner will stay hot."

It served as a relaxer. We all laughed and then I prayed for the Deans, their home and our evening together. During dinner Branch told us that he was raised in a devout Christian home, was a believer until his early teens when, as he put it, the false piety and hypocrisy turned him sour. He then went through a period of deep rebellion. As the conversation wore on, I sensed that Branch was listening intently as I talked about my experience in the Christian life. Soon Branch began to open up about his own spiritual hunger. It was a thoroughly friendly and sociable evening. We were back at our hotel by 11 P.M.

When Fred picked me up early the next morning, I told him what a pleasant time we had at the Deans. He was apologetic. "I guess I was worried for nothing," he said, steering us through early morning traffic to the film studio.

The evening with the Deans soon faded in our minds as one pleasant interlude in an exhausting period of travel that spring. We didn't know how uncanny Fred's perception was and that a ticking time bomb had been set that night which would detonate months later when we least expected it.

The soaring sales of *Born Again* in the spring of 1976 were in sharp contrast to the slowing down of our prison work. The second class of prisoners in February had in no way measured up to the quality of the first class. There had been no damaging incidents and individually many in this class showed good leadership promise, but something had been missing.

What was God trying to tell us? Deep down, I think I knew, but I wasn't sure I was ready to face up to it.

Meanwhile we heard of growing resistance to our program from both wardens and chaplains. Then came a sharp setback. One of the disciples in the second class—"Slim," a tall, outgoing young black— escaped from the Atlanta prison shortly after he returned from Washington. He had been quickly recaptured, but it made no sense. Why do it the hard way from a maximum security prison when he could have walked away anytime while in Washington?

What troubled me most of all was the continuing division. John Staggers, with his usual honesty, told me that I had shown little concern for his work at Lorton. Several meetings with him did nothing to break the impasse. If there was no solution, then perhaps this was God's way of steering my life in another direction.

Harold, Doug and I met for a final session on the matter early in April. As we sat down together in the lower floor meeting room at Fellowship House, I felt a sense of freedom about it and was prepared for a major step. "Brothers," I began. "I think there is only one answer. Let's ask John Staggers to take over this ministry. It's only been a part-time project for me. I'll continue to help, raise money and do anything I can."

It was not a tactical ploy. I felt convicted that I wasn't right for the work. I had been wrong in not making a stronger effort to understand John. We both ended up being frustrated.

Harold shook his head. "I love John Staggers like few other men alive, but he is not the one to take this over. Nor does he want it." Doug agreed.

"Okay, then," I answered. "Let's turn it over to Bill Glass. We've been working together. He is a good man; he has a great heart and a solid prison ministry."

That idea made more sense. I had talked with Bill about working together. He was interested, but we'd never gotten down to details.

"What will you do, Chuck?" Doug asked.

"Business maybe, or practice law in Massachusetts." Nothing would make Patty happier, I knew.

Doug pondered the idea. "It's true that you can serve the Lord in business or law or whatever." We had all agreed that going into full-time Christian service can sometimes be stultifying with the ministry becoming so confining and consuming that the individual loses a sharp spiritual edge.

Harold sat back, thrusting his thumbs under the straps of his farmer's overalls which he sometimes wore to meetings. Then his midsection began to rise majestically; it was always a sign that something was about to erupt. "Now wait a minute, men," he thundered. "Chuck had a vision. He and I went to see Norman Carlson; amazing things began to happen. Chuck has offered everything he can to John; we cannot let a family upset frustrate this work. No, sir, that's wrong."

With that he rocked forward, put both hands on his knees and drew his huge frame upright. He stood over my chair. "What does God want you to do, Chuck? Whatever it is, I'm with you."

Harold is the kind of man you want in the same foxhole when people are shooting real bullets.

I was ready to give it all up, but was I ready for the converse—to give it everything I had? I shook my head. "I don't know, Harold, I just don't know."

Patty and I had just returned home from an early Saturday night dinner with friends when the phone rang. It was Harry Dent, who had bailed Chris out of jail the year before, calling from Columbia, South Carolina. Harry had been a good friend in White House days and was now practicing law.

"Chuck, I'm afraid I've got bad news."

My heart began thumping. Visions of Chris hurt in a car accident raced through my mind.

"What is it, Harry?"

"It looks like Chris has been arrested again. It's all over the papers."

"What do you mean 'looks like'?" I was shouting into the phone as Patty grabbed my arm and held it firmly.

"There's a big article about a drug raid. The police nabbed a Christian Cole, the ringleader. There isn't any address, but the neighborhood is the one your son lives in. He probably gave the name Cole so it wouldn't create so much news. I called the police; the kid is out on bail. But, it's too much of a coincidence, isn't it?"

"Yeah, it sure is," I sighed. "Harry, would you ride over to Chris' house? See if he's there, or if anyone knows anything."

Harry promised he would find out for sure, but there was little doubt in his mind or ours. We tried calling Chris. No answer. We called other friends of his. No answer. We called the lawyer who had tried Chris' case in court; she had heard nothing from Chris but clinically pronounced the verdict: "They'll go tough on him a second time."

Despair settled over me. "I've got a prison ministry, all right; it's right in my own family." I looked bleakly at Patty. Tears were welling up in her eyes.

"Maybe it is not *our* Chris," she said, but the words were hollow.

"No sense kidding ourselves. But how could he have done this to us . . . and himself?" There was self-pity and anger here, I realized, mixed with sadness. *How could he have done it? I had lived through the prison horrors. Not Chris. No. It mustn't be.*

Patty and I bowed our heads at the kitchen table and prayed. We couldn't ask the Lord to spare Chris for us. It was too late. We'd only ask for strength to face what had to be faced.

An hour later we reached one of Chris' roommates, Steve. He might have thought he was in the witness box in a murder trial. He swore he knew nothing about it. Chris was away sailing. He would have known had Chris been arrested. No, there was no marijuana in the house. They hadn't gone anywhere where there was any. "Honest! Honest!" he pleaded. I kept bearing down. "Look, I know roommates are supposed to cover for each other, but I want the truth. I'm coming down on the first flight in the morning. Do you understand?"

"Honest, nothing happened." He was almost crying.

Patty and I sat staring at each other. There was at least doubt;

not much, but some. I knew Steve had to be lying; besides, how many people are named Christian? And in the same neighborhood!

"Why don't you call information and just see if there is a Christian Cole listed?" Patty's words broke a long uncomfortable silence.

"That's silly," I snapped, then lunged for the phone. The operator insisted I spell it twice; while I waited for her to return I held my hand over the receiver and whispered to Patty, "This is ridiculous, you know."

The operator's voice was like sweet music. "Yes, Sir, I have a Christian Cole." She gave me the address—it was in our Chris' neighborhood—then the number. Without stopping to think what I would say, I dialed Christian Cole and seconds later a voice came on the line.

"Are you Christian Cole?"

"Yes, Sir."

"Were you just arrested for narcotics possession?"

"Yes, Sir."

"Thank God . . . I mean, I'm sorry, I really am. I wish you well. God bless you."

I couldn't think of anything else to say and so I hung up, feeling silly. Christian Cole probably chalked it up to a crank call.

Patty couldn't resist having some fun with me. "Chuck Colson! You see? You should have trusted Chris. I knew it all along."

Patty and I were in a deep peaceful sleep at 2 A.M. when our Chris called in; it was one time we didn't mind being awakened. He couldn't understand what all the excitement was about. Sheepishly I explained that we knew all along it wasn't "our Chris;" we were just checking. "And Son, we love you."

Some weeks later I was visiting a particularly overcrowded institution in Florida. The guard escorting us reluctantly agreed to let me walk through one of the jammed dormitories. Bunks were piled on top of one another, the way I'd read slaves were brought to this hemisphere in the holds of ships 200 years ago.

"This is wretched," I murmured to the guard.

"Sure is."

"How often do you walk through here at night?" I asked.

The guard stopped walking, turned toward me in astonishment: "Are you kidding?"

"No, I'm serious."

"Well, the answer is, *never.*" He shook his head. This is like a jungle. It wouldn't be safe. There's a gang rape here almost every night."

As his words were being spoken with such finality, my eyes fell on a young lad with long blond hair, dressed only in undershorts, sitting on the edge of his bunk. His head was down and dejectedly he was staring at the floor, arms limp at his side. He was the image of my Chris.

Chills sped down my spine. Then my shoulders began to shake with emotion. *There but for the grace of God could be my son, Chris!*

Then it struck me how selfish my reaction was. Did it matter that it was not my Chris? It might have been Christian Cole; he was someone's son and he needed help. For whatever reason I was here inside this prison where this lad's father could not be, as a Christian I was to care about this young man just as if he were my son.

Encouraging news came about "Slim," the member of our second class who had tried to escape shortly after his return to prison. His life had been threatened by another inmate, we were told, and though he had only months left on his sentence, he saw no other way out. One of our friends in Atlanta was already on the scene to help him. For the second time in a month I asked forgiveness for my too-hasty judgment of another.

Our visits to prisons, however, continued to be discouraging. Two of the men in our first class were from the Petersburg, Virginia, penitentiary, only a two-hour drive from Washington. They had reported real persecution after their return; a militant Muslim group threatened to beat them up, and their small Bible studies had to be conducted in secret. Fred and I decided to visit them as an encouragement.

The chaplain, a veteran of many years in the system and soon to retire, met us at the gate. He told us we could not visit with our inmate friends until we saw the warden who would not be available for an hour.

"Could we tour the prison?" Fred asked.

"Impossible. We can do nothing until we see the warden," he replied.

"Could we visit the chapel?" I inquired.

The chaplain shook his head irritably. And so we sat for nearly an hour in the visitor's area. At last a secretary appeared. The warden was ready to see us.

The chaplain's edginess increased as we neared the warden's office. "I think you should know that Mr. Mustain doesn't care much for these spiritual programs."

"Then will you ask him if we can tour the prison?" I asked.

"I don't know about that . . . we'll see."

Max Mustain was a new warden at the Petersburg facility. He had inherited a tough situation; only a few weeks before, the inmates had burned out one dormitory. The prison was badly overcrowded, racial tensions were high and the majority of the population were young offenders who create most disciplinary problems.

Two assistants flanked him when he entered. None of them smiled. "I'm Warden Mustain." He half rose from his chair, shook my hand and motioned to a straight chair before his large, mahogany desk.

Mustain was tall and gaunt; a neatly trimmed, black mustache and piercing eyes made his appearance even more severe than his gruff manners. After greeting us, he leaned back in his chair and crossed his feet on the desk top. I found myself staring at the soles of two large leather boots. "Well, what can we tell you, Mr. Colson?" he said, breaking the awkward silence.

"How many men do you have here?" I already knew the answer but needed to say something.

"As of this morning six hundred seventy one," he replied crisply without a second's hesitation.

The chaplain sat frozen in his chair and never once joined in the conversation. Nor did the two assistants who stared fixedly at me the whole uncomfortable 10 minutes we spent in the office.

"May we tour the prison?" I asked. Max Mustain shook his head. "Security has to come first."

"Then will you let us see the five Christian men I mentioned in the letter to you?"

He agreed to this. Shortly thereafter they were escorted to the visiting room, and we visited for a half hour with our friends.

The experience was disheartening. Even the chaplain seemed hostile. Then I recalled the advice given us from others who tried to start prison ministries: expect hostility and rejection. To prison officials you are amateur do-gooders who only create problems.

The visit offered little hope for the future. And Max Mustain seemed the perfect caricature of a warden: stern, cold, heartless.

While at a governors' prayer breakfast in a southern state these disillusioning experiences came to a head. The man next to me at the head table introduced himself: a judge of the federal district court. While we were eating he spoke of his admiration for former President Richard Nixon.

"You guys were on the right track," he said, "until all those crazy liberals brought you down."

I winced on the inside and continued to eat my scrambled eggs.

"Especially on law and order issues. Lock 'em up, I say, and throw away the keys."

The eggs stuck in my throat.

He pressed on. "In my district, I sentence everybody to the big house at Atlanta, not to any of those country clubs like Eglin and Maxwell."

I hoped my cold stare disguised the explosion taking place inside me. Since becoming a Christian my temper had become more docile, but it always flashed at that "country club" line. And this man knew nothing about me, I realized.

"Have you ever been there, Judge?" I asked.

"No, but I know all about those places. They're too good for criminals."

The food had lost its taste; I prayed silently for self-control.

My talk that morning dealt on my experiences at Maxwell. I felt a surging of the spirit as my words flowed forth about the needs of prisoners. Frequently I turned to my side, my eyes seeking the judge, who gaped at me in disbelief.

The governor then spoke about prison problems, singling me and our ministry out for generous praise. Though the governor knew nothing of my conversation with the judge, it was as if he were trying to pour ointment on my raw wounds. It only made me more angry.

What was happening to me? The law-and-order judge was no different from millions of other Americans in his approach to criminals. He took a position I had hotly defended only a few years before. Were my political beliefs changing? To some extent, yes. But at heart I was still a conservative on many issues.

Was I going the social action route? That one gave me pause. The injustices in our courts and the barbarism in our prisons aroused my anger and made me resolve to do something about it. Did this make me a do-gooder?

Then I recalled a speech given recently in a conservative church where at one point I said, "I believe in the literal truth of Scripture and the authority of the Bible." Choruses of "amens" roared through the sanctuary. Later I referred passionately to Christ's words that we are to visit those in prison. The sanctuary was silent.

A friend told me afterwards that next to him was a man who had been taking enthusiastic notes throughout the speech. When I urged visiting the prisons, he wrote somberly on his program, "Colson sounds like a do-gooder."

I wanted to shout at them: "Your argument is with Jesus!" But it didn't matter. If believing the literal truth of His words made me a "do-gooder," so be it.

When Fred and I boarded the flight to Washington, I was fighting a real case of the blues. Everywhere I was meeting defeats and upsets. I knew that my conversion had won me many new friends, but did they care at all about the terrible conditions in our prisons? I was trying hard to alert people to a real need. Was anyone listening? Sometimes I thought not.

As we made our way down the aisle of the plane, I saw a middle-aged black man look up and smile. Then he raised his hand, his index finger and thumb making a perfect circle.

"Hey, Mr. Colson. Right on. You are really helping our people. God bless you."

I waved back at him, and as Fred and I settled in our seats, I experienced a flood of overwhelming joy. "You know, Fred, that man's words meant more than all the flowery things the governor said about me this morning."

In an ironic footnote to that day, the prayer breakfast committee never did send us the contribution they promised to the ministry. But the smiling man on the plane handed us an envelope as we were getting off. In it was a five dollar bill and a note saying, "To help you with your work." It was the first public contribution to our ministry.

On the bottom of the note was written the perfect, two-word antidote to any discouragement: "Right on."

> ... *until we have wrestled with God till the break of day, like Jacob: that is, until we have struggled to the utmost limits of our strength, and have known the despair of defeat . . . [until] we have really understood the actual plight of our contemporaries, when we have heard their cry of anguish, [until] we have shared their suffering, both physical and spiritual, and their despair and desolation . . . then we shall be able to proclaim the word of God—but not till then!*
>
> JACQUES ELLUL

10. Wrestling with God

A series of good turns followed the black man's "right on." We learned that Kirk Schenk, the young man in Stillwater Prison who was sentenced to 10 years for a $20 unarmed robbery, was about to be released. It was a great victory over governmental red tape for our Minneapolis friends. Kirk's problems with alcohol were not solved, but at least he would be out of prison where we could help him.

Good reports were coming back as well from seminar graduates. Jackie Butner, from the second class, had begun a thriving fellowship at Lexington, Kentucky. "Soul" Adams, from the first class, was leading something close to a revival at Lewisburg with inmates and guards alike making decisions for the Lord. Some 150 of Soul's brothers turned out to welcome us when we visited this prison. Several men had started an "upper room" service at the Atlanta Federal Penitentiary. The warden at Morgantown, West Virginia, who had been skeptical about our program, wrote us that the chapel was now the center of activity in his prison.

For the first time, Fred reported, we were financially in the black. The Minneapolis men had been disappointed during my three-day speaking stint because only $3,400 was raised of the promised $5,000.

But soon after I returned to Washington, a check for $1,000 arrived from a man who sat next to me at a dinner; other checks trickled in. The total: $5,100. God had made good on my friends' pledge.

Meanwhile *Born Again* had reached the best-seller lists. Book royalties in excess of what was expected would soon be available for the work. Fred began to talk about setting up an office, hiring a full-time secretary and finalizing a nonprofit organization.

"We're not ready for that," I cautioned. So far the prison work had involved only about a fourth of my time. Logic warned me to keep other career options open. Patty wanted it that way. Inner emotions began tugging at me to get more involved, but I held them in check.

Patty met me at the front door one sunny afternoon with joyous news. "Myron and Nancy Mintz are going to have another child," she exclaimed.

The Mintzes had gone through a deep depression the past fall after the tragic crib death of their first child. For months afterwards Myron was subdued, sometimes sullen. Always a prodigious worker, he had plunged himself into his law practice in reckless disregard of his health. To get rid of ugly memories, Myron and Nancy had sold their home and bought another. They took up new hobbies. Gradually they pulled out of the doldrums, though Myron told me wistfully one day that they never expected another child.

Since Myron had become trustee of our family finances while I was in prison and continued this role after my release, we were together often. During one visit to my home, Myron brought several dozen copies of *Born Again* for me to autograph for friends. I was puzzled.

"Myron, you and I have been close in politics, and we are good friends, but this is a Christian book, you know."

Myron smiled. "Sure, Boss. I know that."

"It has a pretty pointed message."

"You mean because I'm a Jew I'm not supposed to like it? I've got a few Christian friends, you know."

"I guess it surprises me how many Jewish people are so attracted to the Person of Jesus," I replied.

Myron stared at me intently, his graying curly hair tousled as always, a large lock over his forehead. "I've never told you this, but when I was in the government several years ago a man came to see me with a legal problem. In the middle of the meeting he stopped talking, looked at me and said, 'You have a problem too. You don't know what to do with your job and your life.' He was absolutely right. Then right there, right in my office, he prayed for me."

"He was a Christian?"

"Yes, like you," Myron replied. "It was only a few days later that you called me about coming to your law firm. Kind of strange, huh?"

"No, not strange, Myron. That's the way the Lord works. Maybe you and I ought to have a talk about Him sometime."

"Me?" He pointed his index finger into his chest, then shook his head. "That's not for me, but *Born Again* I like and understand." He gestured for me to sign more books.

I wondered later if I had failed my friend. Perhaps I should have nudged him a little harder. Before large crowds I had learned to give altar calls but face-to-face encounters with old friends were often awkward, something I knew the Lord would have to resolve.

The decision to hold a third prisoner seminar in May was made soon after the meeting where I offered to turn my prison work over to John Staggers. My giving it up seemed to remove the tension. Even John acted relieved. He declined the responsibility, though, saying he would concentrate on his work at Lorton Prison, leaving the seminars to us.

There were confirming signs that we were back on the track. The selection process went almost effortlessly as Paul Kramer encountered little opposition to our choices from prison administrators; every selection for the second class had involved strenuous negotiations.

Paul was growing fast on the job. Unsure of himself during those first months out of prison, seeing less of me than he had expected, the unaccustomed loneliness had been hard on him. Prison tends to deaden a person's ability to make decisions and act. Coming suddenly into freedom and responsibility can be a traumatic adjustment. Now he was growing stronger by the day, helped by Bible studies and a caring group of people at Fellowship House.

An important dimension was added to the third class in the person of a brilliant instructor, George Soltau of Dallas, Texas. George, a third-generation Reformed Presbyterian minister, volunteered his services and gave real professionalism to our teaching. Because of his background in prison work, he also made us aware of one common thread which ran through the lives of most inmates: a history of continuous rejection. Often it begins in infancy with a broken home or alcoholic parents or parental beatings. The rejection continues through school and inevitably produces an encounter with the law. Since prison is society's ultimate rejection, many years of confinement leave the individual's sense of self-worth so battered that he or she simply cannot comprehend God's love. A person's inability to accept himself becomes an obstacle to accepting others, including Christ.

Soltau's experience was that it wasn't too hard to persuade a convicted criminal, who is honest with himself, of his own sinfulness and thus his need for repentance. But it is hard for him to believe that he can ever be forgiven and that he can achieve self-worth. This then encourages criminal conduct: one with no self-worth tends to see no worth in others. Life is valueless; a crime against another produces no guilt. It is a vicious and unending cycle and once caught in it, the criminal has almost no way out but through the drastic transformation produced by genuine conversion.

Soltau's insights caused us to reshape the curriculum. Several lessons would deal with the characteristics of God and how man is made in His image. Once the prisoner could learn to love himself, we felt that he would find a previously undiscovered ability to love others.

The third class of prisoners arrived safely in Washington, studied hard and proved to be an intelligent and trustworthy group with the most potential for leadership of any class so far.

At a time when I needed encouragement the mail from readers of *Born Again* began arriving at home in stacks, often 40 to 50 letters banded together. One of the greatest joys of my life was to sit at our kitchen table each day reading them.

A husband and wife were reconciled after six months of separation when each of them were given copies by friends. Another couple wrote that they had found the courage to acknowledge they were alcoholics, sought help and now believed they were on the road to recovery.

A criminal defendant awaiting trial wrote, "Your book had a profound effect on my decision to plead guilty." An inmate at Soledad Prison in California reported, "Midway through your testimony, I began crying, and as I cried harder I hurriedly got up and put a coat over the small window in my cell door so men passing by wouldn't see me. After twenty-four years in institutions (I'm 40) I don't think I've ever felt such an unexplainable feeling of happiness."

Letters came great distances. A 37-year-old businessman and senator in the Philippine government wrote how the book had led to changes in his life. Breaking ties with the New People's Army, an underground Communist organization, was his first step. Then he summoned his 70 employees together to announce that his business would thereafter be a Christian enterprise and as evidence gave them a salary increase. Finally, he went home to his wife from whom he had been separated.

Another letter from the British Virgin Islands told about "Soloman," a trusted employee in the small business of an American couple. Employee theft was apparently a big problem on the island, but Soloman was considered to be above suspicion. One day he arrived at the couple's home with *Born Again* under one arm and a brown bag under the other. "Here," he said, handing the book to his employers, "please read this and then forgive me. You'll understand." Then he handed them the bag which he explained contained all he had stolen from them. Inside was $8,000 in damp and musty bills.

For 40 years an unyielding mechanism inside me had kept tight control over every one of my surface emotions. They were weaknesses which had to be held in check. But ever since the tears flowed so freely and joyously that August night in 1973 outside Tom Phillips' house, I felt not a tinge of embarrassment about them. When the Holy Spirit spoke powerfully through letters like these, I often found myself weeping.

One unforgettable one opened with the same confession:

> *Born Again* has stirred me with hope that I can find meaning and purpose for my life. I have never been moved to such emotion on the subject of faith and Christ. I couldn't stop the tears which so many of the incidents you related brought to my eyes. I was ashamed of myself for such lack of control. I moved to another room so my family wouldn't notice this strange reaction. At one point—your testimony at Brother Blow's Tuesday night service—I actually began sobbing. I was startled and shaken by my lack of composure and yet, at the same time, happy that I could feel such emotion.
>
> Then, I prayed. I prayed for guidance in how I might truly accept Christ and become, at least, a "baby in Christ."
>
> I've achieved "success" as it is commonly measured and have a loving, Christian wife and three bright, healthy, straight-arrow children. Still, I'm the mid-40s guy you describe, afraid I'm losing my grip, unhappy, perplexed and ashamed before God that I am not happy because I'm so fully blessed. I have gotten up in the middle of the night to stare across an empty living room, consumed with anger toward my "enemies" and planned how to manipulate and maneuver them as well as to ponder how I am being manipulated and maneuvered.

To me, your most important message is that acceptance of Christ and understanding of its meaning is a continuing growth experience. Somehow, I have always felt it must be a one-time, cataclysmic occurrence from which point forward a person has totally "different" feelings, attitudes and behavior toward others. But now I think I understand these are only awakenings. I'm truly excited and I desperately wish to be born again.

Sincerely,
Alan Steuber
Wayland, Mass.

I answered Alan's letter immediately and sent a copy to Tom Phillips who lived in the next town, suggesting that Tom invite him to his regular fellowship breakfast. A few weeks later I received another letter, which read in part as follows:

Dear Chuck,

The past five weeks have been the most remarkable and wonderful weeks of my life. When I felt compelled to write you after reading *Born Again* I looked upon it as some sort of emotional catharsis. I realize now my letter was a cry for help and I now understand the way Christians respond to such a plea.

When Tom Phillips contacted me I was startled, even a little wary. It was one thing to write a letter, but was I ready to discuss these new and strange emotions with a man I didn't even know?

I have been attending a weekly prayer breakfast with Tom these past four weeks and it has been thrilling. The first time there I had something of the same reaction you expressed in the book. "Do grown men really sit around in a public restaurant and openly discuss their deeply personal experiences, talk about Jesus Christ as if He were sitting at the table with us, pray aloud?" But they do and now I do also. Brotherhood in Christ. I *know* what it means!

I also know what it means to be a "baby in Christ." I have so much to learn, so much growing to do. But each day is a wonderful experience as I read and search for truth and understanding in prayer and discussion with my new Christian friends. I'm like a starving man suddenly placed at a banquet table. I haven't yet disciplined myself. I devour every piece of Christian reading I can lay my hands on.

God bless you,
Alan Steuber

Reading Al's letters were like reliving my own conversion, the fresh excitement, all over again. His letters renewed my spirit in a very profound way because I knew that no matter how many discouragements I'd faced, no matter what the cost, no matter how hard the road ahead, it was worth it all.

Another exchange of letters was to be as influential in my life but in a far more sobering way. There was a young man named Yuzo Dort who had written a long letter to me in care of the publisher. In it Yuzo recounted his life history. Born in Japan, he was educated in the U.S., and for the last three years had been a professor of economics in New Hampshire. Then he explained:

> I am originally a Japanese who had no chance to be exposed to Christianity until I was legally adopted by a *real* Christian family in America who had no children. This was when I was 28 years old. Even after I lived with my adoptive parents and found that Christianity was something wonderful, I could not commit myself to Christ. I have asked and prayed God to bring me the Holy Spirit and change my heart as a Christian. I go to different churches on Sundays almost regularly. But nothing has happened . . .

The rest of the letter was an appeal for prayer and to be born again. Elsewhere in the letter Yuzo mentioned that he was unemployed. Then came a second letter:

> I have become a Christian . . . my faith in Christ is not as strong as yours but am trying hard . . . it is indeed wonderful to be born again! On the contrary to my present situation without a job for such a long time, I feel very secure. It is a priceless feeling.

For some reason, perhaps the childlike enthusiasm so powerfully conveyed in his adopted language, Yuzo's letter stuck in my mind. A few weeks later I pulled them out of the stack and wrote a short reply. Then as an afterthought, I sent his letters to a friend who might help him to find a job. I prayed for him as I sealed the envelope. Soon a reply came from Yuzo:

> Thank you very much for your personal letter. The day it arrived I was so low in my spirit that I had almost lost my faith in the Lord. To tell the truth, I was even thinking of finishing up myself. I have tried all possibilities in finding a job but was rejected by them all. After such a prolonged period of unemployment, I started thinking of myself as worthless.
> It is not too much to say that your letter saved my life. I will continuously keep looking for a job with my trust in God.
> Enclosed please find a check. Since I am unemployed I do not have

much, but please let me do something for your ministry. I also wish to express my sincere appreciation, in some way, for your giving me the opportunity to be born again.

> Sincerely yours,
> Yuzo Kunimi Dort

The words "I was thinking of finishing myself" leaped up at me from the page. A flashing, feverish sensation spread all over my body, like tiny pinpricks piercing my flesh followed by near nausea. "What if . . ." I mumbled to myself, "what if I hadn't written Yuzo?" I put the letter down and stared at the far corner of the room. *What if? What if?* The words bombarded me until I felt limp.

In the envelope was a check for $100. I scribbled an immediate reply. "I appreciate your check more than I can tell you," I wrote. "I do not believe when a gift is given in the Lord it should ever be refused, and so I am holding it. But I do not intend to cash it until you have found employment."

I didn't have to wait long. A few days later, I heard that Yuzo had a job. The check was the first of what would become a monthly tithe by him to the prison work.

These letters, and the awesome responsibility toward our prisoner graduates, began drawing me toward a major decision.

But there were still Patty's deep concerns. Throughout my pressured years in the White House and during the intense strain of the Watergate months followed by my prison sentence, Patty had drawn on a deep reservoir of strength to comfort and reassure her beleaguered husband. In the process she proved herself a remarkable woman.

But in some ways the past 16 months of our post-prison life had produced the most wrenching strain of all. Though she seldom complained, our once quiet house was often in near bedlam. Mail covered two large desks. My secretary from Fellowship House often worked in our basement. There was a steady stream of visitors; Fred and Paul Kramer were two who met there with me regularly. Phone calls came at all hours; many which Patty had to handle were invitations to speak or appear at rallies. Patty's loving nature and patience were being sorely stretched.

Beneath it all were brooding concerns about our future. Patty sensed what was happening in my life and she resisted it. One night during a rare dinner alone together, she stared at me somberly.

"You just aren't an evangelist, Chuck." She had said it before, but the bluntness of her words now startled me. I realized that I had been talking nonstop all through the meal about one appearance where many people had responded to my invitation to come forward.

I put down my coffee cup, wiped my lips with the napkin, stalling for time. My pride was showing too, pricked by her words, and Patty realized this.

"I mean, you're good at whatever you do, Chuck, but you can't make this your career."

"I suppose not," I sighed. I realized suddenly that the heavy volume of complimentary mail, the adulation of people after speeches, the VIP treatment were all getting to me. It was such a contrast to the vibrations of hate I had experienced for so many months that I was literally soaking it up.

"I'm not sure I really belong in this with you," she continued.

I was surprised somehow that Patty, whose poise and charm were equal to any challenge, should feel inadequate in this area. "Honey, you come first. We'll work it out together," I assured her as I reached for her hand across the table.

In a few weeks we would be leaving for a trip to Europe. Perhaps this would give us both a fresh outlook on life. Certainly by August 1, I needed to make a firm decision about our future.

Events were happening so fast that it was hard to find time to think. But I had to, for much was at stake. For example, what had I learned so far through the prison work?

For one thing, the controversy between John Staggers and myself had continued too long without either of us dealing with the real issues. Had I guarded too closely my true inner feelings? Even in small Christian fellowship groups when sincere effort is made to lay bare one's soul, our defense mechanism is so preconditioned that we let others see only what we want them to see. The result is that the internal bruises remain tender for too long a time.

The confrontation with John, as I reflected upon it, had resulted in my learning two of the most important lessons of my young Christian life.

The first dealt with what Christian unity really means. In his epistles Paul talks repeatedly about the need for Christians to be of one mind and one heart. The new churches in his time were constantly embroiled in disagreements with the integrity of the Gospel often at issue, so unity over central articles of faith had to be a prime concern for Paul.

A lot of Christians, myself included, believed that unity meant achieving real togetherness at all costs, as if being of one mind in everything was the very object of the Christian life.

Two prominent political figures I knew boasted that though they differed greatly, even on moral questions, they could always achieve perfect oneness in their Christian fellowship. They accomplished this by never discussing the issues which might threaten their harmony. But is this spiritual unity or merely superficial sociality?

It can't be right, I decided, for Christians to put aside all differences and submit blindly to one another for the sake of apparent unity. Such unity would be frustrating and eventually deadening. The result would be mindless conformity.

In time I saw that what Paul was dealing with in the young churches were disagreements which were fundamental; some were split over who Christ was. Unity had to be a prime goal because the integrity of the Christian faith was at issue. The truth of the Gospel could not be compromised then as it cannot be today. Followers must unite on this.

But Paul did not mean we were to stifle disagreements or achieve peace in every relationship regardless of the cost. His own actions demonstrated this.

He risked rupturing the young church by facing down Peter on the issue of circumcision; he must have felt he had no choice, because again that issue dealt with the fundamental truth of the Gospel. Through a wrenching experience, Paul himself later broke with Barnabas, who was the very person the Holy Spirit had used to call Paul from obscurity and launch him into service.

Unity is *a* goal of the Christian life, I concluded, but it is not *the* end in itself. Unlike a covenant relationship entered into in the sight of God such as marriage, which the Christian *must* honor, the relationships formed among different individuals may not always result in the same kind of unity.

With John Staggers and me it was important that we approach our differences lovingly, with tolerance for one another's views, speak openly and honestly; and then surrender to God any disharmony which might remain. We can be in one body, part of His family, united in belief, and yet labor in different fields. Sometimes that is exactly what God wants. For helping me learn this teaching—and the sudden freedom which came from it—I was very grateful to John Staggers.

The second lesson was as important. In order to gain something, it must be given up first. Mature Christians understand this, but it is a jolting discovery for the new believer. And it is contrary to every human instinct. Jesus says, "Whoever loses his life for My sake, shall find it"—the absolute antithesis of what most people in our acquisitive society are conditioned to think.

All my life I labored for success, wealth, acceptance and power. The more I obtained, the less I discovered I had. Surrendering everything in absolute brokenness, however, was the beginning of finding the identity and purpose for which I had battled so hard. In giving up my life to Christ, I had found it.

The same thing happened with the prison work. For nine months I struggled to control it, though in our fellowship we never wanted our real desires to appear that obvious. Yet the harder I reached for the reins, the more elusive they were to grasp. When I stepped aside, gave it all up in honest relinquishment, the Lord gave it back.

"Dying to self," "honest repentance," and "taking up the cross" are phrases that so many new believers find to be incomprehensible or once comprehended, painful and hence forgettable. No one wants to "lose" his life or suffer as Christ did. The verses we Christians choose to remember are the promises of what God will do for us, not the conditions He demands in return. I was discovering this to be a very one-sided way to look at our relationship with our Creator.

Then I realized something with a shock: If the prison ministry was my call, my hesitation was like ignoring God's demand. August 1 had to be a firm deadline.

11. The Gospel Overseas

Fathers are said to have a particularly warm spot in their hearts for daughters. This is certainly so with me. At 18 Emily had become a beautiful young lady with long, flowing blonde hair and sparkling blue eyes. As a high school graduation present, we invited her to accompany Patty and me on a trip to Europe.

Born Again was being translated for publication in Germany, Holland, England, Sweden and Finland. The European publishers invited me for television appearances, press conferences and a few speeches, a six-day swing through six countries, but even that should be less arduous than my recent two-month tour through the States.

We flew to England in early June. Patty and Emily stayed to vacation in London while I took a flight to Brussels where I received my first shock.

A Christian layman, Fred Ladenius, and I were sitting at a corner table in one of the charming little bistros that line the picturesque cobblestone streets of this old world city. My host was a big, square-shouldered man in his late 30s, who had recently joined the new office of the Full Gospel Businessmen in Brussels. Probing for information I asked, "How many Christians are there in Belgium?"

Ladenius ran his hand through his flowing blonde hair and looked up at the ceiling for a few seconds. "Oh, I'd say a thousand maybe—if we looked hard."

"Only a thousand in a country of 10 million people!"

Ladenius broke into a wide grin. "You Americans," he laughed, "you don't understand. Things here in Europe aren't like the States. One thousand is good. There probably aren't that many in Spain and Italy combined."

He had to be kidding, I thought. But now Ladenius leaned across the table toward me, his eyes piercing. "The organized church in these countries is nothing but an arm of the state; it is impotent. The governments are moving left. Materialism is god. We are recruiting key Christians across the Continent, setting up, how would you say, an underground. Soon that may be all there is."

My new friend had spent 15 years as a Roman Catholic layman working in the Vatican. During that time he had become involved in the lay renewal movement, traveling throughout Europe. Now he had returned to his native Belgium to build a Christian beachhead in the strategic city of Brussels, where many European and international economic missions are headquartered.

"When you're in Rome, look up Father Morlion. Promise me," Ladenius said, scribbling Morlion's address on a scrap of paper.

"Will he know me?" I asked.

"Yes. He'll be at your hotel the night you arrive. He's sort of our leader—informally." The knowing look of a skilled, cloak-and-dagger operative crossed my friend's face. I thought perhaps he had been watching too many spy movies, but then I remembered how Europeans enjoy being secretive and a bit smug around what they believe to be innocent and naïve Americans.

We walked through darkened alleyways back to the Hilton Hotel. "We're counting on you, Brother," he said before we parted. "Speak out on television and in the papers. People in America—and here, too—will listen to you. We must be working together for what's coming."

It was a sobering introduction to the Continent even though I believed my new friend was exaggerating a bit. Like most Americans I was parochial, my view of the world always seen through the prism of our own culture, going on the blithe and erroneous assumption that almost everyone enjoys the same freedom and openness we do.

At the very moment that Ladenius and others like him were preparing for the worst, a burgeoning evangelical movement in the U.S.

was becoming front page news. Church attendance was rising after 17 consecutive years of decline. Christians, reveling in the new-found respectability of their faith, were wearing it on their sleeves; some were even advertising it in so-called "Christian Yellow Pages." Excesses always seem to accompany revivals. A movement to elect "born again Christians" to public office was gathering strength across the country. The prime exhibit of the "born again" phenomenon, Jimmy Carter, was now front-runner for the Democratic presidential nomination.

My talk with Ladenius that summer of 1976 indicated that the United States and Europe were worlds apart in the practice of the Christian faith. At home it was culturally accepted, even fashionable; in Europe it was barely visible, a tiny minority struggling to keep from being swallowed up by a hostile sea of agnosticism and materialism.

The following morning I spoke to a breakfast gathering of the committed faithful in Brussels. Seventy-five appeared, half of them Americans. Only a few mildly curious reporters showed up for a press conference later.

That Saturday afternoon I flew from Brussels to Hannover, Germany, where I was met by Friederich Haenssler, the first European publisher to translate *Born Again* and its most enthusiastic advocate. A towering figure among European evangelicals, Friederich's muscular frame, jutting jaw and angular features give him a commanding bearing. Though his English is halting, he has such spiritual warmth that we communicated easily and became fast friends.

Each year in the small northern farming community of Krelingen, Germany, a church pastor, Heinrich Kemner, hosts a giant outdoor rally. It is the best known evangelistic event in Germany. Haenssler had arranged for me to speak at the Sunday service. I was allotted exactly 18 minutes and then warned that the program was run with the precision of a fine German clock.

It was a chill, overcast morning when we arrived at the huge outdoor meeting place. Haenssler escorted me to the back of a windswept, wooden platform. The crowd stretched before us across a vast open field, most sitting on crude benches, spilling out under the tall pines on both sides.

At the precise moment planned, Pastor Kemner arose and started toward the microphone. A bear of a man, close to 300 pounds, he rocked from side to side as he moved across the platform and stood before the audience. When he stretched out his arms, his black robes hung straight down from his wrists to the ground; the imposing sight brought an instant hush to the crowd.

By now a healthy case of stage fright was gripping me. It is tough enough with a crowd this size, but this was also to be my first speech through a translator, Winfried Bluth, a knowledgeable and articulate Christian. He and I had spent a short time practicing together, but even for someone with experience, it is a fine art. The two—speaker and translator—have to develop a rhythm, preferably short, staccato sentences, often overlapping with the speaker beginning again just as the translator is about to conclude the previous sentence. Extreme concentration is demanded; pauses can be as deadly for the speaker as for the audience.

The crowd, well over 10,000 I was told, was on its feet lustily singing hymns, the music provided by a small, red-jacketed brass band. A giant, throbbing tuba set the beat, "oompa, oompa," as the booming bass notes sent waves of near martial excitement through the throng.

"Remember, exactly 18 minutes," Bluth whispered into my ear as the crowd settled back onto their benches. Unseen hands were clutching at my stomach; it was far too cold to perspire, so my nervousness, thankfully, didn't show. Pastor Kemner began to introduce me, swinging his robe-draped arms toward me, his deep voice thundering out across the fields. Bluth answered my quizzical look. "He's saying very nice things about you." He might have been saying almost anything for all I could tell.

I followed my interpreter to the microphones. The biting wind was blowing straight at us and I was grateful for the powerful amplifier. I remembered reading how the colonial evangelist, George Whitefield, a scrawny little fellow, had a voice so powerful that it needed no amplifier to be heard by the thousands who flocked into the open fields. Miraculous, I thought.

I began with the only German words I knew. "Guten Morgen." There was an appreciative stirring, but most of the people, huddling together with coats or blankets wrapped around them, sat unmoved. The stares seemed stern and forbidding. I began racing through my testimony so fast I sometimes forgot my translator. Several times Bluth was forced to cut in, glancing at me with a warning expression.

Then we settled into a seesaw rhythm. Still there was no acknowledgment from the audience. I found myself longing for a Baptist "amen" corner or just a simple grin or nod in response to my wan attempts at humor.

Maybe the translator is not getting it right, I thought, as I stared at the row upon row of people sitting as rigid as tombstones. When I described how I asked Christ into my life, Bluth began speaking with obvious passion, but the stares grew even more fierce, I thought. I kept looking at my watch; at least we were right on schedule.

Just as I was coming to my conclusion, one of Kemner's assistants moved immediately behind me, a signal I assumed, that my time was up. His standing there brought the welcome thought that my agony would soon be over.

Then he tugged at my coat. "The pastor says take as long as you want," he whispered. "You are really getting to them."

He must be joking, I thought. My expression betrayed my feelings. "Please, keep going," he repeated.

Aware of the frustration over a divided Germany into an East and West, I talked about Christ's reconciling power. I prayed that the revival beginning in the United States might spread throughout the world. I finished, picked up my Bible and notes, turned, and started for my chair when applause began in the front. Then it spread across the field gathering force as it rippled out.

The people who came forward shook my hand and smiled shyly. A student at a Bible camp who spoke excellent English unlocked the mystery of the crowd's apparent stoniness. "Mr. Colson, we sat in stunned silence because we have never heard anyone in Germany talk about Jesus personally." His eyes were misty as he shook my hand and then slipped away into the dispersing crowd.

German Christians resist any show of emotion. When Billy Graham spoke to a convocation of young people at Essen, the church sponsors insisted he not ask people to come forward; they felt the altar call too demonstrative for reserved Europeans. Billy told me later that now he always asks people to make a decision in European cities and they stream forward.

Pastor Kemner feasted us at his country home overlooking lush meadows and rich, green forests. Plates of boiled meats, homemade sausages, potato salad, fresh vegetables and pitchers of well-aged cider were passed around the huge, rectangular table. It was the first hearty meal I could enjoy since leaving the States three days earlier.

I learned that less than two percent of all Germans attended church. The services are heavy on liturgy, the sermons usually lifeless. Most pastors are employees of the state, politicized and bereft of any spiritual mission. "The church," Haenssler said, "is like a . . . how do you say?" He made a motion with his hands like passing out money.

"A welfare agency?" I suggested.

"Ya, velfare agency. Dot is it." He grinned and nodded.

Haenssler helped me see how dead the church is when it becomes a national institution as it is throughout Europe. In 312 A.D. under Emperor Constantine the process began that a few decades later would make Christianity the official state religion of the empire. The church along with the state then declined in vitality, its influence first co-opted, then corrupted. Entering the Middle Ages the state church grew into the church-state, as the theocracy cloaked civil political muscle with religious authority. Wars for political gain became "holy crusades."

The church's corruption became complete as biblical doctrines were distorted, the church defying and then denying scriptural authority. The lessening moral influence of the church opened the door to renaissance humanism. Societies empty of biblical truth began to seek other answers. Its corruption continued as the church exploitively "sold" forgiveness, the cynical practice called "indulgences," which so incensed the reformers of the 16th century. Though the reformation had far-reaching political consequences, it did not destroy the tradition by which the state maintained its control of the church. To this day official state churches dominate Europe.

I also had some new insights about the situation in the United States. It was against the background of this unhappy European experience that the framers of the U.S. Constitution so jealously guarded the independence of the church from state encroachment. Wasn't this the real but unseen danger, I wondered, in the enthusiastic efforts then underway in America to organize a Christian political effort? Not that it is wrong for Christians to get into politics; that's healthy. But if a Christian political movement succeeded as such, the Christians assuming power would soon not only be subject to the corruptions of politics but would also have to be at least partially responsibile for the political fortunes of the state. The experience in Europe clearly indicated that such a Christian church could lead only to a dead end for the Gospel.

Haenssler was as gloomy about the faithless Europeans as was Ladenius. "Without a great spiritual movement, Europe dies," he repeated several times. "There are forty thousand East German spies in the West. All our people want is money, autos, and time off. They don't know what is happening."

As the biggest Christian publisher in Western Europe, many of

Haenssler's books find their way into Eastern Europe. All of his profits, he said, were being plowed back into printing materials such as tracts which could be spread among the people. When I asked him how he could afford it, he said, "It is simple. Some years ago I gave my business to Jesus." The name Jesus was spoken with such warmth and softness that my spirit was moved.

Since we had to be in Bonn at 9:30 A.M. the next day for a press conference, Haenssler decided we should get up early and drive. He allowed two and a half hours for a 400 kilometer trip. We were strapped into a huge Mercedes belonging to a young man soon to be Haenssler's son-in-law. Only as he put on driving gloves, methodically stroking one finger at a time into the snug leather, did I have any inkling of what I was in for. Then I calculated: 400 kilometers is 240 miles. In two and one-half hours! We would have to average close to 100 miles per hour.

There are no speed limits on German autobahns, and cars travel like low-trajectory artillery shells. The passing traffic was only a blur as I glanced over at the speedometer; we were going close to 150 miles per hour. Our young driver was staring beady-eyed at the road, obviously frustrated that he was born too late to pilot a Messerschmitt, I thought. The mighty roar of the tires was interrupted only by the occasional whooshing noise of another car being passed. It's not hard to understand why statistics in Germany record so few people injured in auto accidents; at these speeds, an accident means instant death.

The angels were with us, however, and we arrived with time to spare. The press conference in Bonn was well attended, but we soon discovered that almost every reporter was from the Eastern European papers. It was explained that the Communists were curious about me and Mr. Nixon. The West German reporters seemed completely disinterested in my current mission.

German television refused to cover us just as they had refused to show the movie, *The Hiding Place,* even when it was offered at no charge. "It is nearly impossible," Haenssler explained "to get on German television or in the German papers with a Christian message." Not even Billy Graham was covered. The German press corps is not just indifferent to the Gospel; it is hostile.

I was disheartened to learn that few Germans knew anything about Alexander Solzhenitsyn or his prophetic warnings to the Western world. When I quoted from Solzhenitsyn's widely publicized BBC interview, many said they were startled to hear he was a Christian. The free German press, I learned, had reported little of Solzhenitsyn and nothing spiritual.

My mind wandered back to the "Today" show and hundreds of interviews like it, to Christian television, to the hundreds of church services televised nationally and locally throughout America. Indeed we take much for granted.

Though we had been together for only 48 hours, I felt a close kinship to Haenssler. "We are putting much faith into *Born Again*," he told me as we were parting. "It can be the breakthrough—if we can start Germans reading it." It was hard to believe that Germans read so few Christian books, had no religious television or coverage in the press and a woefully crippled church.

Haenssler's decision not to call the book *Born Again* in Germany, but *Watergate—As No One Has Seen It Before* was understandable. The phrase "born again" would be virtually unknown in Germany. He did not tell me until we were saying good-by at the airport that the book's cover phrase, "What really happened to the White House hatchet man?" could not easily be translated either. "Hatchet man" is an American slang phrase; in German it means literally that—a forester. The editors came up instead with something Germans could understand: "What really happened to the White House *Hangman*."

"Thanks, Brother," I replied. "Now I can understand why the crowds here were so silent. I'm lucky they didn't stone me."

The situation was different in Amsterdam. The Dutch have a tradition of religious freedom and pluralism. As the old saying goes, when two Dutchmen get together, they form a church; when there are three Dutchmen there will be two churches. As a result the church, while occasionally chaotic, is strong compared to most other European countries.

The press conference at the airport was lively; one of the Dutch television stations did a half-hour special, and the reporters even seemed mildly interested in my conversion. But even in Holland there were grim reminders of the moral deterioration of the West. Since we had a free evening, I asked my hosts if I might see Amsterdam, one of the loveliest cities in Europe and one of the few I had never visited.

"Oh, no," my host seemed surprised at my innocence. "People seldom go downtown after dark," he explained. "Amsterdam has become a sin city, full of narcotics, prostitution and crime." As I pressed the point he became more adamant. "We will have a quiet dinner in the country and put you on a plane in the morning." In the country which had produced such giants as the theologian and one-time prime minister, Abraham Kuyper, and the beloved Corrie ten Boom, tragically this beautiful city had become unsafe to walk at night.

In Copenhagen I faced an intensely hostile battery of newsmen. "Let me tell you about my decision for Jesus Christ," I began when there was a reprieve from the barrage of questions.

"No, tell us about your war crimes in Vietnam," a wiry lad in the back of the crowded room shot back. For 90 minutes the battle went back and forth. Happily some of the spiritual part got through in the next day's papers.

As in Amsterdam, I was told not to walk the streets of Copenhagen at night where flashing lights welcomed passersby to the erotic pleasures of the world's most uninhibited pornography shops. Less than a century ago, the hunched-over figure of Søren Kierkergaard, Christian prophet and great philosopher, could be seen roaming the same streets at all hours. For me it was as if time and 20th-century progress had despoiled hallowed ground.

The reaction of Sweden, then socialist, was similar. Swedish television and press treatment was extensive, but the questioning from reporters was fierce. Sweden was then the haven for a large colony of Vietnam deserters and war resisters. Ninety-five percent of the Swedish people, I was told, belong to the state church; one and a half percent attend. Happily there are small but healthy Baptist, Pentecostal and Evangelical Covenant churches, which, I was told, my visit encouraged.

In Finland unexpected treasures were awaiting. The Finnair DC9, buffeted by strong arctic winds, made a steep nose-down approach to the Helsinki airport. Below us were crystal blue lakes, swollen by a spring thaw, and vast brown countryside as far as the eye could see. The sterile architecture of the small, glass-faced terminal was in keeping, I thought, with the frozen northland and its people. How wrong I was. Valter Luoto, the Finnish publisher, was standing just on the other side of the customs gate when we arrived. A warm smile spread across his round face and both arms were outstretched in a sign of welcome, transcending all language differences.

"Mr. Colson, Brother," Luoto exclaimed as he embraced me, almost lifting my feet off the floor. His editor, a heavyset woman wrapped in a bushy fur coat and carrying a bouquet of flowers, was next; two bulging rosy cheeks protruded under a shock of blonde hair clipped over her eyes. Finns are part Nordic, part Slavic in origin and I was pleasantly surprised to find them exceptionally warm and outgoing. I was never made to feel at home so quickly.

But Finland, a nation of only four and a half million, shares a 789-mile-long frontier with Russia, its neighbor to the east. As a result, official Finnish neutrality over the years has taken on a heavily pro-Soviet cast. The press, some of it obviously Communist, met us in a downtown hotel room.

"How can you, a Nixon loyalist, come here talking about morality? Your Mr. Nixon's war policies threatened world peace. Now that we are finally rid of that tyrant Richard Nixon . . ." As the battering became heckling, I could feel my face flushing.

"Have all the fun with me you want, but Mr. Nixon had the guts to begin strategic arms limitation talks and sign the first agreements to end the cold war. Nowhere in the world should any people be more grateful than you here in Helsinki, sitting on the powder-keg spot where East meets West."

For a moment there was sober silence; Communists respect firmness. The rest of the meeting dealt with my conversion and the power of Christ to reconcile. Much of it made the front pages of local papers. My experience on U.S. talk shows was good training for Finnish television which is beamed into the Soviet Union; Watergate questions evoked answers about Jesus Christ. My new Christian friends were elated.

That afternoon I was taken to the Finnish Parliament to meet informally with the nine members of the embattled Christian Party. When we were escorted into the Senate chambers, I saw their opposition— 30 grim-faced, black-suited senators of the Communist Party. A lanky man in his late 50s, Raino Westerholm, was introduced as the Christian Party leader. A forester and farmer, Raino was one of the most respected layman in the country and considered a leading presidential candidate in the future elections.

Westerholm summoned his colleagues for a meeting in a small room off the Senate floor. It was one of the most exciting hours I have spent anywhere in the world; the fellowship was warm, the prayers, repeated through our translator, moving. Much of our time was spent discussing Solzhenitsyn's speeches to the West. For fear of offending the government, his writings were not translated by Finnish publishers; yet every Christian senator was familiar with them and with Solzhenitsyn's Christian commitment. How ironic, I thought: in West Germany where the press is free, little is known about Solzhenitsyn. In Finland the truth of the maxim—that persecution often strengthens the church—was coming home to me.

That night Valter Luoto had arranged for me to speak at a downtown church. As our old black Mercedes rumbled through the streets of Helsinki, I was reminded of Moscow—large, gray, factory-style buildings, rows of lifeless tenements interspersed with occasional onion-domed structures. Other parts of the city are modern Scandinavian with expanses of reflecting glass, steel and richly polished wood facing.

We drove down a dark alley to what looked like a warehouse entrance, then climbed up a narrow flight of back stairs to the pastor's tiny, cluttered office. Kai Antturi, a short, rugged young man greeted us as all Finns did, with an embrace and beaming smile. Pastor Antturi, I learned, had been arrested many times at the Soviet border. Finnish Christians view their sprawling Russian neighbor to the east with missionary fervor; cassettes, tracts and books, along with a few hardy pastors like Kai, spill over the frozen frontier.

Word seems to spread through the Christian grapevine very fast in Finland. The cavernous but simple sanctuary of the converted warehouse contained 1,500 people. Kai's introduction, interpreted for me by my translator whispering into my right ear, concluded: "Mr. Colson has come thousands of miles across the seas to tell us of the love of Christ. Let's give our brother from America a warm Finnish welcome."

I walked to the pulpit, expecting applause. But the hall was absolutely silent. Surprised, I looked at the rows of round faces peering over the high-backed pews, ladies with black mantillas pulled tightly about their heads, men with black work jackets. There was not a smile.

A warm Finnish welcome, I thought, puzzled. Then I thrust my arms out and clutched my hands together, a symbol of greeting my translator suggested. All at once, as if hundreds of nesting birds were disturbed and their wings began fluttering, hands were raised. Then in mechanically jerky movements, as if hinged at the wrists, they began waving. At my startled expression their big grins turned to friendly laughter.

There were warm smiles and nods throughout my talk. When I finished the hands fluttered again; it was, I discovered, a Finnish custom—a delightful one after the initial shock.

Afterwards we ate together in the home of a doctor: an egg mixture wrapped in potato pancakes, herring, fruit and rich cakes. When we were joined by Westerholm and several of the Christian senators who had been in the church, we had a spiritual feast as well, talking into the early hours of morning. Nowhere in the world have I found Christians so appreciative of their Lord or with a deeper understanding of the true meaning of a community in Christ. There on the furthermost frontier of a spiritually barren Europe is a tiny outpost, a band of Christian men and women, joyful in their faith, persecuted but not oppressed, a living witness to the power of the Gospel. They must be like the Thessalonians of the first century, I thought—another tiny but strong outpost that became a model for the whole Christian world.

As I flew back to London the next day, a sense of exhilaration swept over me. What was it about Haenssler and Westerholm and others that so deeply moved me? In many ways they reminded me of the German martyr, Dietrich Bonhoeffer, who coined the phrase "cheap grace" to describe the then prevalent view of God as an easygoing Father who lovingly excused all sins and failures of His people. All that distinguished the Christian life in this view was forgiveness, a costless arrangement through which believers used God to justify their worldly ways.

Bonhoeffer called upon Christians to make a radical break with the past. "When Christ calls a man," he wrote, "He bids him come and die." Then he added, "Grace is the way to heaven, but he who travels that road must pay the tolls."

The European Christians, though few in number, were living the life of the cross, more so than most of the Christians I had encountered in the States. Had we in America incorporated the "good life" into the Gospel? Some at least seemed to make being a Christian synonymous with old-fashioned virtue, the flag, honest work, success and God's bountiful blessings.

My encounters with these Christians in Europe was sobering. Where I had difficulty maintaining the disciplines of regular Bible study, sometimes finding it inconvenient, Raino Westerholm cheerfully invested his predawn hours studying English so he could spend treasured hours later reading a modern translation of the Bible not yet available in Finnish.

I flew to London to rejoin my family and spend a few days with our friends, Michael and Sylvia Mary Alison. Michael is a dynamic Tory member of Parliament whom I met when he was visiting the U.S. during the tense Watergate days of spring 1974. A short crisis prayer he sent me later was one factor which convinced me I needed to plead guilty for wrongs committed in the Ellsberg episode.

Michael is part of a small prayer group in Parliament, which includes George Thomas, the Labor MP who was then speaker of the House of Commons and as its chief officer one of the most powerful men in British public life. The speaker had invited Michael to bring me to his rooms for a visit.

The Parliament buildings rise majestically from the banks of the Thames—a row of gothic towers, intricately buttressed against the sky, making the soot-darkened structure look like a series of cathedrals. Through the members' entrance we came into a massive corridor under vaulted ceilings. To the left was the medieval Westminster Hall with its marker noting where Charles I was tried during the 17th-century overthrow of the monarchy. Everywhere were reminders of centuries of history.

Michael and I stopped at two tall, leather-inlaid swinging doors where a butler, wearing a black cutaway and white gloves, was posted. He glanced at a sheaf of papers on a clipboard, looked up, threw his shoulders back and said, "Oh, indeed, Sir, the Speaker is expecting you. Right this way, Sir."

He led us through more doors where another butler, this one with a neatly powdered wig, bowed and swinging his arm out, said, "Gentlemen, right this way for the Speaker." Our path took us across well-worn oriental rugs, along red velvety hall runners, past walls covered with the rich leather of old books and under crystal chandeliers. At a richly carved door the butler grasped the brass handle, thrust it open and in a resonant baritone uttered the traditional words, "Gentlemen, the Speaker."

The room was immense. At a table, his back to the towering, leaded-glass windows, a small, wiry man bounded to his feet as we entered. Michael, Oxford-educated and thoroughly British, presented me according to time-honored and formal protocol.

"It is an honor to be here, Mr. Speaker," I began.

"Forget that 'Mr. Speaker' stuff in here. We're brothers. Sit down, sit down." George Thomas placed leather-covered, straight-back chairs close to his.

The Speaker was a short, feisty man, bubbling over with enthusiasm. He was wearing a black vest, breeches and stockings, and a lace-front shirt with white bands. He looked like he had dropped right off the cover of the English humor magazine *Punch*.

"There's a bit of a problem here today," he said casually as he swiveled his chair to the side and leaned back, smiling with a mischievous twinkle.

"What's that?" asked Michael.

"A resolution has been presented demanding that I step down as Speaker." I stared more intently at the Speaker. If the forthcoming challenge bothered him, he didn't show it. A Methodist lay preacher before entering politics, George Thomas had given a speech the day before in his home district. In it, he warned that rising tides of humanism were threatening to drive Jesus Christ out of the British Isles. It was, according to news accounts, a powerful Christian message, but one of London's more popular tabloids editorially demanded the Speaker's ouster for using his high office to advocate a religious position. A group of members were prepared to follow through on the paper's demand.

"This couldn't happen in your country, could it, Chuck?" His brown eyes flashed, then became wistful. "It's a lot different here."

The Speaker questioned me about reports of a new revival in America. "We need it here. God knows, it's our only hope." He paused for a moment and stared out the window. Then he smiled at us. "Prayer is our one defense, isn't it, men? Shall we pray together?"

A palpable peace came over us. The Speaker began, followed by Michael and then me, our heads bowed over a desk occupied over the centuries by some of the most powerful men in the world. But the power that filled the huge sunlit room at that moment was of another kind.

When the resolution was presented against the Speaker in the afternoon debate, he handled it in such a deft, relaxed manner that it quickly died. But it stayed in my mind. How much more costly it is to be a Christian elsewhere in the world, I thought, than in the United States.

The next two weeks brought some welcome rest. In a small, rented car, Patty, Emily and I lazily traveled across France, Switzerland and Italy. Emily, an aspiring art student, beat a wearying path through every museum and gallery from London to Rome.

We arrived in that ancient city under a scorching midday sun. No sooner had we checked into a downtown hotel than Emily had us in tow, cameras slung over shoulders, tourist style, tramping through the Coliseum and other ruins of the once great Roman Empire. We stood on the very ground where the Roman Senate, the world's mightiest political institution, met to enact the laws which would shape the history of the world.

As I stood snapping photographs, my mind flashed back to the Roosevelt Room in the White House, a few steps across a narrow hallway from the President's Oval Office. At eight o'clock each morning a dozen of us, the President's senior aides, had gathered around the antique mahogany table; its polished surface reflected the serious, intense expressions of men who believed the destiny of mankind was in their hands.

"The decision we must make today," Henry Kissinger would often say, "will affect the whole future course of world history." We believed it. Just as the Roman senators, dressed in their flowing togas, believed it nearly 2,000 years ago. Yet here sat their once majestic forum in dusty piles of stone and rubble. Would even this much be left of the Roosevelt Room, I wondered, two centuries, let alone two millennia from now?

I was up early the next morning to meet Father Morlion for breakfast. A big man with a jaunty step and infectious smile, he was certainly not the stereotype of a Vatican priest. I quickly discovered why my Belgian friend, Fred Ladenius, insisted we meet.

Morlion is Belgian born, a skilled linguist and scholar who looked half his acknowledged 72 years and reportedly was even older. His smooth pink skin gave him an ageless appearance. "I met Jesus when I was 17," he told me with as much excitement as if it had been just the day before.

He leaned across the small round table. "Things here in Europe— spiritually, economically, politically—are in as desperate a condition as in the late 1930s." As a papal emissary to Germany during Hitler's rise to power, he had cried out against the dangers of Nazism, but few in the Vatican wanted to hear him.

He shook his head as if reliving the horror. "Hitler had the Germans believing they were God's chosen ones. Insane. So-called Christians can be the most dangerous when they use God for their nationalistic purposes. Guard against this; you must!" he pleaded, and I caught myself thinking of the glib "God and country" sloganeering of the Bicentennial celebration.

"The conditions are right again for chaos—and a man on the horse. We need to build bridges to Christians in America. We need to be

bound together for true strength. We must become real disciples—
you and me and others."

Morlion, who is president of the only university in Rome independent of the state, went on to say that he was in the process of compiling
the names of committed Christians across the continent. Thousands
were already on his mailing list, more being added daily. To each
name he distributed a periodic letter with suggestions for evangelistic
tools and reading.

For two hours I listened to a man of extraordinary intellect interpret
the political, economic and social trends with the historian's perspective. When I asked what he needed from me, he brushed it off. I
was asked simply to be a concerned friend.

"The time is coming soon when we will all need each other," he
said.

There was symbolic irony, I realized, as I glanced through the windows of the rooftop restaurant at the ruins we had toured the day
before. Morlion and I, of different church traditions and nationalities,
were talking of allegiance to a common throne, one that would never
lie in a pile of rubble and dust.

But I wondered: How much time is left for us complacent Americans?

*Believe that you may understand; understand that
you may believe.*

AUGUSTINE

12. Days of Doubt, Night of Discovery

Morlion's words seemed to throb in the pulse of the powerful jet
engines winging us back across the Atlantic. Pictures kept flashing
across my mind as well: Westerholm's lanky frame marching across
the floor of the Finnish Parliament, Haenssler's radiant smile, George
Thomas crouched over his desk in prayer.

What was it about them that so impressed me? Instead of the ostenta-
tious religiosity of many American Christians, there was a no-nonsense,
inner toughness as hard as tempered steel. These men, I realized,
understood the profound implications of the cross, the pain and suffering it entailed as well as the redemption it promised. Their iron-willed
determination to serve Christ was something I admired, even envied.

It seemed paradoxical that such robust faith could be nurtured in
arid lands. Much of the church in Europe was barren. Maybe it was
a reaction to this very thing which hardened their resolve; adversity
often does that, like a grinder which buffs fine gems.

Still, the danger of marrying church and state had been powerfully
impressed upon me during the month in Europe. The thought of what
was once the heart of Christendom becoming a vast spiritual wasteland
sent shivers through me.

I took a yellow pad from my briefcase and began making notes for a speech I was scheduled to give the following month to a gathering of Christian publishers. "Don't use God for nationalistic purposes" had been Morlion's words. Suddenly they seemed prophetic. "The vague deity of American civil religion bears little resemblance to the Christ of the Scriptures" was a phrase from a Senator Hatfield speech which had stuck in my mind. I wrote this on my pad.

Strange thoughts for the one-time marine captain whose love of country made him a zealous patriot. "There is a higher loyalty that must transcend love of one's nation," I continued writing. "God's people, wherever they are, make up the holy nation: black, white, brown, yellow. We Americans can be arrogant and chauvinistic when we think that God has singled us out, that God is on our side and we are a 'chosen people.'" The Nazis proclaimed that in the 1930s.

I shook my head, staring out at the summer clouds drifting below across the vast blue ocean. Could this be so? According to the popular catch phrases of the Bicentennial era, God *had* blessed our nation over all others. And wasn't this precisely because of our religious commitment?

I often concluded speeches with stirring appeals to restore America as the Christian nation its founders intended, discovering that those words invariably brought the crowds to their feet. They were as sure-fire as some of the slogans I'd found so effective in politics.

In the introduction to *Born Again* I wrote, "How magnificently has God honored the covenant of our forefathers"—words, I now admitted to myself, which were intended to arouse the same emotions in the book's readers. Indeed there were covenants, but was it presumptuous to assume God was party to them? Had I been wrong? Until now there had been no reason to challenge my own comfortable assumptions.

I thought back to some of my recent reading. George Washington never once prayed in Jesus' name, and Jefferson took scissors to his Bible to remove all references to Jesus' miracles and resurrection. These were surely not the acts of Christians, though doubtless they were godly men. And though it was uncomfortable, I had to admit that so-called "Natural Law and Inalienable Rights" by definition subjectively defined were not the same as biblical revelation.

The turbines' whine in my ears seemed to focus my thoughts. Yes, I could only conclude, I had been wrong. I was forced painfully to reject what I'd written in the introductory pages of *Born Again.*

Could just one month abroad have so drastically upset long-established thought patterns? Or was something much more profound and powerful working within me?

At home several days later I was sorting through a stack of photographs taken in Europe. Wendell, just graduated from Princeton and working in housing construction outside Washington, was looking over my shoulder.

"What's that one, Dad?"

"That's the remains of the Roman Senate."

"Wow! Imagine that. Looks just like the construction site where I work." Wendell took a big swallow from his soft drink and walked away.

For me the imagery was suddenly overpowering, vividly underscoring the unsettling thoughts which had assaulted me on the plane trip home. *The only lasting kindom is God's.*

Later that same night, after Patty had gone to bed, I sat in my library reflecting on the disquieting discovery of new truths about the Gospel and myself. But what did all of this mean for my own decision? Here it was early July and I had given myself a deadline of August 1 to decide about the prison work: go into it full time or turn it over to someone else.

The moment had come, I sensed, alone with my thoughts and my ever-present yellow legal pad, to get down to serious business—to understand what was really happening in my life.

First, I reviewed what had been the experiences of my Christian life. On paper it became a useful check list:

1. *Conversion:* For me, an emotional experience which broke my proud resistance and convinced me that Jesus Christ is who He says He is. Such a "crisis" conversion is like suddenly stepping from a dark room into a brightly lighted one but is a long way from learning how to live in the new environment.

2. *Fellowship:* Finding support and strength from other Christians who taught me to pray and seek help from the Bible. Their role was that of nursing a baby.

3. *Repentance:* Seeking forgiveness for wrongs committed is essential to any true conversion. Out of this came the decision to plead guilty to the offense of obstruction of justice but awareness of the depth of my sinful nature increases as time passes.

4. *Surrender of self:* Through confinement in prison came freedom, strange though it sounds. Jesus' words, "He who would lose his life for My sake shall find it," became very real.

5. *Compassion:* In prison I also first "heard" His words about the "least of these." On the cross, Jesus took on the suffering of all mankind. Are we not to do the same?

6. *Commitment:* The discovery of what it could mean to "lay down your life for another" when Al Quie offered to serve the rest of my prison sentence.The Christian must be willing to sacrifice everything. I haven't been put to that test, and I envy those whose commitment is so authentic.

7. *Knowledge:* The awareness of how little I really knew about the Christian faith—an important milestone because it started me digging into books on theology, seeking out good teachers, hungering for understanding. Still, the hard questions throw me.

8. *Persecution and adversity:* I knew what it felt like to be hated for Watergate and even occasionally for my Christian faith. Not much compared to others, however.

9. *Gratitude:* Not hard for me, with the loyalty of my family, the faithfulness of friends and the love and protection of God. Yet, though I feel gratitude in my heart, the key question is: How does the Christian translate that into action? Mine is still a superficial understanding.

10. *Service:* What might be some "good works" have begun, but how does one serve God? My struggle is to know His will, and I flounder most of the time.

At a glance, I could see that what had happened thus far in three years as a Christian was almost entirely a transforming work in my heart. Most of my progress, if that is what it could be called, was based on experience and changed *feelings.*

It is in the heart, of course, that most conversions begin. The new believer is like a baby learning to walk: wide-eyed with excitement the child totters about the room grasping and touching everything within reach, grinning foolishly at every new discovery. The baby believer's blissful world is filled with the same kind of exciting new experiences: love of a kind not known before, forgiveness, release of pent-up emotions, inner peace and the like. Emotions of the heart.

So it is understandable that sins of the heart, such as temper, hatred, jealousy and pride, are the first to be affected in one's conversion.

But that is only the beginning, only one part of the transforming process God intends for our lives. If we are to be new creations, much more is demanded: heart, body, spirit and mind.

The mind is the key, I realized, as my eyes scanned the check list. I *felt* things; my problem was *understanding* them. Experiences and emotions can carry a person only so far and often, in fact, can be undependable supports.

I pushed myself away from my desk and walked to the French doors leading to the patio behind our home. The shrill chirping of crickets from a nearby stream seemed muffled by the blanket of heavy moist air which descends on Washington each summer. On the horizon was a hazy orange halo from the distant city's all-night lights. As I stared into the darkness, I began to see, to sense for the first time, the real significance of the startling new thoughts that so unsettled me on the flight home. They were themselves important, of course, as new perspectives weaned me away from old prejudices. The issues I'd been forced to re-evaluate were real ones. But they were only symptomatic of something much more fundamental: God's way of beginning the renewal of my mind and thoughts.

I recalled Paul's words to the Romans: "Do not be conformed to this world, but be transformed by the renewal of your mind, that you may prove what is the will of God, that which is good and acceptable and perfect" (Romans 12:2, RSV). The more I mused on it, the more I realized what a key verse of Scripture it is—maybe *the* key verse for growing up as a Christian.

Back on my desk was a Bible commentary on Romans; I found the place. The first 11 chapters of Romans, regarded by scholars as the finest systematic theology ever written, deal with inner, regenerative experiences such as election and justification—that is, God's work in the believer. Chapter 12, verse 3, and through Chapter 16 are the outward expression and acts of the Christian life. The first two verses of Chapter 12 are, therefore, the pivot, the link between the inward renewal and outward life—the steps the believer must take to translate his faith into everyday living.

The first command—*to present our bodies as a living sacrifice*—is at least easy to understand, if not to do. But the second—*be transformed by the renewing of the mind*—is glossed over in much contemporary teaching.

The Greek word, from which "transform" is translated I discovered, is *metamorphoō;* the English word "metamorphosis" derives from it and means more than a natural, progressive change from one thing to another. Webster defines it as "by supernatural means," as with an egg becoming a bird. The only other time *metamorphoō* is used in the New Testament is to describe the Transfiguration—the exalted occasion when Christ led Peter, James and John to a high mountain where "His face shone like the sun, and His garments became as white as light," (Matt. 17:2, NAS).

Man, though still in the flesh, was given a magnificent glimpse of the age to come: the unspeakable joy literally of looking into heaven. This leap from the sin of this world to the holiness of the next is breathtaking even to contemplate. Yet that is the precise parallel for this passage of Romans: the Christian *must* make a break with the past so radical that his mind is filled with the thoughts of Christ Himself.

A faith which does not do this, which stops with the belief that being "saved" is the whole Christian experience, is dead and denies Christ's concern for all mankind. It is like a baby dying in infancy; the child may be born healthy, but his life will have little or no impact on others.

Grasping this concept was a turning point for me, as it is, I suspect, for many Christians. God, I now understood, was working a powerful transformation in my thought habits and forcing me to *think* about what it really means to live as a disciple of Christ.

And as so often happened when I did this, Al Quie's face appeared in my mind. In January 1974 Al had telephoned me in prison and said he had learned of a little known statute that permits one man to serve the prison term of another. Al knew how heavy were the problems in my family, particularly with Chris' arrest. When he offered to take my place in prison, I was staggered.

Al Quie was then one of the most respected members of the House of Representatives, having spent 20 years in Congress, and had become the ranking Republican on the House Education and Labor Committee, a pillar of integrity, who in 1978 would become governor of Minnesota. I couldn't believe that he would endanger one of the most illustrious careers in American politics. "I've been led to do this," was his explanation.

I knew at that moment beyond all possible argument that Christ lives. He was real in Al Quie's life. He had to be. Nothing less than the presence of the living God could make a man risk so much for another.

Months after my release I learned that Al Quie had known one special fear all his life. Ever since his third grade class had been taken to visit a local jail, the thought of being imprisoned haunted Al. A carrier pilot during World War II, Al is not the sort of person who has many fears. But at the time he offered to serve my term, he still had a genuine terror of confinement behind bars. It's interesting how God deals with our special weaknesses.

Next to the Romans commentary on my desk was the volume that had become almost a Christian textbook for me: Bonhoeffer's *The Cost of Discipleship*. Sacrifice and suffering, a costly break with the pre-Christian life, nothing less than death to self, to Bonhoeffer were indispensable elements of the Christian life, and his own life was lived true to his preaching. Though an outspoken foe of Hitler, Bonhoeffer in 1939 chose to return to Germany from his safe haven in America. If he did not join his people to suffer with them through the war, he reasoned, he could not pastor to them in their recovery afterwards. He spent most of the war years in prison until his execution in 1945. It was not that he chose martyrdom—his letters from prison make that plain—rather he was simply obedient to Christ's call. "Only he who is obedient can believe," Bonhoeffer wrote.

That was the word I had been searching for: *Obedience*. I wrote it on my pad in large capital letters. That was behind Al Quie's offer to take my place in prison, and behind the acts that had often changed the course of history.

It was after a bad day fishing that Peter heard a stranger call out, "Put out into deep water, and let down the nets for a catch" (Luke 5:4, NIV). *Absurd*, he probably thought, but he obeyed, and became the great fisher of men.

Luther's obedience to God's word is what caused him to stand alone against the world and begin the mighty Reformation.

Wesley spent 50 years preaching, even as the surging tides of apostasy in 18th-century England seemed to wash his words away. His willingness to obey his God led to one of the great awakenings of modern times.

A young member of Parliament, William Wilberforce, heeded Jesus' call and opposed the barbaric slave trade, resisting the entire British Empire; his faithfulness and that of a small band of companions, prevailed through 20 years of struggle. Slavery was ended in his lifetime.

This was the quality—a tenacious, single-minded commitment— that I had seen in Haenssler, Westerholm and the others in Europe.

Everything about their lives reflected unswerving *obedience* to Jesus.

But what did all this have to do with prisons? A growing and imposing list of negatives were arrayed on the "con" side of my yellow pad: painful and unrewarding work; hard to raise money; no one cares; tough to get in; my own painful memories relived every time I went inside. Then there were Patty's fears and the sober warning to myself that going into the ministry would keep me in the public eye, a target of all the lingering poisons of Watergate.

Yet the longer the list of negatives grew, the more unimportant they seemed to be because the conviction deepened that that is where I *must* be. It wasn't a choice, I was beginning to understand, that could be weighed out rationally and logically. My decision would have to *turn* on the central question of *obedience*.

Would Jesus go there? I asked myself, already knowing the answer. Prisoners are the most despised of society. But Zacchaeus was one of the most despised men of his time and Jesus chose to dine in his home. Jesus' keynote sermon was taken from the prophet Isaiah, "He has sent me to proclaim release to the captives" (Luke 4:18, RSV). He spent His time with the sick, the poor, the sinful.

Many Christians, I knew, believed our sole task was to point others to salvation; that is, to preach the good news. But what is this news? Jesus forgave sin *and* fed the hungry. They aren't mutually exclusive. He did both. Can an obedient follower do less? The words on my pad were screaming back at me. *No, of course not!*

Something else was becoming clear. Now I understood why people always seemed to find Christ in those very places—in prisons, at death beds, in hospitals, in the gulags, in rat-infested ghettos. The richest spiritual experiences I have known have not been in vaulted cathedrals surrounded by stained-glass windows but in the filthiest prison cells. Christians will miss the greatest blessings if they isolate themselves from the reality of the world in which God lives.

What's more, He tells us we will be judged before God's throne by how well we have cared for suffering humanity. "What you have not done unto the least of these," Jesus says, "you have not done unto me" (Matthew 25:45, NIV). These are hard words, but as one who believed in the authority and truthfulness of Scripture, I could not duck them.

Was I being called to prisons as my particular response? Again: of course!

In the depths of my heart I had become convinced that I had gone to prison for a larger purpose than just getting my own life turned around. Prisons are holes of living hell, I mused, then scribbled on the bottom of the page, "obedient discipleship offers me no other path." I wondered why it had taken me so long to understand. I underlined the words and laid the pad and pen on my desk top. It was now very late at night; the sky was beginning to lighten, signaling the coming of a new day. The same thing, I realized, was happening in my life. If only Patty were beside me . . .

Between speaking dates in the northwest, Patty and I decided to accept Senator Mark Hatfield's invitation to spend a few days by ourselves at his seaside home in Oregon. The sea has had special importance to me all my life. One favorite spot was a high point of rocks north of Boston. I'd sit there for hours as I tried to sort out the problems involved in making a career decision. Always the greatest of problems seemed insignificant compared to the vastness of the ocean. The surging waters and deep, irresistible movements gave perspective; even then I sensed that there was a power beyond man's.

My decision for Christ was made as I watched the sea churn against the rocky coast of Maine. Now with another life-changing decision to be made, the sea would once again be my ally.

The Hatfield home is located on a bluff of land looking down on miles of unspoiled beach. Cool, gray wisps of fog were floating up from the sea below when we arrived. After charcoaling fresh salmon steaks bought at a local market, Patty and I pulled our chairs in front of the cheery fireplace. Yellow flames from burning driftwood licked the blackened bricks, while the thumping roar of the waves set the stage for a perfect night of reading and rest.

Patty curled her feet under her and began poking through the pages of a novel Fred and Winona had given her. I became engrossed in Malcolm Muggeridge's *Jesus*, a brilliant modern treatment of the Lord's life.

As I reached for my coffee, I noticed Patty staring wistfully into the fireplace. "Any thoughts you want to share?" I asked.

Patty smiled. "I think so, since they're about you and me." I waited, loving the way her eyes always telegraphed her feelings and moods. This night they were sparkling.

She continued, "Well, I've watched you these past couple of months and I've realized what's happening. Before, I wasn't so sure, but I am now."

"Sure of what?" I blurted, always restless with people who speak in riddles.

"You know full well, Chuck Colson. You can't fool me. Six months ago you were all caught up in the glamour of your book, television appearances, public speaking. But you weren't really into it. Now it's different. You're serious. Prison work is your life, isn't it?"

Wanting Patty to express her own feelings, I dodged a direct answer. "I don't know. What do you think?"

"I've been thinking about it a lot." Her forehead wrinkled as she tried to be very precise. "First, we've always had a good marriage even when things were so rough. But lately it's been even better, and I've been thinking about why this is so. I've come to a conclusion which may surprise you. I think it is so much better because Christ is in it. He really does make all the difference."

She paused for a moment while I resisted the urge to hug her. "I see now that God wants you to be in a full-time ministry. We can't deny that, and we shouldn't, no matter what our preferences might be. Furthermore, I know you feel this way too."

Patty knew me too well. She had seen right through me. "Well, Honey, yes . . ."

"I knew it," she cut in. Then her intent expression relaxed. She broke into a big smile. "Well, I just want you to know that if that is what you want, I'm with you all the way."

I tried to restrain my excitement, but I think I must have come straight out of the chair, pulling Patty up into my arms. This courageous woman, who so wanted a quiet home and privacy, was picking up her own particular cross and would be at my side whatever came.

"So where do we go next, Chuck Colson?" she asked, looking straight into my eyes.

"Into the prisons, Honey—into every prison in this country," I quickly replied.

"They will never be the same if you do."

"I pray to God that you're right—that He will see to it that they never are the same again."

When James Calvert went out as a missionary to the cannibals of the Fiji Islands, the captain of the ship sought to turn him back. "You will lose your life and the lives of those with you if you go among such savages," he cried. Calvert only replied, "We died before we came here."

DAVID AUGSBURGER

13. Sticking My Neck Out

When Fred and Winona Rhodes arrived two days later to join us, we told them of our decision. Fred was as excited as I had been and hurried to get his briefcase.

Soon we were seated on the sun-soaked patio, Fred with manila folders by his chair and a yellow pad in hand while I ticked off what we would need: an office—very simple—secretary, staff people—hopefully an ex-prisoner or two . . .

I saved the toughest for last. "What about our articles of incorporation, tax exemption and all of that? The paperwork could take us a year."

"I've got all the forms; nothing to it," Fred quickly replied.

"Wait a minute, Fred." I looked at him suspiciously. "I just made my decision. How could you have them?"

Fred stared back sheepishly. "I knew this day was coming. I thought I'd be ready."

Fred, in fact, had never been in doubt, though I gave him some trying moments. "Remember God is calling you to work in the prisons," he would frequently admonish me, usually when he thought I was being enticed by the glamour of big public events.

Several times Fred had passed me notes after especially triumphant evangelistic speeches. "Good job," he would write, "but future platform appearances should be accepted only as they relate specifically to what God is calling you to do."

Once he left a note in my hotel room just as I was to meet with a famed European evangelist who he thought might try to persuade me to go into a preaching ministry. "I do not believe God is calling you as an evangelist. Rather He has given you a special jubilee message to proclaim to those in prison. You must stick to this . . ." These wise words deflated my ego but helped steady my course.

After we finished drawing up a rough organizational plan, we started into the house for lunch. Fred stopped and stared at me for a moment. "Brother, I love you for sticking your neck out this way," he exclaimed, throwing his arms around me.

He didn't know how soon I would indeed be sticking my neck out, at least for one group of prisoners.

Leaving our wives at the Hatfield house, Fred and I left the next morning for Seattle and the Bill Glass crusade to be held in the oldest federal prison, located at McNeil Island in Puget Sound. The decision, finally made, left us exuberant. "I can't wait to speak to those men," I told Fred as we stepped off the plane.

Bill Glass greeted us wearing a warmup suit, which is his standard garb for prison appearances. An all-pro tackle and one-time captain of the Cleveland Browns, Bill is a hulk of muscle with a flashing grin and teddy-bear gentleness. He retired early from professional football to go into full-time evangelism, much of it in the prisons.

The Glass crusades consist of testimonies from Christian athletes, lively music, singing and special performances from champions in all walks of life. The inmates turn out in great numbers for what is always a first-class event. Whenever he senses the audience is right for it, Bill preaches, as hard hitting from the podium as he used to be on the gridiron.

A ferry boat operated by the prison met us about noon and took us from Seattle, past the Puget Sound Naval Shipyard, by the city of Tacoma, then around Point Defiance to McNeil Island itself, an egg-shaped piece of land about four miles long and two miles wide. The trip there takes 20 minutes.

It was a beautiful day, a mild, southerly wind fanning ripples in the sparkling, clear waters. Bill Glass briefed us as we soaked up the sun; the attendance had been excellent the night before, the men were in good spirits and about 60 counselors were on hand, most of them veterans of earlier crusades. Some of the inmates had made professions of faith.

When the boat docked we walked up a path toward three granite buildings, surrounded by a wall. There were two security gates leading into a series of large prison yards. Strange that security would be so tight, I thought; even if a prisoner slipped through the wall he would never make it alive to the mainland. Though not as well known as Alcatraz, the now defunct island fortress in San Francisco Harbor, McNeil is a maximum security institution, equally tough to escape from.

When we arrived in the compound, much of the prison population was gathered in open air bleachers by the softball field. A flatbed trailer had been drawn up in front of the stands. On it was a podium with microphone, an electric organ, plus a dozen chairs. Members of the Glass team took seats on the platform. Fred and I sat with about 700 prisoners in the sunshine.

Bill Glass' voice boomed across the yard to open the program. I was making notes for my talk while the ventriloquist drew whistles and the strong man grudging applause. Fred and I had prayed that morning, claiming this forsaken island for Jesus Christ, so I wanted this to be a powerful message.

When Mike Crain, the karate and kung-fu expert, was introduced, up jumped a husky figure who began to pace back and forth on the stage shouting and waving his arms. I knew a little about karate, nothing about kung-fu, but I was about to learn. Mike had on black makeup, black shoes, black socks, black pants, black long-sleeved shirt and a black handkerchief around his neck. A round patch of closely cut, jet black hair topped his head.

First he asked guards to place two long slabs of ice on two cinderblocks. Each must have weighed a hundred pounds. For several minutes he danced before the ice, brandishing his fist. Then "thud!" He dealt the ice a mighty karate chop with his hand and the ice broke into two pieces. Heavy applause.

Next he invited a guard to lie down on a table on his back. A watermelon was then placed lengthwise on his stomach. Out came a samurai sword. "This must be the kung-fu act," I said to Fred who was staring at Mike with wonderment.

The prisoners were now all with Mike. "Slice the screw in two," they chanted. (Guards are given unflattering labels in every prison.)

Mike winked at the audience, nodded his head and donned a blindfold. The crowd was hushed. Then he began to swish the sword through the air with quick deft strokes.

Twice he circled the guard, making savage feints at the melon. The guard was sweating. Who wouldn't be? I thought; this is torture. But the inmates were howling with glee. Finally the sword flashed down slicing through the melon faster than the eye could follow. The melon broke in two, red juice spurted, seeds splattered. Unhurt, the guard shakily climbed off the table rubbing his stomach. Bedlam in the stands. The prisoners loved it.

Next came an act in which Mike lay on a bed of spikes while the guards piled cinderblocks on his stomach. Another guard was handed a sledge hammer by one of Mike's assistants. He leaned back, the hammer behind him, and then in the mighty swing, broke the cinderblocks on Mike's stomach. For some reason Mike was not even scratched. Amazing body control, I thought to myself.

After this demonstration, out came the samurai sword again as Mike moved to the microphone. "I understand that Charles Colson is in the audience and is going to take part in the program soon. Mr. Colson, will you stand up, please."

Alarm bells rang inside me, but I had no choice but to stand; the prisoners applauded politely.

"Chuck Colson, I have long wanted to meet you. Will you come up front, please?"

Fred looked at me helplessly, and we both groaned. Slowly I walked to the platform and up the steps.

Mike Crain greeted me effusively. His grip was like an iron vice closing on my sweaty hand. Then he turned his back and smirked knowingly at the audience.

"Mr. Colson, you have been good to come up on the stage and be a part of my act. And I want you to know that I'm looking forward to hearing your speech in a few minutes. Now what I want you to do right now is very simple. Will you get down on your hands and knees facing the audience?"

I didn't like what was happening, but fear or cowardice in any form spells instant rejection in the macho environment of a prison. I was trapped. Slowly I got on my knees, then on all fours, arching my head back so I could see what was happening.

"Thank you, Chuck Colson." Mike then reached over to a small handbag and pulled out a brown object about six inches long and three inches wide. He told me to look at the ground; then he placed it gently on the back of my neck.

It was a large Idaho potato.

I tried to smile. This had to be a gag, I thought. He was testing me, seeing how far he could go before I protested. Obviously, Mike was going to pretend to cut it in two with his sword *on my neck.* But that would be far more dangerous than slicing a watermelon in two on the guard's stomach. Certain that he would stop at the last minute and determined to call his bluff, I tried to relax.

The thought of getting up and walking off the stage crossed my mind. I didn't know it then but only a few weeks earlier Dallas Quarterback Roger Staubach found himself in the identical predicament and did just that. But Roger's life was football, mine now was prison work. I couldn't walk away.

Mike Crain was now going into his act, prancing about the stage, flashing the samurai sword. He stopped at the microphone, grinning. "Chuck, my Republican friend, I forgot to tell you. I'm a Democrat, a passionate, ardent Democrat. Just can't stand Republicans."

Loud cheers from part of the audience.

Now the feints began toward the potato perched on my neck as I thought: *What if he isn't kidding! He's not really going to split that potato on my neck as he did the watermelon. He could slice my head off—at the least, a nasty cut. How can I stop him? But the prisoners would hoot me out of this place if I chickened out.*

My skin was prickly and I felt the strength being sucked from my body as though a giant exhaust fan was at work. Afraid I might start trembling, I tried every calming prayer I could think of. And if this madman cut at the potato, my shaking might throw him off. I sensed that the audience was standing up to see if the White House hatchet man himself was going to be axed.

The shouts from the inmates goaded Mike on. "Chuck, I'll confess something else to you," he shouted. "I've long dreamed of this moment, hoped that somehow I would have you in my act. Ah, ha! Now here we are—just the two of us."

There were more dance steps, some banzai yells, then several practice swishes of the sword. I could not turn my head without dislodging the potato, but my eyes were straining in their sockets. I could see Mike's black shoes, coming at me and then retreating.

He was stomping his feet now and each step sounded like a rifle shot. Woosh! I heard steel whistling through the air and felt faint pressure on the back of my neck. One quick, jab downward and two pieces of potato spun across the floor. There was loud, thunderous applause.

My hand flew to my neck. I really expected to feel blood. It was like the time when I narrowly missed having a serious auto accident and my body was so weak I couldn't drive for a while. I wondered if I would be able to get up on my feet.

Regardless of how I felt, the prisoners loved it. And they loved it too when I slowly drew myself up and staggered to a chair. Now they knew that I could take it as well as dish it out, but they would never know at what price I had won their respect. When Bill Glass then got up and introduced me, the prisoners stood up stomping and applauding.

If only I had five minutes to get my composure. But there was barely a minute or two. When I got up to speak, my stomach hurt, my voice was weak and cracking, my thoughts were disoriented. For 10 minutes I struggled to gain my composure. But it didn't matter. Mike Crain's escapade so enhanced my credibility, the inmates hung on every word I uttered. When I told how I came into the presence of the Lord, they were attentive, thoughtful. When I shared my own experiences in prison, there were appreciative nods and even applause.

For an hour or so after the program, Fred and I were surrounded by prisoners. Along with members of the Glass team we heard confessions, prayed aloud in the yard for special needs, and helped many make decisions for the Lord. Only when the prison loudspeaker called the inmates back to their cellblocks did the huddle break up.

When we were on the ferry, heading toward the mainland, Mike came up to me. "You were a good sport, Chuck. Hope I wasn't too rough on you."

"It's quite an act, Mike," I replied through somewhat tight lips. "I just hope you're a teetotaler. You sure cut it awfully fine."

"I've no problem with drinking, Chuck. But I have cut nine people. You're a lawyer. Do you think I should take out insurance on my act?" Mike was smiling, but the experience was still too vivid for me to return it.

"No, we lawyers have a doctrine known as assumption of risk. Any idiot who allows you to slice a potato in two on his neck," I answered, "would be thrown out of court if he tried to sue."

There were long periods of silence that night as Fred and I drove the darkened roads back to the Hatfield home.

"Quite a debut for our new ministry, wasn't it?" I murmured. "I didn't think I'd be sticking my neck out quite so soon."

"Good lesson," Fred was squinting for the turn in the road.

"You know, Fred, we Christians kid ourselves. We tell each other that once the Lord blesses something, it's all one big bowl of cherries. That's not what I'm discovering." I thought of something, flipped on the car light and thumbed through the pages of my Bible.

"Listen to this." Then I read Luke 14:28. " 'For which one of you, when he wants to build a tower, does not first sit down and calculate the cost, to see if he has enough to complete it?' " (NAS).

"Calculate the cost," mused Fred, "I guess that applies to us, because what we want to do won't be easy. Today was nothing. Just a good example of what's to come."

How right he was!

*The plain fact is that if Simon the Zealot had met
Matthew the tax-gatherer anywhere than in the company of Jesus, he would have stuck a dagger in him.
Here is the tremendous truth that men who hate
each other can learn to love each other when they
both love Jesus Christ. Too often religion has been
a means of dividing men. It was meant to be—and
in the presence of the living Jesus it was—a means
of bringing together men who without Christ were
sundered from each other.*

WILLIAM BARCLAY

14. Love and Hate

Before returning to Washington, one sentimental reunion was
planned—a visit to the San Clemente compound of my friend and
one-time boss, former President Richard Nixon.

In the 18 months since my release from prison, we had been in
occasional contact by phone and letter but had met only once—a
short meeting at San Clemente late in the summer of 1975. Then
Mr. Nixon, still recovering from his near fatal bout with phlebitis,
had sat with his leg propped up on a high footrest throughout my
hour's visit. Twice a navy paramedic had interrupted, once to give
him pills and another time to check blood pressure. Although Mr.
Nixon kept smiling stoically, I sensed that discussing the White House,
Watergate or my time in prison was as painful for him as the throbbing
in his leg.

A staff member told me that his strength was now back to normal,
and I was eager to see him again. Fred and I drove a rented car
from Los Angeles. A small, green sign with white lettering, "Avenida
El Presidente," marked our turn off the bustling San Diego freeway;
it was the only surviving memento from San Clemente's glory days
when it boasted the world's most illustrious citizen. Gone were the
"Welcome, Mr. President" streamers from the rooftop of the town's

central motel; also gone were the red, white and blue bunting and presidential portraits from store front windows.

How fleeting is fame, how twisted the turns of history! This little seaside resort, its streets once crowded with excited tourists, straining to catch a glimpse into the back windows of speeding black limousines, surrounded by police escorts with flashing red strobe lights, was now sharing in the silent shame of a fallen leader's exile. But for the bronzed bodies of surfers and bathers drifting toward the beach, the scene would have been like a still-life painting.

At the end of a long, tree-shaded road were two unmarked, five-foot-high solid wood gates. Fred got out of the car and walked to the single phone fastened on a post as a cyclops-like television camera perched atop the gate, its lens glistening in the morning sun, stared impassively. Fred self-consciously announced us to the mechanical sentry and stared into the speaker waiting for a response. When there was none, he turned toward me and shrugged his shoulders. Such a silent pantomime is probably the one source of amusement for the gatekeeper sitting in the distant control room. A minute later my name must have cleared, for slowly the huge gates swung open.

The sprawling Spanish-style structure, once known as the Western White House, sits on a high promontory overlooking an endless expanse of blue Pacific waters. It is protected by a high wall to the north and a coast guard station to the south where temporary offices had once been constructed for the President and his staff. As we drove past deserted sentry boxes once manned by marines in starched khakis and polished brass who snapped white-gloved salutes, memories crashed over me like waves on the beach a hundred feet below.

"All things pass away," I muttered quietly as I stared at the untended stalks of brown grass bending in the breeze where manicured lawns had been. It seemed no less desolate to me than the rubble of the Roman Empire's ruins which were still fresh in my mind. It was lonely, eerie, and I felt sadness for Mr. Nixon and his family.

Then a thought struck me. How foolishly man struggles to preserve his monuments and glorify his works! It is futile and has been from the tower of Babel to today.

A secret service agent led us to the main building, a long, one-story, stucco structure that more resembled an economy motel than the offices of the United States President. Ken Khachigian, once a member of my White House staff, greeted us warmly and walked with us through a small reception area, past two empty rooms, one of which I had used as an office when I was in San Clemente, and into the President's wood-panelled but spartan office.

Richard Nixon, wearing a dark pin-stripe suit just as he did in the Oval Office, was on his feet. "Chuck, well, good to see you, good to see you." There was a bounce in his step and no sign of the limp I had noticed a year earlier as he came across the room and clutched my hand in both of his.

"You may remember Fred Rhodes, Mr. President . . ." I began.

"Of course, of course, let's see now, you were at the Veteran's Administration, weren't you, Fred? Deputy administrator, if I remember."

"Yes, Sir," Fred was beaming.

"But what I seem to remember best . . . " Mr. Nixon continued as he put his index finger to his lips and paused a moment, "yes, let's see . . . early 1972. That was a great sermon you preached at our worship service. Mrs. Nixon liked it especially."

Fred, speechless, looked like a small boy who just won first prize in a piano recital. Nixon was unchanged. He had the same uncanny memory I'd known in the White House. His aide could not have briefed him in advance, as we used to do, for he had not known Fred would accompany me. Despite the torment of Watergate, his fall from power and a debilitating illness, the sharp edge of his knifelike mind had not been dulled.

Fred excused himself and the former President and I talked alone for almost two hours. Mr. Nixon stared at me intently as I recounted my experiences in Europe; he was fascinated by the attitudes of foreign leaders and asked several questions; his own intimate knowledge of people and issues always astounded me.

Then, feeling surprising freedom, I shifted my subjects and outlined what was happening in my life through my Christian conviction and the work I was undertaking in prisons. Mr. Nixon leaned back in his chair, his right hand propped under his chin and supported on the chair arm. The sun streaming in through the oceanfront windows behind him highlighted the grey flecks throughout his hair, the only visible sign of aging. In the White House Nixon had quickly grown impatient with lengthy explanations, but this day he interrupted only once. "Explain that," he insisted when I passed too quickly over one point.

I could not remember any time in the White House when Mr. Nixon had more perception of mind or clarity of speech than he did this day. I had gone to San Clemente—as I would do several times again—to be helpful to him if I could. But this visit would have far more impact on me, I suspected, than on him.

We said good-by, then drove through the gates. Just outside Fred pulled the car to the side of the road so that we could pray, as we had done at the same point on the way in. We both were burdened for Mr. Nixon and his family and asked the Lord to impart grace and strength to them.

As I looked up from my prayer, I was startled by the realization of something. "You know, Fred, it's amazing. I felt different with him today."

During the thousands of hours I had spent with the President of the United States, I never quite lost my awe of the office or the man. Today it was as if God had stripped away the phony glamour of world-exalted position and made transparent the trappings of power before which I am all too inclined to kneel. I could look, man to man, into the eyes of a fellow human being and care for him as a person, not as a famous or important world figure, but for himself. As if to underscore the lessons so vividly revealed to me in Europe, the visit to San Clemente wiped away any vestiges of doubt about the source of Power that really matters.

But as we drove back to Los Angeles that hot summer day, I tried to probe the reasons behind the intense hatred aimed by so many at the former President; for a lot of this hate had spilled off from the President onto me. Feeling the frightening effects of it myself, though I received only a small percentage of what the former President had, I could understand what he had been through.

In November 1972 Richard Nixon had been elected President by the largest margin of votes in U.S. history. Within a year waves of hatred from millions of people were crashing down on the White House. Since then, best-selling books, news stories and comedians had excoriated him, dissected his drinking habits, speculated on his mental capacity, ridiculed his mannerisms. Woodward and Bernstein's second book shamelessly described his sex life with Mrs. Nixon, who was to suffer a stroke some weeks after its publication.

The President had become, like all of us, prideful, he had made mistakes, he had lied to the people, he had tried to cover up wrongdoing. The public was right in feeling betrayed, but why the consuming, continuing hatred?

One national television personality on a coast-to-coast network program boasted, "I have hated Richard Nixon since 1946."

Yet Americans also consider themselves a forgiving people. Every time we win a war, we forgive the people who were our enemies, even though they killed the cream of our manhood. Then we make it possible for the defeated country to become prosperous.

Is it arrogance and pride that brings on such hatred? These are the sins most often laid upon Richard Nixon.

Germany under the Kaiser in World War I and under Hitler in World War II were totally arrogant and hateful regimes. Yet even though Americans suffered many killed or wounded, we were quick to forgive Germany after being victorious in both wars.

"If only Nixon would repent, come clean, admit all he did," protested one national commentator after another. It is a common refrain echoed by Christians and non-Christians alike. I used to wonder about this myself until I understood that according to God's word our willingness to forgive Mr. Nixon should have nothing to do with whether he repents of his sins or not. We ask God *to forgive us as we forgive others.* He makes no conditions that the others must repent, only that we do ourselves. In fact, only as we forgive others will God forgive us.

I went back again to the question: "Why the blind and passionate hatred of Richard Nixon?"

In addition to his betrayal of public trust, some say it came through hostile press coverage. Others would argue it resulted from the unhealed wounds of Vietnam. All these things are true in part. But if that were all, wouldn't the hatred subside after the man left office? The reason it continues, I mused, must be due to something far deeper.

In my mind, I reviewed Mr. Nixon's background. He rose from humble beginnings, worked his way through college, became a naval officer and as a relatively young man won a seat in Congress. It was a classic, pull-yourself-up-by-your-bootstraps story so admired by his generation. Nixon was the man who embodied as well as preached the work ethic, material success at any cost and by any means. Thus his success reassured millions of Americans whose memories of the great depression had bred deep insecurity. Defeated once for the presidency, he fought back and won. His comeback was the crowning proof that the American way was what we always wanted to believe it was. Mr. Nixon became a hero because he was a mirror image of us—or of what we wanted to believe of ourselves.

The Vietnam war came and with it a youth culture which rejected hard work, materialism, power and worldly success, all the things Mr. Nixon represented. Then followed Watergate and his betrayal of trust. He was wrong, all of us in the White House were, no doubt about that. We broke our trust. The many good things Nixon accomplished were washed away by that one perfidy.

But there was more than the crimes of Watergate that went wrong. Suddenly what Americans saw about Richard Nixon, they looked in the mirror and saw in themselves. And they didn't like what they saw and were.

This must be the real reason, I thought, as we turned off the San Diego Freeway onto Century Boulevard and toward our airport motel. Richard Nixon had become the hate symbol of American life. People have always been reluctant to see their own sins and punish themselves, so it is convenient to have a symbol like the former president to chastise. In a way we can cleanse ourselves by heaping our anger and venom on him. I remembered a similar situation in another era. Charles I in England, whose political woes three centuries ago bear fascinating parallels to Nixon's, was beheaded. There must have been times when Mr. Nixon probably thought of that as a more merciful fate.

It will continue, I thought, until the self-purging is complete and historians begin the inevitable revisionism. In the meantime I prayed again for the Nixon family and for my nation which I love and cherish.

Back in Washington our new ministry came together like pieces of a jigsaw puzzle. Fred located an office in a converted townhouse five miles outside Washington in the Northern Virginia suburb of Arlington. For $350 per month we had two large rooms and one small one, enough to crowd in seven people. Fred found surplus file cases and typewriters. My son, Wendell, a proficient carpenter, was commissioned to make desks from flush doors. Within a week—and for only a few hundred dollars—we were in business.

Since we were so much a part of the Washington *fellowship* and would be dealing with *prisons,* the name Prison Fellowship naturally evolved, with Fred designated president. Within weeks, thanks to our friend and former IRS accountant, Al Hagen, we received a provisional nonprofit status from the Internal Revenue Service.

For Paul Kramer, the office, makeshift furniture and all, was an especially welcome sight; he had been working out of his small bedroom at Fellowship House, papers and files piled high on his bed and dresser. Whenever someone called him to the telephone he had to bound down two flights of stairs.

God's hand seemed evident in the choice of people as well. Jackie

Butner, the pert, young ex-bank embezzler and graduate of our second group of inmate disciples, joined us as our first full-time secretary. Because of her accounting background, she took over our financial accounts as well.

"Isn't this placing too much temptation before Jackie?" someone asked me. Possibly so, but the whole ministry was based on trust.

Gordon Loux, enthusiastic, tough-minded, well organized—formerly a young executive at Moody Bible Institute—came on full time to manage our day-by-day operations. Though it meant taking his three children out of school in Wheaton, Illinois, and leaving a beautiful older home which he and his wife, Beth, had just finished remodeling, Gordon felt the call to our ministry.

There seemed to be confirmation that God was in this decision too. Harold Hughes, grieving over the recent death of his daughter, Carol, who had succumbed in her long battle against cancer, decided to sell his home in McLean and move to a farm on Maryland's Eastern Shore. The week before Harold was to list the house with brokers, Gordon and Beth arrived in Washington to look for a house. In four days they found nothing they liked or could afford. They were about to return to Chicago, empty handed and discouraged, when I mentioned Harold's house; it was love at first sight. The price Harold set was, unknown to him, almost the precise figure Gordon had set as his maximum. The deal was closed with a handshake. A few days later Gordon sold his Wheaton home.

We also needed a good researcher. Hearing of a recent college graduate who wanted to volunteer his help for expenses only, we set up an appointment. The next day Mike Cromartie, sporting a full beard, was seated across from me. There was a time when I associated young, bearded men with anti-war, pot-smoking hippies, but Mike turned out to be an answer to prayer. Bright, studious and energetic, he began to organize a library, prepare research and speech materials.

Nan Martin, a young girl from North Carolina who had been living for a year at Cornerstone, the Christian student center at the University of Maryland, walked into our offices shortly thereafter and offered to work for $150 per month. Lisa Whitney, a Wisconsin school teacher, who had been led to us through the pages of *Born Again,* volunteered to give us her summer vacation. Margaret Shannon, a talented government careerist, spent long nights and weekends organizing our files and office systems.

Soon the office was surging with activity, volunteers arriving each night to catch up on filing and three-month-old mail. Fred led us in daily devotionals, sitting in a circle on the floor of my office. Being on the floor was a helpful reminder of how dependent we were upon the Lord. Besides we didn't have enough chairs.

The fourth class of prison disciples was scheduled to arrive in mid-August. All of us were excited by the advance reports on the men chosen, especially one inmate from Mississippi.

Leighton Ford, Billy Graham's associate, had visited Mississippi's Parchman Penitentiary, one of the toughest and most overcrowded maximum security institutions in the country. There he met Tommy Tarrants who so impressed him that he called to urge us to include Tommy in a training course.

In the early 1960's Tommy Tarrants, obsessed by hatred of blacks, Jews and Communists, became an extremist. Expelled from college, he went underground. A crack marksman and explosives expert, Tommy became a coldly efficient terrorist, joining the White Knights, the most violent wing of the Ku Klux Klan.

Trapped by the FBI while attempting to bomb a Jewish business-man's home, Tommy and a friend were caught in a gun battle. His friend was killed and Tommy's bullet-riddled body was rushed to the hospital where the doctors gave him little chance to survive. Mirac-ulously he recovered and was later tried and sentenced to 30 years in prison.

Prison, in Tommy's words, was like "living in a sewer." After a few months he escaped. Again there was a gun fight which left Tom-my's accomplice dead; Tommy was back in prison, this time in a solitary cell for one year. There, his reading progressed from extremist propaganda to philosophy to the Gospel. Though labeled "the meanest man in prison," Tommy met Christ one sweltering night in his lonely cell.

Guards and inmates alike soon noticed the change in him. The intensity of his hatred was redirected to a passionate hungering for the Lord. Tommy became a model prisoner and soon a leader among inmates.

Getting Tommy released to attend our fourth prison seminar was a major problem. A call to Governor Cliff Finch finally cut through the paperwork. Tommy's furlough into our custody was approved, his first time out of prison in seven years.

The fourth class arrived on a steamy Sunday night. Paul Kramer, steadily gaining in self-confidence, took charge. Harold Hughes was in rare form, challenging the men to deep Christian discipleship. Around the table in the second floor dining room at Fellowship House were determined expressions, set jaws, every eye on Harold, most men taking notes furiously.

The reports during the first week confirmed our initial instincts. Led by Tarrants, a voracious learner, the group was so studious and mature that instructor George Soltau had difficulty staying ahead of them in classes. Fred and I were heartened; this was the first class since our decision to plunge full time into our ministry.

Then came an unusual phone call. "Chuck, you won't believe this one." Fred burst into my office, waving a piece of paper covered with notes. "Billy Graham wants you to talk to a new Christian and give him a little coaching."

"We can do that. What's the big deal?" I answered.

"The big deal is that the new convert is Eldridge Cleaver—one-time bomb-throwing Black Panther, that's who!"

In late 1975, Cleaver, a fugitive exile for eight years, voluntarily returned to the United States and surrendered himself to stand trial for his role in a 1968 Oakland shoot-out with police. Sketchy press reports indicated that Cleaver had experienced a conversion in an Oakland, California, jail. I had written Cleaver an encouraging note but had no answer. Art DeMoss, head of a Pennsylvania insurance company, was so convinced of Cleaver's sincerity that he flew to California and put up a $50,000 bond to bail Cleaver out.

When Cleaver agreed to appear on "Meet the Press" the following Sunday, DeMoss was concerned. Though Cleaver was highly articulate as a revolutionary political leader in the 1960s, to speak about a personal spiritual experience before millions of television viewers could be a frightening prospect for anyone. After a meeting with Billy Graham, he was advised to talk with me. We set up the meeting at Fellowship House for the Saturday night before his television appearance and invited Harold Hughes to join us.

A dinner with the 11 members of our inmate class was also planned at Fellowship House for that Saturday. Since Cleaver had spent eight years in prison, Fred and I agreed it would be good for the inmates and Cleaver to eat together.

Naïvely, I never once gave a thought to Tommy Tarrants, the one-time klansman terrorist who had so violently hated Cleaver and everything he stood for!

To be truthful, I had felt almost as strongly about Cleaver myself. Memories of the fiery-tempered militant, shouting obscenities at the police and all whites, were burned into my consciousness. I recalled one telecast in particular when the Panther boss screamed at a crowd, "Kill the pigs—rape the white women." Though the Lord had moved strongly in my life, it would take a few extra doses of His grace for me to stomach Cleaver, conversion or no conversion. Still, I knew I had to do it.

Accompanied by his wife, Kathleen, Nancy DeMoss (Art's wife), and a young woman lawyer, Maxine, who had been active in radical groups, Cleaver arrived at Fellowship House shortly after 5 P.M.

"Eldridge, I've been looking forward to this." I stuck out my hand.

"Me, too," Cleaver replied, shaking it firmly.

Tall and imposing, Cleaver's features were those of the angry man I'd seen in photos and on TV a decade earlier. Though unsmiling and stern, the few words he spoke were in a voice so gentle I had to strain to hear them.

Cleaver and I retired to the paneled library on the first floor, the room in which our prayer group now met every Tuesday morning. Once seated I took measure of the muscular figure across from me, outstretched hands planted firmly on each knee. Another place, another time what I saw would strike terror into a person's heart. His eyes were narrow slits, eyelids drooped and his head cocked back. The way his nostrils were upturned, I imagined they once belched forth fire and smoke.

As we talked, the fearsome expression did not change. I realized it was a legacy of a life lived in prison, exile and terrorist enclaves in the darkest parts of the world. Cleaver was measuring me, too; whatever he might know of my conversion would not quickly overcome years of distrust and hate implanted in the depths of his soul.

The conversation shifted aimlessly in search of common ground. Finally Cleaver's experiences began to unfold. He had fled the United States in fear of his life: to Cuba, North Africa, China, the Soviet Union, North Vietnam. He became a darling of the Communist world, a propaganda showpiece. But then disillusionment began to set in. Communism in practice was far from the ideals of Marxism about which he had studied, its repression of people far greater than Cleaver had seen even in the worst of American ghettos. As his intellect grappled with the exposed bankruptcy of Marxist idealism, the memories of home grew more and more alluring.

One night Cleaver was alone at his home on the southern coast of France, sitting quietly on a balcony, gazing into the blue-black sky dotted with thousands of sparkling pinpoints. His eyes were drawn to the full moon; suddenly Cleaver jerked upright in his chair. The face of Mao-Tse-Tung was engraved in the center of the moon's bright yellow light. He rubbed his eyes and squinted again. Now it was Lenin; then Karl Marx. It was a parade of his Communist heroes, shapes shifting slowly from one into another. Cleaver was stunned; what bizarre tricks was his mind playing?

Then against the moon's glow there was the unmistakable face of Jesus Christ. Something exploded inside Cleaver. He found himself on his knees, sobbing and shaking uncontrollably, reciting the Lord's Prayer and the 23rd Psalm which his Christian mother had taught him as a child. But he despised Christianity! For years he had considered it a tool used to control and placate the masses, part of the repressive machinery which he fought.

Emotionally drained, Cleaver went to bed. That night he slept better than he had in months, awakening the next morning refreshed and unashamed over his strange and bewildering experience of the night before. Something was changed inside him. The anger, the rage, the hostility, elements that had motivated his entire life, were strangely diminished. Had he gone soft?

Something else was different too. He wanted to return to the United States even if it meant going to prison. When he told his wife, Kathleen, she was startled, then overjoyed. Then Cleaver shocked his lawyers by ordering them to arrange for his voluntary surrender to the police. American officials when informed were equally perplexed, several demanding to know "what kind of deal" Cleaver wanted.

Cleaver's story had me spellbound. Months later in a California jail, still puzzled over the changes inside him, Cleaver was called upon by a visiting prison chaplain of Mexican descent. "Eldridge Cleaver, I want you to meet Jesus Christ."

The chaplain handed Cleaver a New Testament. "Jesus Christ, this is Eldridge Cleaver."

When the chaplain left, Cleaver disgustedly threw the book on his bunk. The bold statement about meeting Christ had triggered old hatreds. "What nerve," he grumbled to himself, tucking the book under his mattress so that other inmates would not see it.

A few days later, members of the God's Squad, a group of young prison workers, came by with a copy of *Born Again,* the story of a man Cleaver passionately despised. This time he had trouble concealing his anger and again hid the book in his cell.

Time passed. Weeks later, with nothing better to do, Cleaver began to read the Bible. Similar to that night under the French sky, he felt a strange stirring inside. Then he opened *Born Again* and came across the passages about my inner disquiet and restlessness as Watergate heated up.

"That's what happened to me," he had shouted. On page after page he discovered remarkable similarities between his experience and mine.

By now I was emotionally involved with this imposing man. The figure across the coffee table no longer looked threatening. What I had heard, told softly in simple words, was an authentic description of another of Christ's miracles working in the unlikeliest of people.

Eldridge Cleaver was now my brother. I told him so, and for the first time in our meeting, there was a trace of a smile on his lips. When Fred interrupted us with the announcement that dinner was about to be served upstairs, I realized I hadn't even explained to Eldridge and his party our plans for the evening.

"Hope you don't mind eating with eleven convicts, Brother," I quipped.

"Hey, man, you'll make me feel right at home," Cleaver said with a broad grin.

Then I remembered Tommy Tarrants. How stupid of me! We had deliberately not told the inmates about Cleaver's visit in case he preferred anonymity. If it was hard for Cleaver to accept me, what about a klansman who bombed the homes of blacks?

"Wait here. I'll be right back," I said and then bounded up the stairs, two at a time. Tommy was in the kitchen, his tall gangling frame leaning over the stove. "What's up?" he asked.

"Tommy, there's a new brother here for dinner with us. I want you to meet him."

"Sure, Chuck." Tommy wiped his hands on the white apron covering his front. "What's his name?"

"Eldridge Cleaver."

"Ah—sure," he muttered weakly.

Eldridge was gracious when I introduced the two and briefly outlined Tommy's background. "We both have a lot to live down, don't we?" Eldridge said, gripping Tommy's hand and looking straight into his eyes.

As I stared at the two men standing under the glow of the chandelier in the center hall, for a moment I was frozen in time. This could have been the first meeting between two of the original apostles, Matthew and Simon the Zealot. Matthew was a despised collaborator with the Roman Empire, Simon a fervent Jewish nationalist working for the violent overthrow of the Roman oppressors. Anywhere but in the company of Jesus, Simon would have thrust a knife into the hated Matthew.

The dinner was unforgettable. Harold Hughes gripped us with his explanation of discipleship. Several inmates including Tommy Tarrants told of their own experiences with Christ. Cleaver stared at Tommy, trying to look into his soul. Maxine, who had explained that she was a nonbelieving Jewess, sat wide-eyed, hardly touching her food. Sensing that the deeply spiritual talk might be offensive to her, I walked around the table to where she was sitting. "I suppose we may seem a little strange to you, a little crazy perhaps."

Maxine looked up. "Well, if you are, then the whole world ought to be crazy like this."

After dinner several of us including Tommy adjourned to the library where Harold Hughes and I spent the next two hours coaching Eldridge on how best to handle the tough questions of skeptical newsmen.

"Brother, just remember one thing," Harold summed it up. "Don't be embarrassed talking about Christ, even when they give you those smug or disdainful looks."

Harold, taking Eldridge's hand on one side and Kathleen's on the other, suggested we pray together before going our separate ways. Those seated around the room joined in as the circle closed. The prayers flowed—for Eldridge, his family, those on the panel of "Meet the Press," the inmates from six prisons, and for our ministry together.

What a strange collection of people: the one-time Nixon loyalist, a recovered alcoholic and liberal Democratic senator from Iowa, a member of the Black Panther Party and avowed Marxist revolutionary out on bail, and an ex-Ku Klux Klan terrorist doing 35 years in prison. Here were men who represented opposite poles culturally, politically, socially; it would be unthinkable in the world's eyes that they could come together for any purpose. Yet on this night they prayed together, wept together and embraced—joined together by the power of the Holy Spirit in a fraternity that transcends all others.

What we see, and like to see, is cure and change. But what we do not see and do not want to see is care, the participation in the pain, the solidarity in suffering, the sharing in the experience of brokenness. And still, cure without care is dehumanizing as a gift given with a cold heart.

HENRI J. M. NOUWEN

15. Fallen Brother

Paul Kramer burst into my office late one afternoon, his expressive eyes filled with hurt.

I braced myself for some bad news. "What is it, Paul? You look like you've lost your best friend."

"You're pretty close . . ." He walked to the window and stared moodily outside. "Corbin is back in prison."

Lee Corbin was the burly ex-marine and one-time con man with the irrepressible grin who had become our close brother in Maxwell prison. He had been out on parole for 18 months. Just six months before, Paul and I had been with him in Chattanooga; pictures of our joyful reunion in a bookstore were carried on the front pages of local papers.

"How could he have done that?" I nearly shouted, slamming my fist on the desk in disgust and anger. My mind churned. Corbin was one of the heroes of the prison chapters of *Born Again*. Millions had read about him, believed in his conversion, and now he had let us down.

Paul read my mind. "Chuck, our brother is in trouble and needs us." His words made me suddenly want to crawl under my desk. I was concerned with myself and the credibility of my book, not Lee Corbin.

"Sorry, Paul . . . thanks. You're right. Okay, what do we do?"

"He has a hearing in the federal court in Aiken, South Carolina, next Monday for parole violation. My guess is that the judge will give him five years for sure, unless—unless you are there. Maybe you can help him get a reduced sentence."

I grimaced. This was Wednesday. I was flying to California Saturday, scheduled to speak to the California Bar Association Sunday in San Jose. To get to Aiken by Monday morning would mean flying all Sunday night.

"Your brother needs you."

With a sigh I agreed. We booked my ticket on a flight not-so-affectionately known to cross-country travelers as the "red-eye." A friend of the Fellowship would be there to meet me.

I left a day early for a visit with Jim Fuller, the industrialist who had offered me a tempting business opportunity but had flared so at my mention of Jesus Christ. He and I had become good friends. Our relationship was now well established on mutually understood ground rules. I would not try to persuade him to accept Christianity and he would not try to talk me into going into business.

The day I arrived Jim and his wife arranged a small dinner party at his home. Two of the guests were obvious believers who, twice during the evening, referred to Scripture verses which fitted the subject under discussion. Fuller even asked some questions about them.

Later that night after the guests had left we sat alone in Jim's study. Only one lamp was lighted, but the room was bright from the orange flames leaping from aged, oak logs. "The good that I wish, I do not do; but I practice the very evil that I do not wish." I must have looked startled because he was precisely repeating words from Chapter 7 of Romans and they came up totally in the context of what we were discussing.

"Surprised?" he asked. "Well, I learned a lot as a kid. That verse stuck with me because it certainly does describe the condition of all of us, doesn't it? Sad but true."

"But there is a way out," I said.

Jim smiled. "I know what you're thinking, but people can do the right thing if they really want to. And without God."

I shook my head.

"Yes, they can," he insisted. I knew Jim was struggling with some ethical questions in his business. Though enormously successful, he had acquired more property than he could comfortably finance and was feeling a cash pinch.

"Do you have a Bible?" I asked.

"Yes, there's one in my bedroom. I read it sometimes in bed at night," he replied.

"May I read you something from it?" I asked.

Jim looked hesitant, then got up. He returned with a well-worn King James version, part of its leather binding hanging loose. He handed it to me and I read aloud all of Romans 7 and the first verses of Chapter 8. Then I handed it back.

He said nothing, his expression neither approving nor disapproving.

"I'd like sometime to try and relate that chapter to the dilemma you face in business—and in all your life."

He shook his head, stood up, and threw some rumpled notes from his pocket into the fire. "Remember, we have an understanding about that," he smiled.

"Whenever you want to pursue it, Jim, I'm available. It's up to you." My role was to relax, be a good friend, and allow the Lord to do His work in His timing.

After our evening of coaching and fellowship, Eldridge Cleaver had appeared on "Meet the Press" and handled himself with poise, explaining his new faith just at the end of the program. Cleaver's conversion then became a major news story, and he was being besieged with offers to speak and write about his experiences. A feeling of uneasiness swept over me. Once in this same position myself, I had been dismayed by the way a few Christians had used me for their own purposes. I wrote Cleaver warning him about some of the dangers he faced.

In San Jose my speech to the bar association was received politely but without enthusiasm, especially when I urged the assembled lawyers to volunteer their services at nearby Folsom and San Quentin Prisons. A few seemed interested, but I sensed that many were hostile to me and suspicious about my motives. When Fred and I headed for the airport afterwards, I felt weary and oppressed. And now I faced an all-night flight to South Carolina.

Though we had agreed always to travel in twos, I prevailed upon Fred to fly straight home from San Francisco. Wanting to spare him the exhausting rigors of the night flight to Atlanta and then Augusta, I persuaded him that I would get on the plane and fall asleep.

Once on the jumbo jet I walked briskly down the aisle, heading for the last row. I slid into the window seat, flipped off my overhead light and tucked a pillow into the corner. Then I turned my head toward the window, trying to doze off before the plane was airborne, a trick I'd learned in my years in politics. In a few moments I was aware of someone sitting down beside me. I was determined not to look over but to concentrate on getting to sleep. There was a rustling of seat belts, then a cough.

"Pardon me."

Pretend sleep, I told myself. But it was no use; the gentle tapping on my arm could not be ignored.

I squinted out of one eye at the smiling face of a middle-aged man. "Yes," I mumbled.

"Pardon me, but you look like Chuck Colson."

"A lot of people say that." I smiled back and turned away again, burying my head in the pillow. *It might work,* I thought. *And I hadn't lied.* Seconds of silence passed, then the words, "Are you?"

He had trapped me; there was no escape. I drew up in the seat and stuck out my hand. "Yes, nice to meet you."

"I know you probably need sleep, but I just want to tell you how much I respect your views."

He was a friendly person who was only being nice. "Thank you. I'm glad we're flying together. You probably want to sleep too, don't you?"

He nodded, and I started to close my eyes again. "I sure wish I had what you have," he continued.

I thought about ignoring his last sentence, then my conscience began to speak. *You go and preach to thousands, but you don't have time for the needy man in the next seat. Hypocrite!*

For more than two hours we talked. The man poured out his life's troubles: marital tension, boredom in his work as an engineer with a large company, the trappings of success but no fulfillment inside. He stared at me intently as I recounted my own experiences with Tom Phillips, Doug Coe and Harold Hughes. He was not ready to make a commitment at 40,000 feet somewhere over the prairies of Kansas, but he promised to begin meeting in his hometown with a group of Christian businessmen whose names I gave him.

Bleary-eyed, we prayed together. He then fell peacefully asleep while I fitfully napped the last third of the journey, praying that I could somehow keep my eyes open in the courtroom with Lee Corbin the next morning.

Frank Gagliardi, a friend of Fellowship House, is a deputy sheriff in Aiken, South Carolina. He was waiting as I stumbled groggily down the ramp at the Augusta airport in early morning fog and drizzle.

After a short ride north, we stopped at an Aiken motel long enough for me to change my shirt, try to smooth the wrinkles out of my crumpled suit, shave and splash cold water on my face.

Aiken is a quiet southern town, mercifully spared so far from the urban onslaught of the 20th century. A reporter and photographer from its one paper greeted me on the steps of the courthouse—a square, red-brick, colonial building surrounded by towering oaks. When I explained that publicity might hurt my friend's case, they nodded agreeably; the reporter held the large wooden door open for me while the cameraman snapped one picture.

Inside the small courtroom were four men from Frank's prayer group seated on a back bench along with a few spectators. One lonely government lawyer, leaning back in his chair, was thumbing through a sheaf of papers. A matronly clerk sipped coffee at a table below the judge's dark mahogany bench.

"This honorable court is in session. All persons having business . . ." The bailiff's words pierced the peaceful silence of the courtroom.

Everyone rose. A respected but tough-minded young judge we had appointed during the Nixon law and order days strode into the room, stepped up onto the bench, and gently motioned those in the room to be seated. On the other side of the room a door opened and a craggy-faced marshal, carrying the handcuffs which he had just disengaged from his prisoner, led in Lee Corbin, followed by the young criminal lawyer we had hastily hired.

Lee, drawn and pale, was dressed in a faded green sport shirt and baggy rumpled pants which looked like he had slept in them. With his curly red hair and broad shoulders, he was still a commanding figure. When he saw me, he grinned, then struggled to hold back tears.

The gavel rapped, the clerk crisply read the dockets and the prosecutor began reading the "rap sheet"—a long litany of Corbin's petty swindles, credit fraudulently obtained, check overdrafts and installment contracts broken. My heart sank; if true, Lee had drifted back into old habits. How could it have happened? What had gone wrong? After the months of agony we had endured together at Maxwell, how could a man risk losing his freedom again?

As the voice droned on, my mind went back to the calls we had received from Lee after his release from prison. He had seemed to be doing all right, but obviously this had been a front. Of course! He had been crying for help, only I hadn't heard him. He had been supporting himself and his family on nickel-and-dime chiseling schemes. It wasn't money he needed when he had called; it was fellowship. Why hadn't I gone to see him? Why hadn't I invited him up to spend time with Paul and me? Why? Why?

It wasn't Lee Corbin who had failed; it was I, his brother, who was too busy to offer him more than dollars. It wasn't Lee Corbin who was waiting to be sentenced in that courtroom but Chuck Colson, the so-called Christian celebrity. Only it was Lee Corbin who would be spending something up to five years in clammy cells.

Painful questions wracked my conscience. Had I become self-important just as in the White House days? Grandiose schemes for the cure of prison ills all across America wouldn't be worth a thing if they blinded me to my commitment to care for one person in need. Had I so quickly forgotten Al Quie's example? Al had been willing to go to prison for me, but I was so busy I couldn't even spend time just to be with Lee when he needed me.

The words from the probation report were like stinging needles being plunged mercilessly into my skin.

Lee's lawyer, who had only a few days to prepare, made a valiant effort to answer the charges, but the evidence was overwhelming. The judge's fingers were tapping impatiently on the polished wood desk. Frank Gagliardi leaned over to me. "We're lucky he can only give him five years."

"Your honor, this is highly unusual, but with your permission I would like to call on someone who is here today to testify for the defendant." The lawyer was now desperate. We'd agreed in advance that I would speak only if the lawyer decided there was nothing to lose. "Mr. Charles Colson, who is from Washington, is a friend of the defendant. He has a few things to say, if you'll permit it."

The judge looked away, expressionless. "It is unusual," he said reflectively. My heart, which moments earlier had sunk to my shoelaces, was now throbbing excitedly. I would take the blame; I deserved it; maybe the judge could understand.

"All right, Counselor, we'll hear from Mr. Colson."

I pushed through the swinging gates and walked before the bench. The memory of the last time I had done this—when I myself was sentenced—sent shivers up my back.

In a short appeal for my friend, I traced his calls after we were out of prison and my failures to help Lee. If the court in its mercy would give us another chance, this time I wouldn't fail, I promised.

As I was nearing the end of my remarks, the judge leaned forward, obviously impatient with my monologue. "Mr. Colson, I have a few questions for you."

Startled, I forgot the point I was making. "Well . . . of course . . . Your Honor." My mouth was dry; my body stiff from the sleepless night before.

The judge reached into his briefcase and to my astonishment pulled out a familiar black and yellow jacketed book, a copy of *Born Again*. I stood frozen. He must have known I was coming. And I hadn't even bothered to reread what I had written in my own book about my friend. My depression deepened.

"On page 296 of your book, Mr. Colson, you quote the defendant admitting he had 'swindled so many people, he could never find them all.' Is that correct?"

"Uh, yes, Sir, I think that's correct."

"On page 324, you describe how you talked the defendant out of trying to escape from prison."

"There were extenuating circumstances—his family, Your Honor."

"On page . . ." It went on and on. Each reference from the book was pounded home like nails into a cell door of the jailhouse. Lee was sure to get the maximum sentence. I had sent Corbin a copy of all references to him in my book before publication, asking him if he approved the copy and the use of his name. His answer had been ringingly positive: "Tell it like it is."

Grudging admiration for the judge was mixed with the sinking realization that I had failed Lee in another way—I should have been more sensitive about what I had written.

When the questions mercifully ended, I made one final plea.

"Thank you for coming, Mr. Colson," the judge said.

I walked limply back to my seat.

Corbin then came forward, admitted his guilt and asked only for the court's mercy. His lawyer stood at his side looking on helplessly.

There were long moments of silence as the judge stared at the papers in front of him. I could see Frank's prayer group in the back, heads bowed. The sun was breaking through the morning clouds and a shaft of light from the high windows fell across the courtroom.

"In view of the appeals that have been made here today," the judge looked toward me with a faint smile, "and my belief that you do want to straighten your life out, Mr. Corbin, I am sentencing you today to fifteen months."

As the gavel cracked I felt a sudden relief. Truthfulness and humility had been honored. Corbin turned to us with tears rolling down his cheeks. The marshals looked startled as I threw my arms around my friend.

"Forgive me, Lee," I pleaded.

"Forgive you? I love you, Brother. I can do 15 months standing on my head. Thank you. Thank you. God bless you."

The handcuffs snapped. "Get word to my wife," he called out as I watched him led away.

Frank Gagliardi and the other Christian friends surrounding us rejoiced over prayers answered. But for me that jarring hour in the Aiken courtroom was an experience I prayed I would never forget. Better to stand steadfastly with one man than, failing in that, to win all the world's most glittering trophies.

My painful learning process was to continue. At home in Washington I received a call from Fred Rhodes. "There's a letter here from an attorney in Atlanta," he said tensely. "He claims your description of the Fulton County Jail in *Born Again* is false and libelous. I think we have a real hot potato in our hands."

> *Our ideas about institutionalizing [problem people]
> are based on what we might call "the toilet assump-
> tion"—the notion that unwanted matter, unwanted
> difficulties, unwanted complexities will disappear if
> they are removed from the immediate field of vision
> . . . Our approach to social problems is to decrease
> their visibility: out of sight, out of mind . . . When
> these discarded problems rise to the surface again—
> a riot, a protest, an expose . . . we react as if the
> sewer had backed up . . . and immediately call for
> the emergency plumber . . . to ensure that the prob-
> lem is once again removed from consciousness.*
>
> PHILIP SLATER

16. A Day with Daddy King

My first reaction to Fred's call was one of amusement. How could
a person be sued for libeling a jail? Most are cesspools of filth, inade-
quately equipped and poorly maintained. I opened *Born Again* to page
320 and reread the following paragraph:

> . . . The Fulton County Jail in Georgia is a favorite dumping ground
> for men from Maxwell. There in the overcrowded, hundred-year-old institu-
> tion, broiling hot in the summer, icy cold in the winter, 16 men have
> sometimes been locked in one, open, 20-foot-square cell for days. There
> is only one toilet, one wash basin, no windows, and four tiers of wooden
> slabs for beds. The inmates may be drunken vagrants, murderers awaiting
> trial or federal prisoners in transit. I met men who after a few days in
> such holes were in severe shock . . .

Reading the letter from Robert G. Young, the Fulton County attorney, quickly sobered me. It called the passage libelous, challenging
the facts one by one. "An asset of the Fulton County Jail is a committee
entitled Friends of the Fulton County Jail composed of outstanding
Atlanta citizens," he wrote. "They meet . . . in order to make the
jail a more humanitarian place along with donating gifts to improve
the facilities . . . On behalf of these people and the members of the

Board of Commissioners of Fulton County, we demand an immediate retraction of the quoted statement to appear in all the major newspapers throughout the country . . ."

If Atlanta had a committee of citizens interested in improving the conditions of its prisons, I wanted to be their friend and supporter, not an enemy. But how could my facts be so wrong? *Born Again* had been in print for eight months. Though a few reviewers had treated it harshly, no one had assailed its credibility. I had gone to great pains to insure accuracy, submitting galley proofs to people I had written about and then making extensive changes to accommodate any objections. I knew that doubts raised about any part of the book could undermine the whole book.

After going over my files of notes on the book, I asked Fred Rhodes for advice. "I can't figure it, Fred. All these months and now they challenge us. I have careful notes. A dozen prisoners told me about the Fulton County Jail, including Paul Kramer."

We invited Paul to join us, and he studied the correspondence carefully. His eyebrows arched up as he read over the paragraphs about good conditions in the jail.

Paul put the papers down and looked at Fred and me. "The place was a rotten hole. The first three nights I had to sleep on the floor. Then I was given a mattress. It was a week before I had any bed linen, never any clean clothes. In the 30 days I was there, I had no recreation. The jail was just as you described it."

"When were you there?"

"I think it was in March 1974."

"Maybe they've improved things since then," Fred interjected.

The whole matter would soon die away, we concluded, but it was agreed that I should check out the facts. If I was wrong I would write a letter of apology to the county officials and make corrections in future editions of the book.

What we learned later was that the condition of the Fulton County Jail had become an issue in the local sheriff's campaign for re-election. The description of it in *Born Again* was being thrown in the incumbent's face by his challenger.

Two days later, the issue exploded across the front pages of Atlanta newspapers:

"Colson Challenged on Statements About Local Jail."

"Libelous Statements on Local Jail Charged to Colson."

The stories left no doubt that the word of Atlanta's civic officialdom was to be taken over that of a Watergate villain. The next morning, phone lines into our office were jammed, good friends calling to urge me to correct the mistake, local politicians angrily demanding an apology. Other newspapers were calling. The lawyers sent copies of their demands to federal prison Director Norman Carlson, U.S. senators, the *Washington Post* and others. My publishers consulted their lawyers.

Paul remained adamant: the jail had been a horror. He even called some ex-prisoner friends who emphatically agreed with my description.

When I called the chairman of the Fulton County Commission, he was polite but firm. "You've made serious charges about *my* jail, Mr. Colson."

"If they are untrue, I'll apologize," I assured him.

"You've done a lot of damage," he spoke gravely.

"But you fellows have created the publicity," I countered.

"Just doing our duty to set the record straight."

"Will you accept my apology?"

"Well, this is all in the hands of the lawyers. Mighty serious business, they tell us."

I couldn't believe what I was hearing. The whole thing was like being in a wild chase scene from a slapstick movie, where a speeding truck races out of control through streets filled with traffic. I could see lawsuits and a hot political issue continuing for months, a whole city up in arms, it seemed, over one paragraph in a book. Meanwhile, our work in the prisons would surely suffer.

"Look, I'll fly down there tomorrow and tour the jail. Let me see it for myself and then I'll tell the press if I'm wrong. That's all I can do."

He seemed startled by this suggestion. "Oh, I don't know about that. I'll have to see if Nick Eason, the chief jailer, is in town. I'll call back and let you know."

There was no call that day or the next. I phoned again the third day but could reach no one. Finally the commissioner called back setting a date for my visit but not until a week later. Paul didn't like the sound of it. "In a week they'll renovate the place." But neither he nor I realized the trap that was being set.

It was a rainy, overcast morning when Paul and I pulled up outside the front gates of the Fulton County Jail, an unimposing brick building which, but for the barred windows, looked like a high school. The jammed parking lot didn't alert us, but then we saw three TV equipment trucks with cables strung across the ground, police cars with lights flashing and a string of cars and vans with radio call letters painted on the side.

"We're in for it," I sighed.

To one side of the jail was a fenced recreation area the size of a basketball court. It was filled with prisoners, some tossing balls.

"Look over there." Paul nudged me as we walked toward the jail's entrance. "Doesn't it seem strange that the men are playing in the rain? Those guys are going to have recreation today even if they drown."

The rain was coming down steadily. Many of the inmates were huddled against the fence holding jackets over their heads.

Paul and I entered a large, plain reception room. Standing in the center of the hall, flanked by a group of people, obviously local officials, was a nearly bald, bull-necked man.

"I'm Nick Eason." He stuck out his hand and general introductions were made. "The press would like to see us before we begin the tour. Follow me." He marched us all toward a door to the right. As he swung it open, lights and noise exploded. I had not seen so many newsmen in one place since the impeachment hearings. Cameras were grinding, mikes thrust in my face, bodies shoving. Everyone seemed to be shouting questions all at once.

Eason took charge. "Quiet down . . . clear the way," he said with such authority that the crowd parted on both sides, opening a path in the center of the room. There we saw a plain wooden desk. A large black man was seated behind it, his arms folded.

He was an imposing sight with his black suit, dark tie, and white shirt. Beneath closely cropped grey hair two penetrating eyes were fixed upon me. An uneasy silence fell over the room, all eyes and cameras focusing on this dominating presence.

"Daddy King," Paul whispered to me.

So this was the father of Martin Luther King, the revered civil rights leader of the '60s. I started to speak, my voice cracking, as I approached the desk. "I'm happy to see Dr. King here. I'll . . ."

My sentence was clipped short, left hanging in the still air as King jumped to his feet and in the voice of an Old Testament prophet pointed his finger at me and began shouting: "What right have you to write about a prison you never visited! How dare you do this?"

The cameras were turning and I could see that "Daddy" was starting to preach a sermon. He was Jeremiah and I was the wicked despoiler of the temple. *This can't be happening,* I thought to myself. *Surely, it's a bad dream.*

Once again, I tried to say something, but nobody was going to interrupt Daddy King until he had completed his speech. Paul stood frozen at my side, a terrified look on his face.

The scolding black man finally stopped. The cameras turned to me. "I came here to visit the jail," I said quietly. "If I've made a mistake, I'll admit it."

Daddy King was unmoved. "I've been in prisons all over the South, young man. This is the best one there is. And you had the audacity to defame it and all these fine people in the book you wrote." He swung his arms in a great sweeping motion as if to embrace all the "Friends of the Fulton County Jail" assembled in the room. Nick Eason was now smiling triumphantly.

This has to be a nightmare, I told myself, wanting to run out of the room and splash cold water on my face. Who was defending what? The former Nixon law and order apostle who had taken up the cause of downtrodden prisoners was being assailed by the father of the great civil rights champion. Who was Daddy King representing? Certainly not the white southern establishment?

"All right, folks; you heard the man," King thundered. "Mr. Colson is here to have a look at our jail." His head shook from side to side as a wry smile crossed his face. "He's certainly entitled to a look."

I turned to Nick Eason who was still grinning. "Could we make the tour without the press?" I asked. From experience I knew that cameras, mikes and reporters with notebooks inhibited any real dialogue with prisoners.

Eason ignored my request. "This way," he commanded the press. Later I was just as glad.

As we waited for the cameramen to get their equipment ready, Daddy King approached again, a smile on his face. "You're going to see a handsome prison," he said.

"My concern is for the prisoners," I replied. "If my coming here can help them, fine. I'm willing to eat some crow."

With that the elder King gave me a pat on the shoulder. "That's good. That's good. We all make mistakes. Even us Christians."

He grabbed my arm as we started the tour and whispered in my ear, almost conspiratorially, "I know what you are doing. It's good work. Keep it up."

"Thank you, Sir," I replied.

First stop was the prison kitchen. "Have you ever seen a brighter, cleaner kitchen than this one?" Eason asked.

I shook my head and went over and sniffed the wall. "A fresh paint job does wonders," I smiled. He ignored that, and we continued the tour.

Halfway through one of the upper tiers of cellblocks, we ran into a local Christian layman who was part of a visitation program. "Mr. Colson, God's timing is so great. Four prisoners have just accepted the Lord. Will you come back and pray with them?"

I asked Eason if he would let me see these prisoners alone. He agreed but was unable to stop the group of newsmen and women from following us. They didn't intend to miss a thing.

We walked the narrow catwalk past cell after cell filled with men clutching the bars, not one of whom spoke. Everywhere was the smell of fresh paint and disinfectants. Finally we came to one cell at the end of the walkway. With cameras and mikes pressing in behind me, I met the four new Christians, one with tears running down his cheeks. It was awkward. How do you pray with new Christians when television cameras are turning?

I turned my back to the camera and the four men pressed up against the bars. "Lord," I prayed, "we know that You are here with us amid this confusion. Thank You for touching the lives of these men, forgiving them their sins. Now fill them with Your love." The four men seemed oblivious to the cameras; their eyes were glistening in the lights.

The parade continued down another cellblock with single cells on the right, each holding eight to ten men. The press took it all in, even as we came to one cell where an old man was sitting on an open toilet. I tried to hurry them past, but the cameras kept grinding mercilessly. Conditions were obviously better than I had described them in my book, but several reporters later told me they were shocked to see open toilets and so many men crowded into one cell, staring out vacantly like animals on display in a zoo.

Nick Eason suddenly stopped in front of one cell and jabbed his finger through the bars into an old man's chest. "How do you like it in this jail?" he demanded.

The pale-faced old man's lips quivered. "Just fine, Chief. Fine jail you have," he answered in a quaking voice.

"You see there, Mr. Colson? You heard him." Eason grinned at me as the cameras turned.

At one point I whispered to Paul to talk with Eason while I fell behind, stopping at several cells, hoping the men would talk. Unlike any prison I had visited, the men were strangely mute. Finally, one man furtively motioned me close to the bars and whispered, "Hurry back. Because of your visit, they've painted, cleaned things up and given us decent meals. The TVs are fixed and we got new linens."

When we started toward the maximum segregation unit, Daddy King excused himself. The jailer explained that the man who had killed Daddy King's wife was confined there; this shocking murder had made the front page of papers all over the world in the summer of 1974 and reminded me all over again of the multiple tragedies this elderly man has had to endure. I felt a surge of sympathy for him.

Eason was uncomfortable taking me to the maximum security cell, and I soon saw why. Most of the men incarcerated there were severe mental cases. Mrs. King's killer had everything in his cell spread out on the grimy floor in a weird design. When he saw us, he excitedly tried to describe the laser beams which were slicing through his cell, his bulging eyes rolling upwards as if they were trying to escape their sockets.

"He belongs in a hospital," I said to the jailer.

"The court ordered him here," he replied with a shrug of resignation.

Once we were reassembled in the reception room, the reporters, more subdued now, started asking questions. The tour had been good for them, most of whom had never been inside a prison before. In answer to one question, Paul started describing the conditions of the jail when he had been imprisoned there in 1974. At that the shouting began all over again.

Eason jumped up and demanded that Paul apologize. "Don't let that man leave here saying something like that!" A clerk ran for the prison record book; seconds later he returned with the log for the very month Paul was in the jail. I had to grudgingly admire Eason for doing his homework.

Paul was now backed into a corner, surrounded by angry partisans. "We're not here to fight with you," I protested. "There are problems in every jail in this country. If our visit here calls attention to prison needs, then it has been very worthwhile."

"We have no problems in this jail," Eason replied and his supporters shouted their approval.

"I don't believe it," I retorted. "What about federal prisoners passing through here who have no change of clothes? Why are they kept here for weeks before they are moved? Why can't they make telephone calls to their families?"

In the hubbub that followed, it developed that federal prisoners were, in fact, given no clothes. The county officials assured the reporters that changes would be made. More questions brought out additional promises; a library would be built in the next year; more money would be requested for improvements.

I quietly rejoiced. The county officials were so proud of their jail and so anxious to prove their point to the press, they were making all kinds of promises they would now have to keep.

I was asked to sit at the desk and make a final statement. "I've been given a complete tour of this jail," I said. "Some of the things I wrote in my book are obviously in error and I apologize to the prison authorities for this. The next edition of the book will have the corrections. Instead of accepting what other prisoners said about this jail, I should have checked their statements out myself. Obviously this jail is not a hundred years old. But it is not a good jail."

"This is a good jail," Eason shouted.

"I have yet to see a good jail," I continued. "It is terrible to herd men together like cattle. If you treat men like animals they become animals. We need a program that will help get prisoners straightened out and back to their families so they can become productive people. And with God's help that is what my life is now committed to."

Daddy King walked over and put his hand on my shoulder. "I like a man who will admit he's made a mistake. Mr. Colson has done that, and he is forgiven. Let's hope some good comes out of it. We've had a fine day here at the jail. Now let's go and have a good lunch together."

Licking our wounds, Paul and I dragged ourselves to the Atlanta airport for the flight back to Washington.

To be a Christian means being vulnerable, I was learning, and being willing to admit error and perhaps to be made out to be a fool.

"Colson Offers Apology" was the headline in the next morning's paper. "I'll eat crow," was the caption under my picture. But after describing my prison tour, the story went on to detail how I had accepted Jesus Christ and was now giving full time to a prison ministry. *People* magazine had a cutting swipe to this effect: For Watergater Colson the end still justifies the means. He says he doesn't care if he makes a mistake if the result is helping prison conditions.

From all the press reports, it seemed that suddenly all of Atlanta was aware of its jail and anxious to do something about conditions in it.

I was learning, too, that the Lord can use mistakes and humiliation as effectively as success.

The Good Shepherd suffered. Why should we be lambs who are petted and protected? The practice of positive thinking—now better known as possibility thinking—or even by nights of fervent prayer, cannot permanently prevent the river from rising. Neither should we expect that when the river rises God will whisk us out of the flood with his heavenly helicopter. Biblicists ought to anticipate trouble but not be shaken by it.

VERNON GROUNDS

17. Problems Strengthen Us

Despite setbacks involving Lee Corbin and Atlanta's Fulton County Jail, our prison ministry was growing so fast we could barely keep up with the demands on us. A fifth class of prisoners held in November 1976 went smoothly. With a few exceptions graduates of these classes had become faithful disciples in their prisons. Many of those from earlier seminars had been freed and were back in the world helping our program, some beginning ministries of their own.

As our volume of work increased Fred spent more time in the office while Mike Cromartie began to accompany me on trips. Mildly concerned about how some people might react to my having a bearded companion, I needled Mike some about his beard until one day he presented me a sheet of paper with three pictures posted on it, each with full beard: his, Dwight L. Moody's and Charles Spurgeon's. I never kidded Mike again. Meanwhile as we traveled together, pitfalls seemed to be in every situation.

One night Mike and I were seated in the rear three seats of a Boeing 727 returning home from Chicago. The plane was only half full. Mike was on the aisle, papers and books piled in the seat between us. I was absorbed in an article.

"Pardon me, could I join you?" A sweet voice broke my concentration. A smiling young woman, squeezed into a snug-fitting red dress with plunging neckline, was leaning across Mike and pointing at the seat between us. Mike reddened as he discovered his nose two inches from her shapely but top-heavy front section.

"We're working, Lady!" he protested.

She ignored Mike. "Mr. Colson, you don't remember me, but I met you in a TV studio in San Francisco when you did the 'Katherine Crosby Show.'"

"I'm glad to see you again," I murmured. Then pointing to the books and papers Mike had feverishly spread over the middle seat, I explained that we had work to do.

"What I really want is a picture I can send my mother and dad, if you don't mind. They love you." She smiled shyly and fished into her purse for her camera.

"Why, of course," I replied, thinking she simply wanted a shot of me.

"Now, young man," she looked at Mike, "if you'll just move into the aisle, I'll get the stewardess to take a picture of Mr. Colson and me." Her eyelids fluttered.

Warning bells went off inside me. I had visions of a picture of me and this young coquette appearing in newspapers throughout the country. Mike sat rigidly in his seat.

"It won't be necessary to call the stewardess," I stammered. "Mike can take the picture. Ah—give us time to finish these papers, say 10 minutes."

It worked.

"Oh, thank you so much. My folks will be so pleased." She smiled enticingly and walked away. We had borrowed some time.

"Her folks, I'll bet." Mike was stern. "Why didn't you just tell her no?"

"No, Mike, think of a better way. She might be sincere."

"Well, she can't take that picture. It could be blackmail. There are newspapers that would love to run a picture of you and some bosomy chick."

"Think, Mike," I pleaded. My mind was groping as the minutes ticked by.

"I've got it." The inspiration came all at once. "You take the picture, Mike, but get it out of focus."

"It won't work. I saw the camera. It's an Instamatic."

"Aim it to the side of us or at our feet."

"Perfect." Mike beamed as he headed up the aisle to summon the girl. A minute later they were back, the girl settling into the seat next to me. Any doubt about her intentions were removed when she immediately snuggled up against my shoulder and crossed her legs, gently pulling her skirt back from her knees. I watched Mike nervously as the camera trembled in his hands. *Make his aim bad,* I prayed silently. The flash exploded the dimly lit cabin.

"Again, please," she ordered, edging even closer.

Again I prayed; the camera was fluttering in Mike's hands. *Flash:* it was over.

Mike bowed courteously as he handed her camera back. She offered to send us copies, but I assured her she needn't trouble herself. As she walked away, Mike began to grin.

"I snapped the empty seat next to her. Wasn't even close," he whispered proudly.

But Mike couldn't help me avoid an unpleasant episode in San Francisco. He was leading me through a crowded doorway from the ballroom of the Fairmont Hotel where I had just spoken to a breakfast meeting of the Young President's Organization. The YPO allows no media representatives in its meetings, so I was not surprised to find a reporter waiting for me outside the door.

"Can I ask you just a few questions, please?" The bushy-haired young man with smoldering dark eyes and a camera slung over one shoulder looked like he was from San Francisco's Haight-Asbury hippie section. But, I thought, all people. even newsmen, dress casually in California. He carried a large bag: camera equipment, I assumed. We walked to a quiet corner of the lobby.

"Mr. Colson, Anita Bryant says there are more homosexuals per square foot in this city than anywhere else in the country. What do you say?"

"I don't know; I haven't taken a census," I replied.

The young man was scribbling in his pad. His eyes never looked at mine. "Some people say this is the most sinful city in America. What do you say?"

"I like it; it is a beautiful place. Besides, I came to speak, not to judge the city."

There followed the usual spate of questions about Watergate, Nixon and then some obviously intended to belittle President Carter's faith. He was visibly annoyed when I defended Carter as a sincere Christian. Never once did his eyes meet mine.

Soon Mike was dutifully tugging on my arm. I found myself feeling sorry for this angry young man; his inability to look me in the eye made me think that he felt guilty about something. "Good luck," I said, shaking his hand firmly, as I was leaving.

Mike and I made our way through the crowded lobby toward the elevator.

From afar came a shout. "Mr. Colson. Just one more question."

Mike was holding the elevator door open when the reporter burst through the crowd. His face was contorted, his muscles straining as his right arm—holding something, I couldn't tell what—drew back.

The first thought that flashed to mind was *He has a knife!* Instinctively my hand went up and I started to crouch, a judo response that had been drilled into me in the Marine Corps.

It was too late. Something hit my face hard, stunning me. There was instant darkness and I heard a lady's shrill scream above the shuffling of feet and shouting. "Oh, poor Mr. Colson. Help him! He's been hit."

So I have been shot, I remember thinking. *This must be how it feels.* There was no pain. People were holding me up by my arms, for which I was grateful. When I removed my glasses, I discovered that I could see again. And also that it was not blood but chocolate meringue pie that covered my face!

Meanwhile Mike had sprinted across the hotel lobby and tackled my assailant just as he was about to escape through the brass-framed glass doors. When I had removed the chocolate from my eyes, I saw that Mike, who probably weighs 160 pounds wringing wet, had his arms wrapped around the young man. Grunting ferociously, he was hauling his catch one step at a time back across the lobby.

It was a comical sight and I almost burst out laughing. But then I raced toward Mike, shouting, "Leave him alone! Let him go!"

Mike looked hurt, like a hunting dog that had recovered a downed bird only to be told it wasn't wanted.

"Don't hit me," the young man pleaded, still caught in Mike's grip.

"I won't hit you. Mike, let him go."

"Jesus told me to do it; He told me to hit you," the reporter said, obviously near tears.

"Let him go," I insisted. Mike released his hold, the young man hurried away, and I headed for our room to get cleaned up.

The young man, who was a reporter for a counter culture newspaper and a gay rights activist, immediately called a press conference and boasted that he had tricked me into not hitting him by claiming, derisively of course, that Jesus told him to do it. He explained his action by saying that he wanted to tell his grandchildren that he had "hit a Watergater." Some legacy.

When I came back down to the lobby 20 minutes later a woman was cleaning the elevator.

"What happened?" I asked innocently.

"Some nut threw a pie in here. Said Jesus told him to do it. I wish Jesus had told him to clean it up, too," she sighed disgustedly.

The media played the story his way with news accounts and television reports going all across the country. And so an angry young man, hungry for attention, found the bizarre action that would get his name into print. Unfortunately, this kind of publicity encourages other sick and alienated people to go out and commit strange acts, hoping to appear on television.

When the house detective asked me to press charges, I refused and also discouraged local police from taking extra precautions for our security. Then I wondered: Did my attitude toward the episode have any relation to what I had been reading just the day before in Bonhoeffer's *The Cost of Discipleship?*

His words, "Violence stands condemned by its failure to evoke counter violence," had stuck in my mind. Maybe they had restrained my otherwise natural inclination to flatten the young man's nose.

The pie throwing episode seemed more and more humorous, indeed trivial, as time passed. Yet it raised once again the question of how Christians should respond when attacked. Learn to suffer persecution gladly, we are told, though it goes contrary to every instinct of human nature. "Evil becomes a spent force when we put up no resistance," is another Bonhoeffer admonition. How hard it is for us to identify with Him who without faltering or striking back walked to His cross to die between two thieves. It is in moments of silent suffering—which is how that experience is shared—that the believer is drawn so very close to the Lord. Bonhoeffer, like the early apostles, understood this.

Where do we see examples of this today? The believers did in Amin's Uganda and do today in some Moslem and Communist countries, but few of us have ever encountered real persecution for the Gospel's sake.

The most common persecution for American Christians takes a subtle form. Walking into a disbelieving world and announcing, "I believe," produces the inevitable snickers, the sideward, knowing glances, the eyes rolled upward, the, "Oh, one of those," reactions from nonbelievers. Syndicated Washington columnist Nicholas von Hoffman likened my conversion and others to "a socially approved way of having a nervous breakdown."

After the 1978 Jonestown massacre in Guyana, *People* magazine featured an interview on cults. Included in the article was a picture of Eldridge Cleaver and me. Referring to our conversions, the caption read: "By their own accounts Charles Colson and Eldridge Cleaver underwent dramatic changes when they were 'born again.' " Our experiences were lumped with the cultists.

The reactions can be nastier than mere mockery or derision, as some new believers discover. One night I received an especially heart-warming call from a vice president of a stock brokerage firm who said, "I've accepted Christ and it is the most marvelous experience of my life." Some months later, I joined him when his small weekly prayer group met on Wall Street. He was accompanied by several fellow workers whom he had led to the Lord.

Then I heard he had been discharged from his company. "An economy measure," he was told and indeed the stock market was being pinched at the time. But the more likely reason was that his up-front evangelism cost him his well-paid post. Soon after that, this businessman went into full-time Christian service with Campus Crusade. "All that's happened has been a blessing," he told me later.

Make no mistake about it: there is a cost to being born again. Arthur Taylor, named president of CBS some years ago before his 38th birthday, lived up to his "whiz kid" reputation and increased the profitability of this powerful network. He also committed his life to Jesus Christ one day during a quiet luncheon in his office. Those of us who knew Taylor rejoiced; he was in a strategic position to reduce the amount of sex and violence being beamed through television into millions of homes. Taylor tried to do this, pioneering a "family viewing time" plan as one alternative.

But Taylor's ideas encountered brutal opposition. He was soon embroiled in law suits and was dismissed with a terse announcement by CBS which stunned the industry. Taylor's wholesome entertainment projects were then quietly dropped.

Anita Bryant's courageous stand against the gay rights movement resulted in major entertainment contracts being canceled and constant threats on her life wherever she went.

Few public figures have been more self-denying than Billy Graham, who draws a modest annual salary and shuns the riches his worldwide fame could easily produce. I know personally the extremes to which Billy goes to insure that nothing will cloud the message he gives the world. Yet recently he too was attacked in the press for a "secret" fund, though it had been properly incorporated and its statement a matter of public record from the beginning.

The desire to tear down people who represent high moral character and the advancement of spiritual values is evidence of an insidious sickness historically peculiar to times of moral decay. "We wait in ambush," British journalist Henry Fairlie writes, "for the novel that fails, for the poet who commits suicide, for the financier who is a crook, for the politician who slips, for the priest who is discovered to be an adulterer. We live in ambush for them all so that we may gloat at their misfortunes . . . we feel cheated by our newspapers and magazines if no one is leveled in the dust in them."

Since persecution is to be expected, should Christians withdraw monklike from the world and live in small, isolated communes? That's not what Christ tells us to do. But speaking our faith boldly is seldom easy. Perhaps the most difficult experience I ever had was on the Lou Gordon television program.

For years Gordon's interviews from Detroit, syndicated around the nation, were famed for the controversy and occasional shouting matches they produced. Gordon's questions were always caustic, biting and often irreverent. Guests have been known to walk off the set in the middle of a show. Lou made no effort to disguise his biases which were many. Of his many causes, he pursued none with more unrelenting passion than his hatred for Richard Nixon and all those around him.

My book publisher scheduled me for the show in the spring of 1976. But Gordon was stricken with a near fatal heart attack and hovered near death; later he underwent open heart surgery. A substitute interviewed me.

Gordon wrote several letters, pleading with me to return. So eager was he for a crack at my jugular that I suspect my agreement to do the show with him hastened his recovery. When I appeared months later, Gordon was trim and lean like a trained boxer, obviously well briefed and itching for a good free-for-all, no-holds-barred fight.

When the director flashed the signal for the program to start, it was like a bell for the first round. Gordon came out swinging.

"Mr. Colson, I'm glad you're here to answer for yourself because you've been discussed on this program many, many times."

"Not all bad, I hope."

"No, always bad. I can't think of anything good I ever said about you," he snapped.

Gordon began like a machine gun, firing every tough question that the most compulsive Watergate addict could conjure up. My answers just intensified Gordon's fury; the blue veins running through his temples were throbbing, his neck was turning a purplish red as he repeatedly cut in with a new question before I could finish answering the one before.

Never had I been interviewed by someone trying so hard to be obnoxious. For Gordon, this was not an interview or an act as it is with some TV personalities; this was a holy crusade to smite the most despised enemy. Several times I bit my lip to keep from the kind of slashing replies that had once been second nature to me, the reflex of one who had loved debating contests in high school and college.

When I finally brought the subject to the power of Jesus Christ, it looked like the top of Gordon's head would erupt. Then he hit me an unexpected blow. "Do you suppose, Mr. Colson, that God caused your father to die while you were in prison as a punishment for your lifetime of sins?"

For a moment my anger flared. My dad was my closest friend, a wonderful, decent, kind man, still a model for my life. I loved him deeply. *Why should anyone have to put up with this?* I asked myself as I stared into Gordon's eyes. He stared back: absolute contempt passed between us.

Every human impulse wanted to strike back at him and the perfect answer was on the tip of my tongue: "I understand that you had a near fatal heart attack a year ago; maybe God was punishing you for your hate, for all the bile you've spilled out on others." I wanted to attack him so much I could taste it.

But then came a calm, gentle nudging, a reminder that His way is not weakness or cowardice. And so, like air escaping out of a balloon, the words came. "I don't believe that about my dad, Lou. Ours is a loving God."

It wasn't a strong response either verbally or theologically. But the crisis passed, the tension broke and the rest of the interview was almost relaxed. Gordon leaned back in his chair, spent, as I gave large parts of my testimony which millions would see on the screen.

For weeks, I relived that painful moment, alternately wishing that

I'd torn into him for the sake of my dad's memory, and then thanking God I hadn't.

Then I forgot about Lou Gordon until one day four months later when I picked up *Time* magazine. Skimming through it, my eye stopped on "Milestones."

Died: TV interviewer, Lou Gordon, age 60, of a heart attack.

Life really is but a "vapor", I thought. Suffering persecution gladly has the added advantage of freeing the believer's conscience. Had I struck back with the answer that jumped into my mind, I'd have regretted it the rest of my days.

Meanwhile I hoped that more peaceful times lay ahead. How wrong I was.

If you can meet with triumph and disaster,
And treat those two imposters just the same;
If you can bear to hear the truth you've spoken
Twisted by knaves to make a trap for fools,
Or watch the things you gave your life to, broken,
And stoop and build 'em up with worn out tools,
Yours is the earth and everything that's in it,
And—which is more—you'll be a man, my son.

RUDYARD KIPLING

18. Aftermath of Dinner at the Deans

Sunday, November 18, 1976, began as one of the too-infrequent quiet days Patty and I treasure. After church we spread the Sunday papers out on the living room floor, made a fresh pot of coffee, started a fire and slumped into our favorite chairs.

The rustling of leaves in the brisk fall wind outside and the crackle of dry, burning logs were the only sounds. The silence was soothing. I needed a day like this. Months of demanding travel had left my nerves ragged. Patty gently reminded me how edgy I'd become.

The *New York Times* was first, followed by the *Washington Post* and *Washington Star:* sport pages, the news and then editorials, in that order. Choosing to read or not read is one of the luxuries I could now enjoy after all those years in politics when I absorbed and analyzed every scrap of news and political gossip.

The cover of *Parade* magazine, the *Post* Sunday supplement, advertised an article about *Blind Ambition,* the recently published book by John Dean, once my arch-foe during Watergate days and later my companion in prison. Reading it strained the friendship we'd developed in prison and afterwards; I was disappointed the way some of the old accusations against me were rehashed in the book. John and I had talked in prison about one particularly bizarre tale, which I believed he knew to be untrue. Yet there it was in his book as fact.

"Won't bother with that," I mumbled, casting *Parade* on the floor. Then curiosity overcame my peevishness. I picked it back up, flipped it open and began skimming the article.

My eye caught my name buried in the body of the text. I jumped over a few paragraphs and started to read.

> One night, however, the Colsons, Chuck and Patty, were in Los Angeles promoting his book. They came up for dinner and Colson got very drunk . . .

All at once it was as if flames from the fireplace were searing my cheeks. "Oh no," I groaned. I read the sentence again: "very drunk."

Patty bolted out of her chair and was now reading over my shoulder, steadying the paper with her hand. She read the rest of the article aloud in the most dolorous voice I'd ever heard, like someone mechanically reciting an obituary, and that is what it could be—for me and for Prison Fellowship.

The article purported to quote Taylor Branch, the young editor and ghost writer we'd met that night at the Deans' house. It continued:

> They had come up for dinner, and Colson got very drunk. He had been to six prayer breakfasts, and John Dean was very nervous about Colson's religious conversion and rediscovery of God, because John himself is heavy into EST (Erhard Seminars Training), a self-improvement course . . .
>
> When we sat down to dinner, everybody was uncomfortable. Colson was sitting there as if he planned to say the blessing. John, who hadn't said a blessing in thirty years, was wondering what to do. Finally, he said, "Chuck, would you like to say the blessing?" Then Patty Colson broke into the widest grin and said, "John, you got an hour?"
>
> Colson was so embarrassed he couldn't even talk. But his wife kept making these jokes. She'd say, "I know Chuck's very sincere about this religious business, but he was also very sincere about the Marines. And of course he was very, very sincere about Nixon."

The story went on in the same tone to describe further conversations about the White House years. Patty fell limply into her chair, a whipped look on her face.

What could either of us say? Silence can be serene, and it can also be heavy.

Patty's first words were a relief. "But it is so unfair—it is not true."

Twenty-seven million copies of *Parade* (I remembered the statistics precisely from White House days) were now in living rooms all across America. Images of people reading and looking up in surprise flashed across my mind. Friends embarrassed. Christians feeling betrayed. Enemies pleased.

Patty leaned forward, her eyes filled with pain. "You know, Chuck, this hurts—I mean inside," she pointed to her heart, "more than anything they said about us during the Watergate years."

I nodded agreement.

"Because now it involves the Lord," she went on. "I don't care about us. But He is hurt."

Of course he was right. There had been barrages of vicious headlines during Watergate, some terribly unfair. Each one produced the same sick feeling in my stomach, the same dry mouth. But I remembered none that caused such deep and consuming depression. *Religious phony* was the unmistakable message.

"I'll call Fred," I muttered, pushing myself out of the chair. Fred's dispirited voice told me he'd read the story even before I asked.

"How bad is it, Brother?" The question sounded silly as I heard my own words.

"Bad," he replied glumly.

"Will many people read it?" That question sounded even sillier.

"Everybody in church was asking about it." He mocked a high-pitched voice. " 'Oh, does Mr. Colson have a drinking problem? Dear, dear!' Some have decided your marriage is in trouble."

"Can you come over, Fred?"

Fred said he would. I called Gordon Loux; he too would join us. Patty greeted Fred and Gordon briefly and retreated to the bedroom.

"You were right, Fred," I said. "You warned us not to go to the Deans that night. I should have listened, but I wanted John and Mo to know we are their friends."

"Were," Gordon snapped.

The three of us tried to fathom the motives behind the article. Gordon was certain that John Dean, impeacher of Presidents, was still out to get his old antagonist, the Nixon friend. I couldn't believe it.

Fred had another theory: Taylor Branch, young and impressionable, had ghosted John's book. When he didn't get the credit or money he believed he was entitled to (as the *Parade* story reported), he gave out this interview. Feeding anti-Colson stuff to *Parade* was a sure-fire way to get a hearing.

I shook my head. "I thought we related well to each other that night." Then more pieces came into place. "Wait a minute, give me that article."

Fred handed it across the coffee table. I had been so shaken that I had not bothered to look at the by-line.

"Lloyd Shearer! Of course!" Lights went on. Shearer was a friend of Harold Hughes, a great admirer of his liberal position, but he hated Nixon and me with a passion. Harold had told me of a conversation he had with the *Parade* editor right after my conversion back in 1973. Shearer was enraged, convinced that I was a phony, and had said, "I'll never believe a word that guy says." Subsequent references to me in his articles were vitriolic.

Gordon always takes a direct approach. "Let's call John Dean. Maybe he'll make a statement denying it."

"No, I won't do that." I threw a log on the fire. "I swore I'd never talk to him again after reading his book."

"Not very Christian of you," Fred reproached me. "When we are reviled, we bless, remember? When we are persecuted, we endure; when we are slandered, we try to conciliate."

"That doesn't apply to me. I'm supposed to be the world's biggest hypocrite," I said testily.

Patty had come downstairs and was standing in the doorway. "I'm going to call Mo and find out what this is all about."

"That's the answer!" said Gordon. "Patty and Mo are the ones to handle it."

Patty strode to the desk, found the Dean's unlisted number in a small notebook, picked up the phone and dialed. The three of us gathered around the desk.

"Hello—Mo? This is Patty Colson."

Pause. "Well, we're not doing so well. Have you read the story in *Parade* magazine?"

Pause. "Mo, see if it's in your morning paper. I'll hold on."

Patty turned to us. "She hasn't read it. Doesn't seem to know anything about it." It was only 10 A.M. in California.

Several anxious minutes passed. Mo's voice came back on the phone.

"You've got it? Good. Look over to the second page, bottom of the first column."

We heard a cry coming from the other end of the phone. Patty's face softened. "I'm sure glad to hear you say that, Mo. Chuck is terribly upset because the statement about him is simply not true."

In a few minutes Patty handed me the phone. "John wants to talk to you."

"Chuck," John began, "I don't know what to say. It's untrue. I'll issue a statement. Anything you want. Anything."

I had never heard a man more upset or more sincere. Amazing how God works, I remember thinking at that moment. It had taken this blow to get John and me communicating again. How foolish I'd been.

I thanked John and told him we should talk again when he decided what he could do. Fred said the color had come back into my face when I hung up the receiver.

"Neither of them knew the article was coming out," I reported. "Both were stunned."

Later that same day, we reached Taylor Branch by phone. He was dumbstruck. "I don't remember saying those things," he protested over and over. "In fact, you were the first person to talk to me about Christianity in a way that I could listen to. I'll do anything I can to help."

The *Parade* story dominated our lives for weeks. Long distance calls flooded us. Hundreds of letters poured in.

Most were surprisingly sympathetic. "Tell us it isn't true," was a pleading refrain in many. A few were bitter and angry. One pastor of a large church in Georgia who never bothered to contact us sent a newsletter to his members which included as fact such statements as "Colson receives $5,000 for speeches and turns up under the influence of alcohol."

Alcoholic groups called or wrote wanting to help me with my problem. I was annoyed at the time, but later I appreciated their spirit. These words in a letter from a man who ministers to alcoholics in Florida touched me:

> I'm sincerely hoping and praying that this *(Parade)* story is a falsehood. Since you are so well known I'm sure that you have been given advice and encouragement from many sources. If not, here's one brother in Christ who will be praying that God will grant you victory in this great area of temptation.

At stake were nothing less than the future of our prison ministry, the major film being negotiated for *Born Again,* my filmed appearance on the Billy Graham crusade, a film of my testimony being circulated to churches, dozens of speeches, seminars, retreats, and appearances coming up in the months ahead. "Chapel of the Air," a respected

Christian radio show, was about to make a major fund-raising appeal for our prison work.

The article indicated that I was a phony. This was the question people had been asking since December 1973. Was he or wasn't he? Many now believed the question was answered for them.

Both John Dean and Taylor Branch did make statements on tape and here is a condensed version of the release issued by the World Religious News Department of the National Religious Broadcasters:

Former Presidential Counsel Charles Colson was recently accused of being drunk at the home of ex-White House lawyer John Dean. The accusation was allegedly made by Taylor Branch, the editor of Dean's recent book *Blind Ambition,* and quoted in the November 18 issue of *Parade* magazine. World Religious News has talked with both Taylor Branch and John Dean:

Branch: I am disturbed about the story. It was not a party; we were having dinner at John Dean's home. I do not remember saying what was attributed to me in the article and, in any case, Chuck Colson was not under the influence of alcohol . . . any notion that it was (a) a party and (b) a rowdy discussion is totally false.

Branch also denied quoting Patty as the article reported. Then John Dean expressed the following to World Religious News reporter Mike Muska:

Dean: The event happened in our home, and I can tell you unequivocally that . . . Chuck Colson was not drunk. In fact, I have never seen Chuck Colson drunk.

Muska: What was the general subject of conversation that night, Mr. Dean?

Dean: It was a conversation that touched on our days together in prison. It ended up with Chuck talking with Taylor about his Christian feelings . . . with Taylor saying he too had these feelings which he'd never really expressed publicly before. It was Chuck's attitude and strength that brought Taylor forward to talk about these things.

Muska: Do you think that Chuck Colson's conversion experience is genuine?

Dean: Well, at first I was skeptical, but as I've watched him do the things that seemed so different from the Chuck Colson I had once known, I've become absolutely sure of Chuck's religious conversion and how different Chuck Colson is today than he once was.

These comments helped. But then I began to wonder if we weren't over-reacting. The secular press contained headlines like "Colson Not Drunk" and I cringed. *Where is my sense of humor? Years from now all this may seem very funny,* I thought, *but not now.*

Following release of the Dean-Branch statements, Lloyd Shearer, the writer of the article, was asked by my publisher to make a retraction in *Parade* magazine. Shearer refused, saying that he had reported accurately from a taped interview with Taylor Branch.

"As a reporter, do you generally take one man's hurtful statement about another and print it without checking its truthfulness with other witnesses?" he was asked.

Shearer did not answer.

For the next weeks, the future of our prison work swung precariously in the balance. It was precisely the fear of something like this happening that had given me so much pause when I was trying to decide whether to begin Prison Fellowship. Ten people were now on our team full time. Hundreds of inmates were associated with us. Their fortunes were linked to mine. Yet one devastating article could finish us off— maybe it had.

For months to come the *Parade* article would haunt us. People handed the clipping to me at rallies and meetings, asking if it were true. The question was raised on television and radio interview programs. Anonymous hate letters came. Some people—maybe millions— would never believe the denials; there is simply no way to undo the mischief a lie can produce.

At the beginning of 1977, Gordon Loux, whose tough-mindedness I was coming to admire, took stock of the damage. On careful analysis, the mail was found to be largely supportive. No speeches had been canceled. The prison work was continuing without change. At the end of the year our books balanced, thanks to the fund raising of the "Chapel of the Air," which stuck with us despite the controversy. The damage had not been mortal.

One result of the experience was to cause me to face the issue of social drinking as it related to my Christian witness. I never should have accepted even one drink at the Deans, I realized, and vowed never to do so again in any public situation. In no way did I want to be a stumbling block to others; alcoholism is an epidemic illness in American life and more than 50 percent of all crimes are committed by people under its influence.

In the aftermath of the *Parade* article, I did some sober reflecting. A mature Christian friend had offered advice intended to be comforting: "The article was proof we were doing God's work," he said. "The Lord told us we'd be persecuted so relax and accept it."

As I pondered his well-intentioned counsel, doubts about it kept rising. The *Parade* article may well have been inspired by the editor's hostility toward Christians; then, again, it could be that he respects Christians who authentically do God's work and merely resents those he believes use God for their own purposes. Most likely the lingering Watergate poison made me good copy.

Many times, I concluded, we make no distinction between the persecution which comes to us because of our stand on the Gospel, and criticism which is unrelated to our faith and which we often bring upon ourselves. Ugandan Christians who saw thousands of their members slaughtered because of their faith by the madman Idi Amin know something of real persecution. Georgi Vins, imprisoned so many years in the Soviet Union for practicing his Christian beliefs, surely knows what it means.

But the evangelist who draws public ire because of heavy-handed fund-raising tactics on television may well be subject to legitimate criticism for his own worldly excesses. The Christian arrested for speeding cannot say he was stopped because of the "offense of the cross." The Maryland priests recently convicted for mismanagement of Diocesan funds were clearly *not* being persecuted for their faith.

Yet I have heard some Christians blithely dismiss *all* criticism against them as merely "the persecution we Christians are to expect," as if to validate their actions. When it becomes a cliché repeated over and over again, it is dangerous. For it is untrue and such a conditioned response avoids the necessity of self-examination and feeds the deadliest of our sins—self-righteousness and arrogance.

During this period I found inspiration once again in the life of William Wilberforce who led the campaign against the slave trade. Wilberforce was subjected to a vicious campaign of vilification by slave traders and others whose powerful commercial interests were threatened. Rumors were spread that he was a wife-beater, married to a Negro woman. His character, morals, and motives were repeatedly smeared during some 20 years of pitched battles.

From his deathbed, John Wesley had written Wilberforce, "Unless God has raised you up for this very thing, you will be worn out by the opposition of men and devils; but if God be for you, who can be against you? Are all of them together stronger than God? Be not weary in well-doing." Wesley's eloquent words were enshrined in the young Tory's mind; he never wavered.

I found myself reading Wesley's letter over and over. It is not success but faithfulness that counts; not our glories or humiliations but steadfastness in pursuing God's will. If there had been any question of my continuing the prison ministry, Wesley's words settled the issue for me as much as Gordon Loux's pragmatic analysis.

One night a few weeks after the *Parade* story, when I was still hurting badly, I was praying about it in deep self-pity. Gently, the Lord took me back a few years to my White House days when I had, for very noble reasons I thought, planted a false story in the papers that deeply wounded another person.

The Lord didn't have to say anything more.

*We have had our last chance. If we do not devise
some greater and more equitable system, Armaged-
don will be at our door. The problem basically is
theological and involves a spiritual recrudescense and
improvement of human character . . . It must be
of the spirit if we are to save the flesh.*

DOUGLAS MACARTHUR
(At Japanese surrender in Tokyo Bay)

19. The Deeper Search

When I entered his office, I could tell that Norman Carlson had some
good news. The director of the federal prison system greeted me with
a warm smile and thrust a letter into my hands. Skimming the first
few pages, I could see that it was a critique from Dr. Daniel R. Peterson, a psychiatrist whom Carlson had dispatched to inspect seven
prisons.

"Look at the last paragraph." Carlson, normally cool and impassive,
bent forward like a man waiting for someone to open a Christmas
present.

And that's what it was when I read these words: "Every chaplain
we have talked with," Peterson wrote, "is totally sold on the Fellowship
House program. Inmates who have participated in the experience have
almost universally been instrumental in turning the institutions' religious programs around or revitalizing existing programs. This appears
to be a valuable and dynamic ministry."

I couldn't restrain a low whistle as I read the paragraph a second
time. There had been excellent reports from the 70 inmates trained
and returned to their prisons the first year. But this was the first
independent affirmation—and a ringing one at that.

One of the most heartening aspects of the Peterson report was the
evidence of our growing acceptance by government chaplains. Remem-

bering from my days as a prisoner how strongly inmates viewed chaplains as part of "the system" and how much prisoners who were rewarded by "the system" were resented, we insisted that our volunteers pick the participants. While this kept our credibility with the inmates, some chaplains were understandably resentful. Now it appeared this resistance was being overcome.

Carlson settled back in his chair. "Well done, well done," he sighed as if relieved. His decision to let us take inmates out for discipleship training had involved great personal risk. Even during the *Parade* magazine fiasco, he had stayed firmly with us and our work. Now the decision looked good.

"I tell you what we might think about now," Carlson continued, staring reflectively through the window of his office at a stately row of grey government buildings. "We're opening a new prison in Memphis in a few months. Now there just aren't enough funds for all the programs we need there. I won't have enough until next year's budget. The chapel program is going to be hurting and so I was thinking . . ."

I knew what was coming before the words were out of Carlson's mouth.

"I was thinking," he continued gingerly, "maybe you could find the support to hire the chaplains and put them in, for a while anyway, until we get more money."

Getting our own men inside a prison to live among the inmates would be an unprecedented break with tradition and could turn a prison into a spiritual retreat center, I realized. Carlson had hardly finished his sentence when I practically shouted the answer, "We'll do it!"

The decision was made in the triumphant flush both Carlson and I were enjoying. Perhaps we should have been more prudent and consolidated the good work already begun rather than branch into unexplored territory. Nothing like this had ever been tried; I had no idea where the chaplains would come from—or the money to support them. Yet it was still an opportunity not to be lost.

On that wintry day I could not imagine what was ahead—how the system would react to our invasion of their ranks. I would have savored the hard-won truce with the chaplains if I'd known how short-lived it would be.

The Carlson meeting took place two days before the National Prayer Breakfast in January 1977. An afternoon seminar was scheduled for those interested in Prison Fellowship. People from all over the country, including many Christian leaders, would attend. *Good timing,* I thought, *a good place to break the news about Memphis.*

When I arrived at the large meeting room at the Washington Hilton, people were crowded in doorways, lined against the walls and sitting cross-legged on the floor before the podium. Paul Kramer welcomed the gathering and was followed by several former inmates who told of their experiences with Prison Fellowship.

A hush then fell over the room. Obviously the inmate testimonies were thrilling the crowd, but something was happening, it seemed to me, beyond the stirring of emotions. At least I felt it—a powerful moving of the Spirit deep within me and throughout the mirrored, ornate hotel ballroom.

Then it came to me. I *knew* that the man God had already chosen to be our Memphis chaplain was there, seated in the crowd, unsuspecting, listening, not for a moment entertaining any thought that he might soon be living in a prison.

But that's foolish, my mind argued. The people here were all lay or church leaders. This job was for someone who knows prisons, street work or ghettos. This kind of person does not usually come to the National Prayer Breakfast.

Maybe I was simply caught up in the emotionalism of the moment. Reason stubbornly struggled to regain control. I was often suspicious of the flash revelations I heard others claim, the quick signs from heaven to guide every move. They seemed so close to superstition.

Still, the conviction persisted. I remembered reading how Dwight L. Moody experienced similar convictions and once called someone out of a crowd. Was this one of those times? To announce that the person was in the room might look like blatant showmanship.

Reason dissolved, and I signaled Paul Kramer that I wanted to speak. Paul walked to the podium and introduced me.

"Let me tell you of some exciting things," I began, explaining the Memphis opportunity. The crowd responded enthusiastically even as I told of the missionary-like demands that would be placed on our chaplain. Free of civil service restrictions, he would be in the prison from early morning to lockup at 10 P.M. He would hold no official rank but rather be like an elder brother to the inmates. General Booth, founder of the Salvation Army, wrote his missionaries in India that they were "to get into the skins" of the local people, to become one of them. So it would be with our man.

My heart was racing as I came to the punch line. "This will sound strange, I am sure, but the man God has chosen for this task is in this room right now though I have no idea who he is." My voice was cracking with emotion, but I was confident now. "If God tells you before the meeting is over, come see me; if it happens in the next few days, call me. We have to get to work right away."

I stood silent for a long moment, my eyes sweeping across the rows before me, several times catching startled eyes from the crowd. One curly-haired man in a front seat was staring intently; he removed his glasses, and I thought, wiped tears from his eyes. But no hand went up.

I looked to the back of the room at the bodies lining the walls. No one moved. I turned and walked from the podium to the side of the room where Paul Kramer was standing.

"What in the world are you doing?" he whispered.

"Relax, Brother, he's here," I answered.

Paul stared at me intently, shook his head and then walked back to the mike.

I waited through the rest of the program, watching the audience. No one looked my way. They were caught up with the succeeding speakers.

Mentally, I checked off the requirements for the position: *ordained, experienced in a prison, preferably an ex-con, young, masculine so the tougher prisoners could relate, willing to work long hours and a teacher.* A tall order.

Fresh doubts began assaulting me as I looked at the well dressed, mostly middle-aged crowd—typical prayer breakfast attendees. I knew many of them—pastors of large churches and successful businessmen— not the kind to give up everything to go into prison work.

I was foolish, I told myself angrily. Christians too often get caught up in this kind of thing which is more presumption than faith. *Why hadn't I listened to my better judgment?*

Paul was about to close the meeting when Fred Rhodes passed me a card from the man in the front row who had earlier appeared moved by my description of prison life.

On the front was "Bill Beshears, Minister of Education, First Baptist Church, Warner Robbins, Georgia." On the back, he had scribbled, "I may be the man."

The next afternoon, Paul and I met Bill Beshears and his wife at Fellowship House. Bill was lean and gaunt with an intensity in his dark, recessed eyes. Grace was a handsome woman, simply dressed.

"I don't even know why I was invited to the prayer breakfast," Bill began. "I haven't anything to do with prison work."

Only a few hours before I had checked this out and discovered that I, myself, had added Beshears' name to the prayer breakfast invitation list. A year earlier he had written me an especially moving letter, describing how *Born Again* had renewed his faith and caused him to rededicate his life. His name had stuck in my mind, even though as a minister of education in a far off Georgia church he seemed far removed from my activities.

Grace, seated next to her husband, was white-faced as I explained what was involved in the Memphis prison. The Beshears, we learned, had just finished a two-year remodeling of their house. Their daughter, 21, had recently won the Central Georgia beauty contest and was on her way to the statewide "Miss Georgia" competition. One son was a junior high school student. Grace watched us soberly as the possibility of her family being uprooted became frighteningly real.

Bill outlined his background, his ordination, his years of working with juvenile delinquents. As he spoke in a steady, determined voice, I became convinced of his strength of character. In his mid-40s, he was slightly older than the mental job description I had sketched out during the seminar, but he was vigorous, athletic-looking. He was also a teacher. One by one the requirements were falling into place.

Then came the clincher. "I know what prison life is like, too," he admitted. "I was in jail several times before I was converted. That's why I just couldn't hold back the emotion when you were talking about it yesterday."

Then he drew a deep breath. "I don't know why we are even talking like this," he said, clasping his hands and leaning forward. "It wouldn't be fair to Grace and the kids."

More and more certain that Bill was the man, Paul and I left the Beshears to their own private anguish. They promised to pray about it, talk to members of the family and let us know their decision as soon as possible.

We heard from Bill a few days later. Though soft-spoken, his voice was even more earnest than I had remembered it. "We have had time to think and pray about it," he said. "If you still want us we'll accept your challenge."

Then he explained that one passage of Scripture—Galatians 2:20

(RSV)—sealed his decision: *I have been crucified with Christ; it is no longer I who live, but Christ who lives in me . . .* "Those words convicted both Grace and me. I will go where Christ leads and I guess that's to prison!"

Oddly enough, Bill had come across that Galatians verse while visiting his congressman's office. The passage was written out in my longhand on a prayer breakfast program which the congressman had placed on his desk for any visitor to see.

With our chaplain selected, Gordon Loux hurriedly called together people we knew in Memphis who might organize a community support program. We needed counselors in the prison to help Beshears, a fellowship group in the city to which he would be accountable, local churches to provide help to inmates and financial backers.

My closest friends caution me from time to time about my tendency to plunge headlong into forbidding and potentially perilous situations. In my exuberance to launch the Memphis ministry, I was about to do just that.

It all began harmlessly enough. A Memphis civic group, concerned with the problems of crime, invited me to speak at their regular monthly luncheon. Following this, conferences were set up with several small groups, including one with local pastors.

The luncheon room seemed full of friendly, receptive people. No one bothered to tell me exactly who was there; nor would it have probably made any difference if they had. With increasing fervor I spoke about the historic nature of the executive decision to allow a nongovernment program like ours to come inside the federal prison system. I related our vision for a community-sponsored program for inmates. The room seemed to throb with excitement. The few skeptical expressions I saw did nothing to signal any impending danger.

I lost all track of my carefully prepared notes as I became emotion-filled while recounting some of my own prison experiences; I relived the depression and the helplessness.

"So I know what it can mean to those men inside to have someone they can trust," I said. "In the prison I was in, the visiting chaplain was a military officer stationed at the Air Force Base. He was a fine, decent man, but a friend of the warden and no inmate would confide in him. Government-paid chaplains are part of the system and the system is the 'enemy' to most inmates."

To underscore my point, I repeated a story which I had heard from Eldridge Cleaver. It happened, Cleaver told me, while he was in San Quentin in the late 1950s. An inmate who went to confession was supposed to have admitted his complicity in a celebrated murder case. The priest turned him in, so the story went, and the inmate was convicted and later executed.

Wisdom had gone out the window. It was like placing a stick of dynamite on the podium, quietly lighting the fuse and then naïvely staring at it. The first explosion took place that afternoon.

Several state chaplains were in the luncheon audience, and they followed me to the afternoon meeting. Angered, they demanded to be heard. If I thought I had spoken passionately at the luncheon, it was nothing compared to their aroused feelings. "You have maligned my professional and personal integrity," one snapped at me.

I admitted that my remarks had been too partisan, but this only partly mollified them.

Despite the controversy, the Christian community in Memphis responded enthusiastically to my suggestions. Dr. Adrian Rogers, pastor of the largest church in the city, agreed to be honorary chairman; Dr. Howard Oakley, a Reformed Presbyterian, would head our committee. Several other leaders joined in. A representative core group was formed of committed laymen and pastors. Funds were pledged. A citywide rally was planned to raise more. Paul Kramer would remain for several days to oversee the organizing task.

Paul was troubled as he saw me board the flight back to Washington that evening. "Those chaplains are really mad," he said.

"It will pass, Paul," I assured him. "When they see how much good can be done, they'll be with us."

My response was a naïve underestimation of the fury I had unleashed. Nor could Paul or I anticipate the traps which ironically we had helped set for Bill Beshears in Memphis.

During the days and weeks that followed, angry statements by chaplains had good coverage in the Memphis press. At the same time we received a flood of letters from inmates, reporting every kind of grievance, real and imagined with prison chaplains.

I saw that I had to overcome a bias shaped by my own prison experience; my statements about chaplains had been over-generalized and unfair. Among any group of pastors, one will find them ranging from excellent to poor; so it is with chaplains; so it is in any profession.

My attitudes about chaplains and the institutions they represented were being influenced by the growing realization that, notwithstanding the prevailing 20th-century myth, the institutions of power cannot provide all the answers to mankind's needs. I was deeply impressed by Tolstoy's arguments in *War and Peace*, that the course of history is determined, not by powerful and competent leaders, but by the inclinations, passions, will power, courage and prejudices of the masses. I had come face to face with the limits of government power myself. Orders are issued, decisions made, but often nothing happens; bureaucracy can stifle any program.

In prison the lesson was even more poignant. Prisons do not reform individuals; people rot and decay inside, often learning techniques for more violent and serious crimes later. Consumed by bitterness many vow to get even once they get out. Yet, I saw personally how God's power, transforming lives, could truly rehabilitate.

I was convinced that even a modest effort by Christians at evangelizing a prison could do more to reduce the crime rate than building 20 new fortresses—based on the simple premise that change and reform begin with changed hearts. This was what Prison Fellowship was all about.

This growing conviction that solutions to the world's problems could only be unlocked in the hearts of people caused a hungering to study and learn more about my faith, its doctrines and history. Though I had been reading extensively, I yearned for a seminary training. That was impossible, but the next best thing was arranged. Dr. Richard Lovelace, historian and theologian of revival from Gordon-Conwell Divinity School and a gifted communicator, agreed to do a series of Monday morning teaching sessions at Fellowship House. Others joined me, including a few congressmen. Soon the group numbered more than 20. I was drinking in the teachings like a thirsty man on a desert, rearranging my schedule to be in Washington whenever Lovelace was there. Meanwhile Mike Cromartie began to supply me with informative and probing memos on a wide range of Christian issues.

The studies with Lovelace, and frequent meetings with Dr. C. C. Goen at Wesley Seminary in Washington, deepened my beliefs that the malaise in our society could be healed only by a profound spiritual movement. Major changes in the course of history inevitably flowed from awakenings. I continued to be inspired by the life of George Whitefield and by the writings of Jonathan Edwards which triggered the "Great Awakening" of 1740 among settlers in the colonies. Francis Schaeffer's classic *How Should We Then Live?* showed me the impact Christians have had on every aspect of life down through the centuries.

I yearned to learn more about the great Wesley awakening in England which sparked some of the most sweeping social reforms of modern times. And about Christians like Wilberforce and Lord Shaftesbury who fought injustice in England. These men made me dare to dream about what Christians might do in the prisons of America.

The changes in my life were underscored by an event that took place during this period. Jackie Butner excitedly burst into my office one day. "The White House has called," she said. "You have been invited to speak at next week's prayer breakfast there. I hope you'll do it . . . please!" Paul was right behind her, equally excited.

For Jackie and Paul, both ex-convicts, the invitation had special significance; it was a rare opportunity to talk about prisons to the men and women who shape government policy at the highest level.

A beaming Fred Rhodes joined us and in a few minutes everyone on our team was crowded in my office. From their smiles, I knew they sensed the significance to me personally. It had been three years since I had last been inside those massive gates; in that time I had been disgraced and imprisoned. Going back was a little like the prodigal son coming home.

Yet there were reservations. If the press found out, there would be stories and another rehashing of Watergate. This could hurt our work and embarrass President Ford, whom I'd known as a friend for many years.

Fred, who had regularly attended the White House prayer breakfasts while in the Veteran's Administration, promised he would get me in and out without attention.

On a sunny December morning in 1976, Fred, Gordon and I appeared at the southwest gate of the White House. It was the same gate I had driven through every day for three and one-half years. No reporters were in sight.

The guard greeted me as if I had never left: "Right through here, Mr. Colson. Good to see you again." He held open the gate for me to pass by; only when I pulled out my wallet did he remember. "Oh yes, of course, identification please," he chuckled. "Formality of course."

Nothing had changed. The lawns and shrubs were as exquisitely manicured as I remembered, the building as snowy white. We walked up West Executive Avenue, the one-way driveway which separates the giant gray Executive Office building from the mansion itself. As we entered the basement entrance of the west wing, I noticed that the brass door knob was still polished to a high gloss.

Nostalgia flooded me. How many times had I come through this same door early in the morning on my way to senior staff meetings in the Roosevelt Room? There always was exhilaration on those mornings even though I had had little sleep or was suffering a cold or was worried or had been ugly to Patty at breakfast. Walking in that door was like inhaling a sweet fragrance, the intoxicating sense of being where the forces of history converge at one point at one time. I knew I'd feel it again this morning, looked forward to it in fact.

By reflex, I suppose, the smartly uniformed guard jumped to his feet, a protocol honor reserved for the cabinet and senior staff. I used to breeze past him with barely a nod; this morning I stopped to shake hands and talk with him. He was always one of the friendliest.

But where was the inner excitement, the thrill I had expected? I felt nothing inside, nothing except the realization that I had gone on in life to other things, that the trappings of power I once thought were so important, no longer were.

The breakfast was a marvelous time of warm fellowship. We met in the conference dining room, its paneled walls rubbed to a rich golden hue. The same red-jacketed stewards I'd known so well served us. Presidents seldom attend these bi-weekly breakfasts but there was a sprinkling of high officials along with their staff members.

I spoke about how defeat can be like a crucifixion; without it, there can be no resurrection, and how God could use the darkest things, like prison, to bring glory to Him. I told them, too, that their most profound contribution may not be their service in government but the way they faithfully follow Christ in their lives.

One presidential assistant stopped me at the door as I was leaving. "The boss is out of the building. Would you like to walk upstairs to the Oval Office and the Cabinet Room? There have been some changes since you were here."

I paused for a moment. It was a kind offer. I had spent so much time in these historic rooms that personal memories were buried in every nook and cranny.

"Thank you," I replied, "I really appreciate it, but I tell you what I'd really like to do. The telephone operators were always especially nice to me. Could we visit them?"

The aide escorted Gordon Loux and me through a subterranean

labyrinth to the third-level basement where, in a room packed with equipment, a dozen skilled women manage one of the busiest switchboards in the world. Several were Christians and had written me. We had a wonderful visit.

As I left the White House, I wondered how I could have spent three and a half years in this place and missed so many things that really matter.

Jesus is the prophet of the loser's, not the victor's camp, proclaiming that the first will be last, that the weak are the strong and the fools the wise; that the poor and lowly, not the rich and proud, possess the Kingdom of Heaven.

MALCOLM MUGGERIDGE

20. The Weak and the Strong

I found myself quietly brooding for much of the plane trip back from Attica in early April of 1978. After Paul Kramer and I had such a painful experience absorbing the hatred and anger of inmates, my mind wrestled with a flood of conflicting emotions.

The stark horror of the place, the deliberate dehumanizing of human beings produced a flash of anger. The inmates committed crimes and deserved punishment—most of them anyway—but no human beings regardless of their sins or crimes should be made to live like animals. Small wonder that four out of five crimes in America are committed by ex-convicts. Any man coming out of Attica would be dangerous even if he had not been when he entered.

My anger was mixed with a sense of despair over the futility of the prison system and that so few people really seem to care. The fact is our country is pouring at least $3 billion a year into a system which is failing as well as inhumane. Every expert agrees that prisons do not rehabilitate.

If only Christians could see this, I thought. *They must.* Many of the most glorious reforms in history were led by Christians of conscience and courage, standing against the culture, decrying injustice. Until this century evangelicals were always in the forefront. We must do it again. We must care about the rights of the weak, the poor and the lowly.

Once more I was surprised over the changed emotions inside me. Before my conversion I had been indifferent to the rights of the weak and unfortunate. The high and the mighty ran things, and that's where I wanted to be. If not sitting in the seat of power, then I wished to be right next to it. What was happening to me?

Why did the face of John Perkins now appear in my mind? Mike Cromartie and I had flown to Mississippi to visit John, a black businessman turned pastor, who was working within his community with a host of self-help programs. We walked the streets and sunbaked fields of Mendenhall, the first small southern town I'd ever visited. There were free lunches being served, a health-care clinic, job training, a new co-op store, all financed by Christians—people helping people. The gospel was being proclaimed—John Perkins is a gifted preacher— and being lived. I remember looking into the weathered and wrinkled face of one old man who was contributing his time to work in the garden, and I saw the strength and joy of Jesus living there.

On a recent Sunday I had visited the Sojourners Fellowship in the inner city of Washington. Many there were activists who led peace marches in the 1960s. Oceans separate our politics, but in their church which meets in the basement of an old school, I experienced a unity of spirit that made our differences seem inconsequential. Then we walked past rows of tenements where the Sojourners work and saw the tangible evidence of the Gospel being lived out among the "least of these."

I was discovering pockets like these all across America, simple men and women who loved God, little known Christians working for love and justice in the best tradition of 19th-century evangelicals when the church led the way in social reform.

Why were the faces of these people etched so vividly into my consciousness? Why was I so drawn to them? Perhaps I was beginning to understand God's special concern for the powerless.

As our plane landed at National Airport another thought overwhelmed me. God uses the powerless. The values of His Kingdom are upside down from man's. He uses the weak and the lowly to confound the wise and mighty.

Then I remembered the story of the inmate in the prison chapel who had prayed for Norman Carlson, the director of prisons, sitting right there on the front row of that chapel. Carlson was visibly moved when he told Harold and me about it later during that first meeting in his office. *Of course, of course!* God used a lowly one to touch Carlson's heart. The ministry we have grew out of the simple words of a man wearing brown dungarees, living in a pit of despair, unable to go home to his family, powerless in the world's eyes.

My desire to meet the man, to throw my arms around him and tell him what his prayer had meant was overwhelming. To this day, he has not appeared.

Perhaps it is not God's plan that he glory in what his prayer has meant. The glory belongs to God, not man.

God made this simple truth clear with Gideon who had assembled a mighty army of 32,000 to smash the Midianites. God said, "The people with you are too many for me to give Midian into their hands, lest Israel become boastful, saying, 'My own hand has delivered me' " (Judges 7:2, NAS).

Following God's instructions Gideon reduced his army to 10,000, finally to 300. Though hopelessly outnumbered, the small band of 300 routed their enemy, and the people of Israel could glory not in themselves but in God.

History is full, I remembered, of examples of God using for His greatest work those who seem most insignificant in man's eyes. There was the obscure Christian in Damascus—Ananias—who baptized Paul, the great propagator of the faith. Ananias was unknown before and never heard of again.

Charles Haddon Spurgeon, the great scholar and preacher, whose writings are treasured today, was converted by the testimony of a simple working man whom Spurgeon heard when he stepped into a small church to escape a raging storm.

Dr. Abraham Kuyper, Dutch scholar and theologian, had just finished an erudite sermon when a peasant woman, her head wrapped in a shawl, approached him. "Dr. Kuyper, that was an excellent sermon, but you need to be born again," she said softly. He soon was and thereafter kept a picture of a peasant woman on his desk as a constant reminder.

A butcher in England, Henry Varley, who also was a lay preacher, told Evangelist Dwight Moody, "The world has yet to see what God will do with a man fully consecrated to Him." Moody, who had been led to Christ by Edward Kimball, an obscure salesman in a shoe store, prayed that he might be that man. His ministry then exploded on two continents. Monuments are built to Moody's honor while the names of Kimball and Varley are found only in footnotes.

I like Richard Halverson's statement that "the strong need the weak so they can be close to God's strength." He so often uses people whose names may never appear in the *New York Times* but I'm convinced are printed in bold letters in the "Book of Life."

An example of the powerless moving the hearts of prime ministers was fresh in my own experience. It happened in Ottawa the day of the Canadian national prayer breakfast.

The sky was a magnificent blue that sunny spring morning as I was escorted to the meetings by the veteran politician turned columnist, Paul Hellyer. Paul, a distinguished looking man with graying hair, and I walked along the iron fence surrounding the stately government buildings of Ottawa perched on commanding heights overlooking the river valley. In 15 minutes 600 members of Parliament, senators, and ambassadors from 75 nations, would be assembling in the Parliament building for the breakfast.

"It's sad what is happening over there, you know." Paul gestured toward the province of Quebec across the Ottawa river. "Foolish pride. The French-speaking province wants to secede and be independent." Paul shook his head. "Canada will lose its soul as a nation if that happens."

At that time the separatist movement threatened to rip Canada up the middle. The political debate was acrid between Liberals dominated by Roman Catholics of French ancestry and Conservatives predominantly Protestant and of English stock. Religious differences had dissipated over the years as in the United States, but the gulf created by language and culture barriers remained deep.

Head table guests assembled in the prime minister's reception room. Ursula Appoloni, short, red-haired and very vivacious woman member of Parliament, was chairperson for the breakfast. "I know the Prime Minister will be here. I just know it. I'm so excited." She beamed as we greeted arriving ambassadors, the speaker of the House, members of the cabinet. Limping slightly under the burdens of office and age, but still a commanding figure, John Diefenbaker, the last conservative prime minister, arrived a few minutes before 8 A.M.

The room was full, all guests in place and there was no sign of Prime Minister Pierre Trudeau. He had missed the breakfasts two years running and this year the papers were filled with rumors about his impending separation from his glamorous, 27-year-old wife, Margaret. All the more reason he won't show, I thought, but Ursula's faith was unshaken. Her large brown eyes were sparkling. "He'll be here."

As the bells struck in the giant tower outside, two strapping, red-coated Royal Mounted Police in the doorway snapped to attention. His boyish smile looking slightly wan, Pierre Trudeau breezed into the room, headed right for Ursula and threw his arms around her, almost lifting her feet off the floor. "You know, Ursula, I came this morning *just* because—and only because—of you." Trudeau's great charm had always been the key to his political success.

I noticed that he had snubbed his arch-foe, Diefenbaker, walking past him without nodding. They were symbols of the polarization of Canada: Diefenbaker—Conservative, Protestant and from the West; Trudeau—French, Liberal, Catholic, and from Quebec.

Led by the Mounties we filed into one of the grandest halls I've seen in any of the capitols of the world. Light streamed in from the high, leaded-glass, cathedral windows. A line of magnificent crystal chandeliers hung from the lofty ceilings, carved stone walls were covered with stately portraits.

The Canadians take their annual national worship experience seriously. Unlike the American breakfast, here only government officials are asked to attend and a few outside guests. Members of the press are not allowed in lest cameras intrude on the solemnity of the occasion.

Seated at Trudeau's left, I wondered how he would react to me. One of the unfortunate consequences of the release of the White House tapes was the publication of a very unflattering characterization of Trudeau by Mr. Nixon. The President was privately disdainful of Trudeau's swinging lifestyle and publicly cool toward his sometimes anti-American rhetoric.

If Trudeau bore any grudges, his instinctive political charm overcame them. He was polite and from his questions I could tell that he knew little of my background.

During the breakfast two Canadian senators whom I'd met at Fellowship House walked to the head table. One of them stuck his hand at me across the starched white table cloth. "Hi, Brother, welcome to Canada," he said warmly. "Blessings on you, Brother. We appreciate your coming," greeted the other.

Trudeau looked up from his bacon and eggs. "Those men called you 'Brother.' Is there some sort of fraternal group you belong to?"

"No, Mr. Prime Minister. It is simply a greeting among Christians," I replied.

"Hmm." He looked thoughtful. "In college I studied about the Marxists. They also call each other 'brother.' It's the same concept of brotherhood I suppose," he said.

"No, no," I answered. "Marxists rally around a man and a man's philosophy. Christians follow Jesus Christ who says His brothers are those who do the will of God. We consider this the true brotherhood of man."

"Very interesting, very interesting." He was thoughtful as he returned to his eggs. During the rest of the breakfast we talked about Jesus, the meaning of one's commitment to Him and Christian fellowship. The Prime Minister, experiencing deep alienation in his family and his nation, listened attentively.

During my speech, I felt led at the end to address the issues troubling Canadians. "There are no wounds which cannot be healed, no differences which cannot be bridged," I pleaded. Then I told of the meeting of four incredibly diverse personalities—Eldridge Cleaver, former militant Black Panther; Tommy Tarrants, former terrorist of the Ku Klux Klan; Colson, the conservative one-time Nixon hatchetman; and his old liberal political enemy, Harold Hughes. The only thing we had in common was the depths to which we had fallen—all four of us had been in jail. And though poles apart, we were reconciled and discovered we could truly love one another as brothers in Christ. "No one will ever persuade me that God is not able to reconcile any of us through Christ: here . . . now . . . today . . . in Canada and anywhere around this deeply divided world," I concluded.

There was a hushed stillness in the room that I've come to recognize as one of those moments when God's Spirit powerfully embraces a crowd, and people quietly, reverently reflect on His grace. No amount of eloquence or lack of it has anything to do with it; I have learned that when this takes place, the speaker is only the vehicle. It is God's presence that all at once seems overwhelming.

The speaker of the House then rose to reply for the hosts, a formality strictly observed in Canada. But he discarded his prepared reply and spoke movingly from his heart. There was another hush when he finished.

Seated on the other side of the podium, former Prime Minister

Diefenbaker pushed his chair back, got up and started toward the microphone. Every eye in the hall was on him as he walked slowly forward. The aged leader gripped the podium and looked out over the crowd. Then he spoke.

"I feel we need to pray. Please bow your heads with me."

At the tables filled with ambassadors from every continent, there was a murmur as translators whispered the instruction; then all heads were down, Christian, Jew, Muslim, Buddhist, Hindu and nonbeliever alike.

"Thank You God for speaking to us this day," Diefenbaker began. "I, for one, will pray . . ." then he paused, his voice cracking as he fought back tears. "I will pray this day and each day hereafter," he continued still struggling, "for the Prime Minister."

The prayer, eloquent in its simplicity, was, as he continued, like a charge of electricity crackling through the room. Only the hardest of hearts would not feel the powerful emotion Diefenbaker was experiencing. When he finished, he stepped back from the podium. Instantly Trudeau was up, out of his chair and walking briskly toward him. With 600 government officials frozen in their places watching, the two men embraced.

Like so many new Christians who triumphantly attribute permanent miracles to every anointed moment, I believed this one, unforgettable experience alone might reverse the dangerous direction of Canadian politics. This was presumptuous, of course. There are moments in history when God dramatically intervenes, such as His Son's invasion of earth and the great revivals of recent centuries, but these are rare and of His choosing, not ours.

I'm sure that in God's time the kingdom of the world will become the Kingdom of our Lord; the ultimate victory is not in doubt. Meanwhile the spiritual warfare continues, day in, day out, fought in the marketplace by God's people. And so the political battles have continued in Canada. As I write this, the fragile cords which bind French and English speaking Canadians remain strained and stretched.

A nation's distress may not be instantly transformed, but from time to time God does shine His light into the darkest crevices of His planet, like a flashlight in a black forest, to offer hope and point the way for man to follow.

In that memorable moment in Ottawa the light shone, and a way was charted to man through the unforgettable sight of those two leaders standing before their followers, their hands on one another's shoulders. Remarkably, but not surprisingly, it was the story of a reformed drunk and three convicts—weak men all—which God used to flash on that light.

If Bible-believing Christians can wade against the secular stream by mass evangelistic crusades aimed to rescue otherwise doomed sinners, they can summon up enough courage and concern in public . . . to stand against the culture in majestic witness to the Holy Commandments of God.

CARL F. H. HENRY

21. When the Barriers Come Down

At our December board meeting, Graham Purcell raised the question of giving Christmas bonuses to the staff of Prison Fellowship. It should have been a simple issue, but those that ought to be are often aren't.

Neal Jones, pastor of a large Baptist church in Northern Virginia, who has become both friend and counselor to me, explained why his church didn't give bonuses. Dan Smith, a young law professor who serves as treasurer of our corporation, worried about using funds which came solely from contributions. Bill Jordan, senior staffer on the Senate Appropriations Committee, seemed more absorbed in whether to give out a few hundred dollars of ministry money than the hundreds of billions his committee votes each year. George Wilson, who manages the Billy Graham Association, was always budget conscious. Fred Rhodes sided with tender-hearted Graham Purcell and talked about presents under the Christmas tree. Myron Mintz, the only non-Christian on the board, sat silently soaking in the arguments. Not being a board member, I watched quietly as well.

Soon the debate centered on whether those recently hired should be given the same bonus as those who had been employed longer. Why should someone who just joined the staff get the same as Paul Kramer who'd been working more than a year?

Just as the discussion was becoming contentious, Myron tapped the eraser tip of his pencil on the table. "Isn't there something in the Bible where Jesus says a laborer will be paid the same no matter when he comes to work?" (See Matthew 20:1–16.)

He leaned back in his chair with the most innocent, childlike smile on his face. Neal Jones' uproarious laughter broke the momentary silence. "For thirty years I have been a pastor, and it takes the only non-Christian in the room to come up with the answer—right from Scripture."

Theologians would say that Christ was making the point that everyone is treated the same whenever they enter the kingdom of God, not that everyone gets the same pay regardless of work. But the issue was settled: all employees would be given the same bonus.

After the meeting, Myron confessed that he had been reading the Bible, sometimes two hours a day. "It's fascinating. I'm really learning a lot from it." He almost seemed embarrassed by his own words.

"You know, Myron, there's more than what you can learn in your head."

Myron shook his head. "I know what you're about to say, but I'm not there. I'd like to be, but I'm not." There was a reflective tone to his voice. "I'll be honest about something: I look forward to these meetings more than anything else in my life. They make me feel good, especially the prayers at the beginning."

I didn't press my friend. Only a few weeks earlier, a converted Jew from California was in Washington to discuss one of the proposals to make *Born Again* into a motion picture. We dropped by Myron's office to review the proposed contract.

Midway through the meeting, Myron said something that the visitor took as an evangelistic opening. Within minutes the man from California was standing and leaning across Myron's desk, alternating Yiddish phrases with quotes from Scripture and pointing his finger within inches of Myron's nose. "Myron, Brother, this is your moment; now is the time."

Myron sat stone-faced. To the annoyance of his pursuer, but to Myron's obvious relief, I was able to bring the conversation back to the film.

After completion of our sixth prisoner training class in Washington, Gordon, Fred, and I reviewed our situation. So far, not a single, major incident. Some uneasy moments, though.

Once following a seminar we received a call to say that one man had failed to return to his prison. While the police searched for the "escapee" a prayer vigil began in Washington. The inmate turned up later that same night, having been the victim of a canceled connecting flight in Chicago.

There was one unfortunate happening. A man in our fifth group, named Joel, had been one of our best students. Believing it good for couples to grow together in faith, we allowed married prisoners to have their spouses participate in the seminar if they could afford to come to Washington. Joel's young wife joined him for the second week of the seminar.

Now there was a problem; Joel's wife was pregnant, the prison staff reported. Only it turned out she wasn't really his wife, just a close friend.

For a few anxious days, prison officials threatened to shut down the program. Paul Kramer finally hammered out a compromise with the chief chaplain: families would be permitted to attend only closing weekend worship services; the bureau would certify those allowed to come.

From prison after prison, however, came glowing reports of increased Christian activity inside. "Attendance at both Protestant and Catholic services has doubled, thanks to the men you trained," one warden wrote.

In the Washington area the program produced unexpected dividends from the inmates' ministry to the community. The Baptist women of Washington, D.C., headed by Kathryn Grant, scheduled meals for each class, sometimes bringing steaming dishes of food to Fellowship House, and other times hosting the prisoners in different churches. The arrangement was at first accepted as a generous offer of help and a convenience. But it soon became apparent that the real value came from the personal interchange. Inmate testimonies electrified church groups; attendance at suppers grew. Churches began vying for the groups to visit.

After one especially inspirational program, the Baptist women of Marlboro, Maryland, began a prison outreach of their own. Bible study classes and visitation began in nearby jails, soon spreading into other institutions.

Other churches became involved. St. Mark's Catholic Church in Vienna, Virginia, draws up to 300 Catholic lay persons from Northern Virginia each time the prisoners visit. One evening at another Catholic church the man next to me was visibly moved by the prisoner testimonies. He kept pulling out his handkerchief, apologizing for his cold. Dressed in a gray pin stripe suit, he told me he was a lawyer who never got involved in "religious things," and thought his wife got carried away with all her "religious girl friends."

"But whatever this is," he continued, "I want it." That night he joined in a circle of prayer and to my amazement prayed aloud, asking forgiveness and committing his life anew.

From the church visits came new volunteers for work in the prisons and in our office. Many inmates got on-the-spot job offers. One church created a relief fund for needy prisoner families. A church couple, impressed by the intellect of one young woman prisoner, deposited $100 in a savings account, then promised to raise enough for her first year of college by the time of her release.

Congressman Don Bonker from the state of Washington, whose wife Carolyn volunteered much time to serve as my secretary, invited one class of prisoners, all women, to a meeting in the capitol. Formal invitations were sent a week ahead to 16 of his colleagues in the House and Senate. Thirteen attended, a remarkable response and more than one would expect even for a visiting cabinet officer. Most planned to stay only a few minutes, but when the women began telling of their prison experiences, the congressmen forgot about their pressing business. Ninety minutes passed before anyone left.

The story of one of the inmates, a heavyset black woman named Becky from the Lexington Prison, changed a lot of prejudices. Someone asked her what she had done to end up in prison.

"I was wrong," Becky's round face was doleful as she spoke. "There's no excuse. But you see I have nine children. Their father's gone. I worked as hard as I could so I wouldn't go on welfare. But I never could make it, even at 80 hours a week. Lots of times the kids were hungry.

"Christmas came and well, there were no presents for any of them," Becky couldn't hold back the sobs, "and so I stole. It was wrong but I wanted my kids to have a Christmas like all the other kids have."

There was an uncomfortable silence when Becky finished and wiped her eyes dry. One congressman walked over and put his arms around Becky's shoulder. Later one of my friends, a veteran of many years in Congress and a hard-line conservative, was shaking his head. "Becky committed a crime, but I wonder which is the bigger crime: stealing for your kids or voting a budget which produces such a big deficit it's bound to create more inflation. That's just stealing dollars out of the pockets of little people like Becky. Maybe I am the one who should be in prison." He was still shaking his head as he walked away.

Gradually each class which visited Capitol Hill was changing the stereotyped image of prisoners as evil, violent and dangerous individuals. Some are, to be sure, but the majority are ordinary, albeit weak and troubled human beings. In place of reading cold statistics and impersonal reports about prisons, members of Congress were meeting real human beings they could touch, talk to and often identify with.

Many congressmen offered for the first time to visit a prison; others began corresponding with inmates. Their personal concern, which is growing, is the major hope for long-overdue, much-needed reform in the system.

Meanwhile things were not going well in the Memphis prison and there was no one to blame for it but myself. Telling the story about the California chaplain who had heard a prisoner confess a crime and then turned him in, had been a major blunder. The story, it turned out, was more legend than fact, and gave some of our critics just the opening they had been looking for. Critical articles continued in the local press.

The bishop of the Catholic Archdiocese of Memphis wrote to the federal bureau of prisons stating that unless government-paid chaplains were appointed he might not allow any priest to administer the sacraments inside the prison.

When I called the bishop to apologize, he gave me a 20-minute tongue-lashing, accepted the apology, but said he still could not assure me that he would allow his priests into the prison. What made the impasse so sad was that few churches have been more effective in prison ministry over the years than the Roman Catholics.

The situation steadily worsened. A leading Catholic layman resigned from the committee we organized in Memphis. Congressional friends of mine from Tennessee told me they were receiving complaining letters.

Several Protestant churches balked too. We found ourselves plunged headlong into encounters with critical church bureaucracies; one official admitted to me, "We've got a lot of jobs at stake, you know." There was suspicion about our program. Why should it be otherwise? we decided. We were the new, unknown kids on the block.

Through the spring months fresh accusations were hurled at us: we were not part of *the* church; we were another cult; we favored only evangelicals and wouldn't minister to others; we would endanger prison security. Some, like the suggestion we were anti-Catholic, stung hard. But for the restraining counsel of Fred and Gordon, I would have fought back at the more outrageous things said about us. Theirs was wise advice.

There were times when we would have gladly abandoned Memphis, but the inmates who strongly supported us would have seen our backing down as a defeat for them. There was nothing to do but stand our ground and trust God to see us through. Despite the storm which now swirled around him and his irritation over our handling of Memphis, Norm Carlson made the same decision.

In June, I visited the U.S. Catholic Church headquarters in Washington and issued a public apology to their chaplaincy staff in front of cameras and reporters from the Catholic press. Mass would be held in the Memphis prison, we were assured.

Inside the prison, the situation continued to be stormy. Jesse Ellis, a young, black pastor who had been hired by us as Chaplain Beshears' associate, added to our problems. Jesse's humor was often barbed; he was also outspoken and sometimes uncontrollable. The inmates loved Jesse, but the prison staff considered him officious and were suspicious of his motives.

Two graduates of our second discipleship class were transferred into Memphis, a part of the first group of inmates assigned to this new facility. Both Ike Watson, a black, and Doc Barlow, a white, were strong leaders who soon were developing fellowship groups in each housing unit.

One third of the prison enrolled in Bible study or fellowship meetings. The community response was growing; more volunteers had signed up for duties inside the prison than Beshears could get permission to bring in.

The tension within the prison produced one unexpected dividend. Chapel services were packed. The inmates never doubted whose side the new chaplains were on. Beshears opened the doors of the chapel at 6 A.M. and didn't close them until the housing units were locked down at 10 P.M. He frequently spent his evenings in the living areas, playing basketball, shooting pool or joining in group discussions. Beshears was regularly putting in 16-hour days.

One inmate summed up the attitude of the prisoners. Beshears had taken me one day to the segregation area where security risks and disciplinary cases were held. I peered through the foot-square, glass, soundproof window into one cubicle. When an unshaven older man lying on the cot saw me, he jumped to his feet and walked to the door, motioning to the floor. At the bottom of each door was a grate through which air circulated. We both got on our knees to talk through it.

"I like your chaplains, Mr. Colson. Stick with your men."

"Why are you concerned?" I asked, surprised. I'd talked to many men in the "hole." All were angry and wanted to get out, but I'd never met one before who was so worked up over something unrelated to his own immediate distress.

"Why do I care, did you say?" He was indignant. "Thirty-two years I've been in prison. I've been beaten, tossed in the hole over and over, better off if I had been dead."

His voice softened. "Jesse and Bill are the first people in 32 years who cared for me. I'd give my life for those two." Then he paused as if summoning up courage. "Mr. Colson, I've come to believe in your Jesus through them."

After a few months things seemed to quiet down. Then we had a report that the warden and his staff wanted Jesse Ellis barred from the prison. The warden was livid over a sermon Jesse had preached. Jesse seemed contrite, but the pot was boiling.

Gordon and I left the next day for Memphis.

We were ushered into the office of Warden Hal Hopkins, a handsome, square-jawed man in his mid-40s, who was puffing on his favorite silver-encased, briar pipe. Through the glass wall of his office was a panoramic view of the neatly trimmed green lawn and modern brick buildings of the prison. Memphis, the newest institution in the federal system, is clean, efficient and has humane living accommodations.

"Your Mr. Ellis," Warden Hopkins said calmly, "has preached a sermon that I believe threatens security in this prison. I can't have it."

"Chaplain Ellis tells me it was all taken from Scripture, Warden," I answered.

"I don't know about that, but I know what incites men to riot. He insulted a corrections officer as well." Always well composed and self-assured, Hopkins looked at me with fatherly sternness.

"How do you know what he preached?" I asked.

"Here's a tape. Listen for yourself. I've already sent a copy to Washington." He spun a cassette across his highly polished desk.

"How did you get this tape?" I asked, suddenly concerned that the warden was secretly recording chapel services.

Hopkins tamped fresh tobacco into the bowl of his pipe and held his silver lighter over it for several moments. "Ellis gave it to me," he took a long puff and then added, "*after I asked.*"

"Well all I can do is listen, then I'll be back to see you," I replied. Gordon and I left.

Jesse held two graduate degrees and knew his Bible. The tape we listened to in Beshears' office was Jesse Ellis at his best. He told the inmates the story of Paul and Silas in the Philippian jail. "And so God shook the prison to its foundation," he thundered. "That's what He'll do for you. He'll tear these walls down so you can be free men, free in Jesus Christ." Loud "amens" and "preach it, brother," echoed from the tape.

"I dream," Jesse spoke deliberately, like a locomotive just building up speed, "I dream of the day when there are no more prisons because God will have set all the prisoners free!" The word "free" was shouted with such gusto that the little tape player seemed to reverberate. The inmates cheered.

Jesse couldn't resist a little fun. "Officer Jones here will be out of a job." More cheers. "What is he going to do? All these years he's been walking around just swinging these keys." Jesse was obviously performing, his gangling frame prancing around the altar twirling make-believe keys; the inmates were roaring. "What's he going to do? He'll be unemployed, that's what he's going to be."

Hopkins had interpreted those sentences as disrespect to Officer Jones, but we discovered that Jones was in the chapel, laughing and enjoying it as much as the inmates. It was meant good-naturedly; the officer took no offense.

It was the reference to prison walls coming down that disturbed Warden Hopkins. But it was straight out of Scripture and anyone who once understood it, could hardly see it as a threat of violence. I looked at Gordon, who was still laughing. "No doubt what we do, is there?" I asked. He nodded as we headed back to Hopkins' office.

"Warden, that sermon is exactly the kind we expect our chaplains to preach," I announced, explaining the Scripture verses from which it was taken. "I wish I'd been able to preach that one myself," I concluded.

Hopkins stroked his chin and stared into the sun-drenched courtyard below. "That's your business, Mr. Colson. All I can tell you is that no chaplain *working for me* is going to preach that way *in my prison.*"

There was a moment of uncomfortable silence. "That's why he doesn't work for you, Warden," I replied.

Hopkins stared back, then broke into a grin and knocked his pipe on the ashtray. "Well, thank God for that anyway," he chuckled.

I had a sudden new respect for Hopkins. He was straightforward and he had a dry sense of humor. Our differences at least were always out in the open.

The situation in Memphis cooled off for a while, but to create more understanding for our program, Norm Carlson invited either Harold Hughes or me to address the federal wardens at their annual spring conference meeting in Fort Worth. It was a timely opportunity to state our case—if they would listen, that is.

At one of our Tuesday morning breakfasts Harold and I agreed on a strategy. We would both accept. As an ex-convict my views would be suspect, but Harold had the respect of prison professionals because of his policies while governor of Iowa.

It was a small but select group assembled in the dining room of the Fort Worth hotel: 50 wardens and regional prison officials, accompanied by a handful of wives. During lunch I studied the faces carefully; prison wardens are tough professionals. Most of them started as guards or counselors and worked their way to the top. Several stared curiously at Harold and me but without warmth.

I picked at my food. Having spoken so many times in every imaginable setting, I am seldom nervous. This day, however, my heart was racing. So much was at stake; without their acceptance, even grudging, there was no ministry.

Carlson introduced me. I walked to the podium, greeted by a roomful of intense eyes and unsmiling expressions. The five minutes that followed could best be likened to a person scared and dizzy, trying to walk a straight line after stepping off a high-speed roller coaster. My sentences were disjointed, my thoughts jumbled, and I fought to get words through a mouth that was as dry as the desert. There were no nods or smiles anywhere in the audience, save from the wife of a retired warden. At the end of my five minutes, I mouthed a few well-worn platitudes and sat down to unenthusiastic applause.

Harold was slow starting, perspiring profusely and nervously tugging on his belt, while visions of impending disaster began to crowd my consciousness. The faces arrayed before us seemed granitelike; even some of Harold's best quip lines drew blank stares. It was as if we were running at full speed on a treadmill going the opposite way.

Then slowly but steadily, Harold began to gain ground. Sweat streamed down his face as he thundered, "We've got to care about the souls—that's what we are dealing with—the souls of men."

I've heard it said that Harold could spellbind a crowd reading from the phone book. It was true this day. His voice, deep, resonant and rich as a tuba's notes, seemed to fill the room, gradually commanding their full attention. Expressions mellowed, squirming stopped. The crushing noise of Harold's beefy fist pounding on the rostrum seemed to lift people straight up in their chairs. The eloquence matched the thunder. He talked of brotherhood, the healing of broken relationships through Christ, the hope every human being harbors in his or her heart for an eternal relationship with the Creator. His words sliced through the thickest callouses like a stilletto; men's hearts were being touched.

A roar of approval joined with the applause when Harold finished and lumbered back to his chair, mopping sweat from his brow.

The verdict was no longer in doubt. Several wardens waited in the dining room after lunch, each one assuring us of their cooperation. Warden Hopkins of Memphis was among them.

Harold's speech marked a decisive turning point in the fortunes of our ministry, though an unexpected incident in Memphis a few months later may have been just as decisive. Here is the way it was reported to us by the chaplains and inmates.

One Sunday night Jesse Ellis was preaching in a chapel service crowded with community volunteers and inmates. Jesse's message stirred the congregation and the communion that followed produced a rich time of fellowship between black and white, rich and poor, imprisoned and free. At the end, the chapel seemed to overflow with joy and love.

As the community volunteers began filing out, some of the inmates walked with them. The procession made its way across the grassy compound toward the glass-walled control room and the main gate.

One of the most faithful of community workers was a loving, gray-haired woman in her 60s named Mrs. Rodman. Just as Mrs. Rodman was about to pass the control room on her way to the gate, she turned and hugged two inmates nearest her, Billy Melvin and Lin Brown.

"God loves you boys," she called as she passed through the prison gates.

Two hours later Billy was asleep in his room when the door was unlocked by a guard. "Come with me, Melvin," he ordered. Billy jumped out of bed, rubbed his eyes and hastily threw on the dungarees stretched over the end of his cot.

Minutes later, he was standing in the captain's office as a scared looking Lin Brown was leaving, escorted by a guard. Brown whispered to him, "They wrote me up for kissing and hugging. That's no lie."

Billy was confused at first; then it struck him: *Of course, hugging Mrs. Rodman!* He and Brown had done that at the front gate.

Billy stood before the captain's desk then occupied by a prison lieutenant. Beside him was a corrections counselor.

"Are you authorized to escort guests out of the institution, Melvin?" the lieutenant demanded.

"No, Sir, but I stayed inside the compound," Billy replied softly.

"Don't explain. Just answer. No—right?" the lieutenant barked.

"That's right, Sir," Billy's voice was weak.

"What goes on in that chapel anyway, Melvin? In the darkness, just those candles are lighted. What do you guys really do in there?"

"Communion, Sir, we celebrate the Lord's Supper," Billy replied.

"Come on, Melvin. Is that where the Lord's Supper was held? In prison?"

"It wasn't in prison, Sir, but the Lord knows what it is to be in prison," Billy replied.

The counselor spoke. "Well let's see what He can do for you now. See if He can get you out of the hole."

"You think you can kiss any woman who walks in here, Melvin?" the lieutenant demanded.

"No, sir. It wasn't kissing," Billy replied. "I mean not like you mean. That was Christian fellowship."

"So that's what it is called," the counselor roared. "Ha!"

"The first time I ever threw a man in the hole, Melvin, was for winking at a woman," the lieutenant continued. "Does that tell you where you stand, Melvin?"

"Yes, Sir, it does," Billy replied. He'd been in the hole before; he could stand the long, empty hours, the sterile walls, the unending silence, the tedium. The disciplinary report, however, would cost him the furlough he had earned. There was a heavy, uncomfortable weight in his stomach.

"Well, that's where you are headed for 'unauthorized contact with the public' under Code 702." The lieutenant was writing furiously on the incident report form on his desk. "Well, that's that." He screwed the cap on top of the pen and looked up at Billy.

The counselor had been standing beside the desk, but Billy's eyes had been on the lieutenant and the incident report. There was a sudden loud thud. Billy spun around just in time to see the counselor's body hit the floor, flat, like a post falling over.

The lieutenant jumped from his desk, shouting for help from the adjacent office. The counselor's eyes were closed, his face snow white as if every drop of blood had been drained from it. Gurgling noises came from his throat as his breath-starved lungs started his chest heaving. Billy prayed while the lieutenant pounded his chest and pried his clenched jaw open.

Seconds later, the counselor was on his way to the hospital in the prison ambulance. Billy Melvin and Lin Brown, who had been waiting outside, were hurried back to their rooms.

The incident report was never filed. And nothing could be found wrong with the counselor, apart from a nasty bruise on the back of his head. He had no history of epilepsy or fainting and, in fact, was back at work a day later. Many inmates reported that he seemed changed somehow; he was quieter and more friendly. The tensions within the prison, particularly the hostility toward those in our chapel program, seemed to lessen as well.

A very strange episode, everyone agreed.

It is characteristic of our age that people want to have God but do not want to have the devil. People are inventing gods for themselves . . . their Do-It-Yourself-God-Kits. But they are gods who do not demand much . . . who [do not] punish, [but] absolve them from conflict and doubt, massage them, pat them on the head, and rather like their parents, tell them to run along, get stoned if they will, pick marigolds, and love. So easy it is to love! But above all they are gods who will not trouble them with . . . problems of evil, suffering, and death . . . The recipes are too easy . . . Universal harmony has never been offered so cheaply before.

HENRY FAIRLIE

22. Dealing with Christian Myths

In the early spring of 1977 Patty and I broke away from a string of appearances and prison visits for a weekend in Vail, Colorado. A friend loaned us a beautiful chalet perched on the side of a snow-covered slope looking over the town below.

Neither of us are skiers, but we were so travel-weary it made no difference; all we wanted to do was sit before a raging fire, breathe in the exhilarating mountain air and above all, avoid all contact with the world, including newspapers, television and even the friendly words of well-wishers.

On Friday night Patty and I put on woolly sweaters, squeezed into our boots and ventured down a narrow, icy path into town. While we were reading the menu posted in the window of a cozy little restaurant, several customers about to enter greeted us by name. Others turned around and stared. We smiled and walked on back up the hill. Hamburger, which we had noticed in our friend's freezer, would have to take the place of the quiet dinner out I'd promised Patty.

Late the next afternoon we decided to try again. Back into the boots, sweaters, scarves and gloves. The dazzling white of fresh snow which had just dusted the roads and rooftops made my eyes squint. I had closed the front door behind us and we were walking off the porch when a young girl dressed in skier's garb spotted us. "Mr. Colson," she shouted.

Patty groaned.

"Another night of hamburgers," I sighed.

Wisps of white vapor rose over her bobbing head, as the young girl jogged up the path to our front door. "Oh, Mr. Colson!" she exclaimed. "My husband told me you were here. So glad to meet you." She stuck out an ice-crusted mitten which I shook.

I was surprised at her mention of a husband; she was a sweet-looking, rosy-cheeked young girl, as flustered as any teenager and not more than 16, I was sure.

"Well, I'm so glad to meet you, too," I replied shaking her hand again since the mitten was now removed. "What is your name?"

"My name. Oh, my name. Karen Higgins. Oh, I mean Karen Wheeler. I've been married only a few months," she sputtered, dropping her brown eyes shyly and shifting from one foot to the other.

"Thank you for such a warm greeting. This is my wife, Patty. We're about to take a walk," I said.

"It's a great day for walking," she replied brightly, "but would you mind if I asked you just one question?"

"Of course not, Karen."

"I was just wondering, I mean how is a person sure about being a Christian? I read your book and you don't sound like you have any doubts, but how do you know for sure, I mean?" Her eyes misted as she spoke.

I looked at Patty, who nodded. Karen needed help. We could forget about walking into town. Patty invited Karen inside. As she took her ski parka off I noticed she was trembling, probably half-frozen from waiting outside our house, I thought, or else she was a deeply disturbed young girl. When she took her cap off, her brown hair flowed over her shoulders and halfway down her back.

Karen poured her life out as we sat around the fire: a Christian since she was 12, raised in a devoutly religious family, educated in good schools, married to a childhood sweetheart when she was just 20. So far she fitted the typical, upper middle-class pattern. But then came the shocker. Her older brother, employed in a Christian organization, had always been her hero. But six months before, without warning, he committed suicide. There was no obvious explanation; the tragedy shattered Karen's world.

"He was such a perfectionist that he couldn't take it when he couldn't do everything he was supposed to. He tried too hard at everything," she explained, tears filling her eyes.

Karen kept trying to smile even as tears rolled down her flushed cheeks. She wiped the tears as if angry at the display of emotion. I tried to relax her, explaining that tears were normal, good for her in fact, but her struggle continued.

"I'm afraid the same thing will happen to me," she continued. "I've even thought of . . . I don't know why I'm telling you this . . . I've even thought of suicide myself," she sobbed.

"Why in the world, Karen, would you say that?" I interrupted. "You have everything to live for—a husband you've said you love, friends, Christ in your life, a good home, a whole lifetime ahead of you. I don't understand."

Karen pondered the question, brushed the hair away from her eyes, then she spoke very deliberately, "Because . . . well, because I don't really think I'm a Christian. Some days I'm so depressed I don't feel the joy I'm supposed to. I can't even smile."

"Neither can I lots of days, especially when I'm in prisons," I replied.

"You?" she exclaimed, her eyebrows arching upwards. "But I could tell from your book that you've really *got* it, that's why I thought you could help me *get* it too."

"Karen, there are days when I feel absolutely rotten," I answered, "days when I doubt my own faith, days when I can't stand people, days when I am depressed and angry—those things are normal. But Christ is always present, real, unchanging and He pulls me out of it."

"But all my life I've been told Christians are happy and joyous," she protested. "You mean I can be a Christian even when I can't smile and feel happy?" she said with relief.

"You sure can, if you have truly asked Christ into your life," I replied. "And you are also human. It's not easy to live the Christian life—which is what you are discovering—so don't you believe anyone who tells you it is. In fact, you have my permission to throw your hymnbook at the next person who gives you that simple syrup."

Within minutes Karen seemed at peace with herself. Alternately sniffing, laughing and then realizing how foolish she had been, she would self-consciously stare at the floor. Patty brewed a pot of tea and for the next hour we talked about the reality of the Christian life. It was amazing to watch the transformation as Karen rapidly regained her self-assurance.

She returned the next day to introduce her husband, who now could admit that their young marriage had been on shaky ground because of Karen's emotional turmoil. But this day their spirits were soaring, he told us gratefully, so dramatic was his young wife's turnaround. Karen was liberated when she discovered that she had allowed a Christian cultural myth to control her life.

When Karen first accosted us, I had felt some resentment at the invasion of our privacy. Then I quickly realized that God wants our availability, more than our ability. Patty and I happened to be there when someone needed help. I'm glad we were.

I had another reason to be grateful: there were lessons to learn through our experience with Karen. One was the depth to which 20th-century values have infiltrated the Christian faith.

The modern American ethos exalts worldly success as the overarching goal of all of life's pursuits. The winningest quarterback is worshiped with the kind of reverence the ancient Greeks reserved for their Apollos; millions throng to our coliseums or huddle around TV sets to shout hymns of praise until their voices become hoarse. It doesn't matter that in real life the deified athlete may be a notorious philanderer and wife-beater of despicable character.

The holy shrine of American life is piled high with fancy cars, color TV sets, vacation trailers, outboard engines, gold watches, $400 suits and fur jackets. Books like *Winning through Intimidation,* and *Looking Out for Number One* understandably top our best seller lists when advancement of self becomes life's cardinal goal. Karen's brother, a young super-achiever, was intolerant of his smallest failure, even in his own Christian work. Frustrated by not being number one, despondency overcame him and he ended his life rather than admit inadequacy.

How sad that Karen's brother had not been confronted with the truth that the object of the Christian life is not to be number one but to love God, hunger and thirst after righteousness and do what is pleasing in His sight.

Karen taught me something else: the fearsome hazards of a simplistic gospel. The explosion of Jesus upon one's life transforms the human personality. It often brings peace of mind, contentment, happiness and joy. But to stop there as many do is like comparing real life to a children's fairytale in which the heroes and heroines "live happily ever after."

In giving my testimony before largely secular crowds, I often found myself tempted to promise personal gratification. "Though my world was collapsing around me, threatened with criminal charges, my law practice in trouble, I felt an inner peace, strength, a calm assurance," I would explain in an obvious effort to persuade the nonbeliever of the personal advantage to him of knowing Christ.

What I said was true. Christ did strengthen me through a dreadful ordeal. After my session with Karen, however, I realized that I had given the impression that the believer escapes the fiery trials. I vowed never to use that example again. It can be a terrible disservice, building false expectations and setting one up for the fall which inevitably will come.

So many Christian books have the same happy ending; so much preaching concentrates on the personal blessings of our faith, that it is small wonder really that Karen and others believe that the Christian life is like being lifted on a magic carpet to float over the soot, confusion and pain of the real world to sweet choruses of "Praise the Lord!" I wish Karen were an exception, but sadly she is not. I have encountered hundreds like her.

Karen concluded that a believer is filled with joy and should therefore always be smiling. This bit of folklore drives many Christians to perpetual facial contortions for a smile which will survive even the most dire circumstance. I have known determined smilers who kept their smile intact right through funerals for loved ones.

The joy I see Paul describing in Galatians is not the giddy outward manifestation of worldly happiness; it is the certain knowledge and rich assurance that Christ has claimed us for eternity.

The smiling Christian stereotype was easy for me to shoot arrows at because it was in such contrast to the reality of Christian life inside prisons. It was harder to see the stereotypes I had created in my own mind and to get free of them.

Prison chaplains, for example. While an inmate at Maxwell I saw them as prison officials, government-paid employees whose concern was to please the warden first, serve the prisoners second. This made stereotypes of all prison chaplains—and that was wrong. There are many whose commitment to prisoners comes second only to their obedience to the Lord.

I tended to see prison wardens in the same stereotype mold: tough, callous, cruel. This myth needed to be exploded for me, and it was in 1977.

My warden at the Maxwell Federal Prison had been Bob Grunska, a man who I heard was a Christian but who seemed to me to be insensitive to the problems of his prisoners and unfair in his treatment of us. While Harold Hughes and I were speaking at the Fort Worth Warden's Conference luncheon I spotted Bob Grunska in the audience.

The sight of this tall, stern-faced man startled me. Vivid scenes of my own prison experience collided in my mind while I waited to speak. It was like having a former boss who had fired you on hand to see if you had shaped up in the interim.

Just having Grunska in the audience was enough to rattle me. On top of that I had learned from mutual friends and the prison grapevine that the warden was outraged by what I had written about his prison in *Born Again,* and wouldn't allow copies in the prison library. I had tried to be fair, but a warden could never see things the way an inmate does; the inmates at Maxwell had feared and hated him.

In an earlier chapter I described struggling through my speech well aware that I had not moved the wardens one bit. Harold saved things with his eloquence. Afterwards I saw Grunska approaching, unsmiling. We shook hands.

"Could we go somewhere and talk?" I asked.

"Of course," he replied.

As we walked together toward a small room off the hotel lobby, my mind mentally checked off the things I'd written. *Had I been unfair? Was my writing colored by the passions of prison life, where so much anger at life in general inevitably spills out on those who run the system?*

We pulled up chairs by a small table in the lounge. "Mr. Grunska," I began, "I have heard from others that you were unhappy over my book and I just want you to know I'm really sorry if anything I wrote hurt you personally."

"Wait a minute," Grunska was scowling as if he were about to unleash stored up anger. "Wait just a minute. Maybe I was hurt—I guess I was—but it was good for me. Your book helped me to understand what the prisoners really think."

Then he relaxed and a grin crossed his face. "So, no apology is necessary. It's tough to be a warden. I thought I was doing a good job, now I know I can do a lot better."

My relief must have been written across my face. Grunska laughed. "Relax, the book has been helpful in prisons and in the world. It's sure a best seller in Maxwell."

Then to my surprise he reached across the table and put one hand gently on my shoulder. I stared into the warm blue eyes of a man who could have been my fatherly prep school headmaster. Gone was the image of the tight-lipped, fierce-looking warden striding about the prison compound.

In my surprise I fought back tears. The wall between us was gone as we shared mutual concerns. He told of his upcoming retirement plans, family activities and about the extensive improvements that had been made in Maxwell since I left. A new education building had been constructed, the dormitories totally renovated and air conditioned and partitions erected so each inmate could enjoy the privacy of a small cubicle. "A lot has happened since you wrote *Born Again*." Grunska smiled and then laughed loudly.

We ended our session by praying together, thanking the Lord for the healing work He is doing in the lives of His people. And especially in the two of us.

And so another stereotype was smashed.

During my spiritual gropings I have noticed that in an effort to get across a Christian message many speakers and writers are super cautious about the use of biblical language and even the name, Jesus. When I first began talking to prisoners, I tried to relate by avoiding Christian terminology and being sensitive to what they could understand and accept.

Then I discovered that when you ask the Holy Spirit to speak through you to people, there is a remarkable quickening of communication. It took Billy Graham to explode for me one myth most of us have in the area of the Bible.

It happened when Billy spoke to the inmates of the Memphis Federal Prison. The governor of Tennessee joined him and arranged for inmates from neighboring state and local prisons to be marched in for the event.

Over a thousand prisoners, surrounded by scores of armed guards, gathered on makeshift wooden benches inside the grassy compound under a sunny May sky. I met Billy beforehand and now thinking myself prison-wise gave him what I hoped would be helpful hints. "Don't talk down to the men, Billy. I'm sure you know they resent it."

Billy smiled and nodded.

"Sometimes," I added, "you can work the Gospel in without their realizing it. You know how hard it is to get them to listen to religious talk," I continued.

Billy smiled even more graciously.

When the program began, Patty and I took seats in the third row among the inmates. There wasn't much that could go wrong that didn't. The program started late and under a scorching sun the inmates squirmed uncomfortably. Guards were standing everywhere which always has a dampening affect.

Several of the preliminary speakers made bad jokes, like the man who referred to his "captive audience." That tired cliché is as annoying to inmates as someone running their fingernail over a blackboard.

Just as Billy began to speak, a noisy helicopter swooped in overhead and hovered; a photographer, hired by the sheriff we later learned, was hanging out the open door, snapping pictures. Billy's voice was drowned out so he sat down and motioned for the choir to sing. A prison functionary tried to wave the pilot away, but the pilot thought he was just being friendly so he waved back. Another prison official ran to the radio but no one could seem to get the pilot's frequency. Some of the startled guards had their rifles at the ready in case it was an escape plan; there had just been a popular movie in local theatres about a helicopter escape from a Mexican prison.

When the helicopter pulled away, Billy started again, but the chopper merely made a giant circle and returned to take pictures from another angle. Billy stopped again and sat down. The inmates roared with laughter. Mercifully, the photographer finally ran out of film and the noisy bird departed.

Forty minutes late, Billy began for a third time. That can be disconcerting, but the mishaps took none of the steam out of his delivery. Two minutes into his talk, Billy read the passage in John 3:16. Then he looked out over the crowd and smiled. I bit my lip. *Oh no, I thought, he's going to hit them right over their heads. He can't be serious!*

"Now repeat it after me," Billy said. *"For God so loved the world."* He waited and they responded. *"That he gave his only begotten Son."* The chorus was stronger. *"That whosoever believeth in him should not perish but have everlasting life."* The rhythm was taking hold, the response echoing off the building walls.

Two black inmates in front of me were nudging one another and mocking Billy. *What is he doing?* I asked myself. *This is like a beginners' Sunday School class. These guys will resent being treated like children.* There were titters behind me when the final response was over.

"Those 25 words are the most important in the Bible," Billy emphasized and then with painstaking care he explained exactly what they meant. It was basic, simple, and direct: the Gospel, nothing less or more. The power which seemed to flow through Billy intensified as he continued, his voice seeming to fill the compound. A hush came over the crowd; the titters, knowing glares and nudges stopped.

"If you do not know Jesus Christ, now is the time for you to repent and ask Him into your life. Now just stand up to make your decision."

"I don't believe it," I mumbled, bowing my head and praying for God to touch hearts. *This man has courage!* Peer pressure and hostility toward religion make altar calls tricky in prison. I held my breath. *These men are in the open, guards watching. Will anyone stand?*

Only a muffled rustling disturbed the solemn silence; slowly, I peered ahead at the two black men who had been having so much fun at Billy's expense. They were standing! Two men on either side slowly rose. I looked over my shoulder. Behind me, men were standing; then another man beside me; within seconds they were standing all over the compound—150 by actual count, I learned later.

Before he left I asked Billy if he would join me in walking through the "hole," since men in segregation could not have heard his speech.

"Of course I will," he answered emphatically. For the next 40 minutes we walked from cell to cell. Startled inmates seeing Billy's familiar face peering in through the thick glass slits bounded out of their cots. Billy stopped to talk to each one though it meant sitting cross-legged on the floor to speak through ventilation grates. One man accepted Christ, one on one, with the world's most famed evangelist.

And as for my belief that with some groups I should use cleverness in working the Gospel into my remarks—another myth shot down. The power of the Word, not of man, changes hearts and history. We never need fear to use it—in any situation, as long as we are guided by the Holy Spirit.

The smashing of myths was to continue for me. Another involved Jim Fuller, the high-flying industrialist whose resistance to Christianity had been slowly dissolving. I hadn't seen Jim in months and had missed him as a friend.

When I arrived at his house one night in the spring of 1977, it was late and we had only a short time to talk. His wife greeted me and retired. I began telling Jim stories about prisoners.

Jim was more responsive than usual. The questions he asked indicated a sharpened spiritual perception. *Should I ask him where he stood with the Lord?* I wondered. It was approaching midnight and I was exhausted. If I tried, I'd just botch it again, I thought. Instead, I told him how much I valued his friendship.

As we said good-night, he gripped my hand. "It means a lot to me that you'd want to stop by for a visit." There was a new relaxation and gentleness in Jim which shone out of his eyes. Since I had an early plane to catch in the morning, we agreed that he'd call me at 6 A.M.

I went straight to the guest room, unpacked, and fell bone tired into bed. Six hours of sleep was all I'd get, which usually is not enough.

The pounding in my ears grew louder. The room was pitch black and I nearly knocked the bedside lamp on the floor, fumbling to reach the switch. More pounding, followed by silence. I rubbed my eyes and squinted at my watch; it was just 5 A.M. There must be some mistake. But the pounding resumed at the door.

I struggled out of bed. Never easy to awaken, I was especially groggy this morning. Nearly stumbling over a chair I managed to get to the door and swing it open. Standing there in his jogging suit, a cheery smile on his face, was Jim Fuller.

"Good morning, Chuck. Ready for breakfast?"

"What's wrong? It's only 5 A.M., Jim. There's some mistake."

He looked a bit surprised and answered slowly. "Five o'clock, so it is. Well, we need a little extra time at breakfast, if you don't mind. Some things we need to talk about. Good news. You know what I mean?" He was grinning.

Instantly, I was wide awake. I was dressed in a matter of minutes and joined Jim at the breakfast table. There were just the two of us.

Jim was calm, relaxed and matter-of-fact. "I have concluded," he said, buttering his toast, "that I have maybe twenty-five years left and I want to give them to God."

He spoke with the solid self-assurance of a hard-headed businessman who had studied a complex situation for many months and then made a tough decision. It was an irrevocable decision, no question about that, solid all the way.

We prayed over the food, talked about the future, then Jim pushed his chair back from the table. "I'm grateful to you, Chuck, for pointing the way. Now let's get you to your plane."

Later I reflected over another broken Christian myth. Decisions for Christ are quite real when they are reasoned and unemotional. Sure, we all warm to the pagan who comes to faith with tears, emotional prayers for forgiveness of sins and lavish displays of affection. But just as every snowflake is different, so is every human being.

Fuller didn't follow the standard script for a conversion, but it didn't matter, for God did the regeneration in Jim's heart and mind in His own way and His time, which is as it must be.

As I reflected on why it had taken me so long to commit myself to a prison ministry, I realized that, in part, it was due to another of those myths we Christians unthinkingly create. It goes back to when I first became a Christian. Some close friends, aware of my normally impatient, often impulsive nature counseled me to "wait on the Lord." Mature believers whom I admired used the phrase so often that there seemed no reason for me to question it.

The common colloquial usage of "wait" suggests delay; Webster says it means "put off or postpone." And so, I reasoned, the Bible must mean that before taking action, we should delay. If we wait, God will be able to show us His will.

So like Gideon laying out his fleece I kept waiting, expecting some clear sign from Heaven which would show me what God wanted me to do and even the specific steps I should take. Eventually my own inner agony, study and reflection led me to make the decision to go ahead.

Some months later I decided to find the verse in Scripture and try to understand its meaning. The phrase comes from Psalm 37 which tells us to trust in the Lord and commit our ways to Him. "Those that wait upon the Lord, they shall inherit the earth." Then I saw it. The psalmist teaches dependence, not delay; that is to trust and wait in expectation of *His* triumph when the righteous will inherit the earth. That is far different from sitting around and doing nothing which many, I've discovered, are tempted to do while "waiting."

My study with Dr. R. C. Sproul at the Ligonier Study Center in western Pennsylvania helped me to understand how the believer seeks God's will for his life. First, nothing we do or don't do is going to change what is called "God's Sovereign Will." Such events as the

Tribulation period and the Second Coming of Jesus are already determined and there is no point in our trying to second guess these.

But within those broad parameters is what Sproul calls "God's Preceptive Will," meaning that God has given His people a free will and plenty of room to maneuver. There are clear scriptural guidelines for us. (Go and make disciples, feed the hungry, visit prisons, etc.) Our task then, is to do what is pleasing in God's sight and refrain from what is displeasing.

Does it really make all that much difference to God that one week we are in the Jackson prison and the next in Colorado? Or that one businessman runs his business according to Christian principles while another chooses to abandon his business for another profession? If God cares to be that specific He will let us know. Some people experience very specific "calls"; others do not. But the guidelines are the same. The disciple is like an ambassador; the longer he serves, the fewer cables and instructions need be sent from the State Department.

I cringe now when a Christian tells me, "I'm in a prayer group on Tuesday nights which I know is the one place where the Lord wants me, because I always feel so good when I'm there." I can't believe that person would not feel just as good on Wednesday night. And surely God is pleased whenever we are in a Bible study, probably happier when we go two nights instead of one.

I was slowly learning to beware of the myths and cute little formulas and expressions which become so popular in the evangelical culture. Some catchy phrases are repeated so often they are accepted as the Gospel. The one sure way to test them, I was discovering, was to challenge them, no matter who repeated them or how often I heard them, and then not "waiting" on the Lord but going and picking up my Bible.

It is the one totally dependable source of truth.

Where man is exploited, crushed, degraded by man, the Christian cannot avoid involvement by escape into the realm of spiritual values . . . he is on the side of the little people, the poor. His place in the world is there . . . because his communion with Jesus Christ is communion with the Poor One who knew total poverty, total injustice, total violence.

JACQUES ELLUL

23. Inside the Walls

"Now look, Warden, we haven't lost a single prisoner yet. And no one has given us as hard a time as you have." When Paul Kramer saw me walk into the room, he rolled his eyes upward and gestured at the telephone receiver pressed against his ear.

Paul, I could tell, was in the process of lining up our next class of prisoners. Some warden was obviously being difficult about giving his permission for the release of inmates in his prison.

"Yes, Warden . . . I know, but you see . . . okay . . . but I'm not sure we could do that." Paul was clearly getting nowhere.

He hung up the phone and heaved a disgusted sigh. "That man Ralston is too much. He won't give us anyone."

The federal prison at Oxford, Wisconsin, is a tough penitentiary (average sentence more than 10 years), but Warden George Ralston is tougher. In some prisons inmates through violence or threats gain control. Not with Ralston; he runs a super-tight prison. One inmate a few months before had been furloughed out to attend our Washington seminar and turned out to be a top student. But now Ralston was adamant: he could release none of our choices because their remaining sentences were too long.

"You know what Ralston suggested?" Paul was angrily ripping

off pages from a scratch pad, squeezing them into little wads and hurling them at the wastebasket across the room. "He said that if you guys are so good why don't you bring your teaching team into our prison and run your course here?"

"Stay cool, Brother," I replied. "We'll get plenty of men from other institutions."

Paul shook his head. "I'm not so sure. Ralston is a leader. If he refuses us, the others will start doing it."

Inside I feared that Paul might be correct. Ralston's stand meant I would have to go to Carlson. But I had just seen him about Memphis. Only so many times can an agency head be expected to overrule his subordinates.

Paul was still fuming. "Imagine telling us we should move into his prison."

"Was he serious?" I asked.

"Of course not. It was a clever ploy to get me off his back," Paul snapped.

Later the same day, Fred Rhodes, Gordon Loux and I met to map out our strategy. "What would happen if we took Ralston up on his offer?" Fred asked as a playful smile came over his face. Fred had earned the reputation of being a skilled in-fighter while running the Veteran's Administration. "Let's call his bluff," he said, slapping his hands on his knees in delight at the prospect.

"I don't know, Fred. He'd find a way to back out," I mused. "Besides, we don't have the staff to do it. Oxford is miles from the nearest town. There's a million problems and Ralston knows it."

Fred called for Paul; then Jackie Butner joined us. The verdict was unanimous: Ralston would never let us inside his prison, but Fred's suggestion was our best counter move. Then if Ralston withdrew his offer, there would be legitimate grounds to appeal to Carlson.

Paul was elected to make the call to the warden. Only minutes later he was back. Standing in the doorway he looked slightly dazed. "You won't believe this," he laughed nervously. "Ralston called our bluff. We're to go to Oxford in three weeks."

Preparations were begun at once. The next day Paul flew to Chicago, caught a feeder airline flight into Madison, Wisconsin, and rented a car for the two-hour drive to Oxford.

The Oxford Penitentiary had been constructed originally by the state. Before it was completed, a new governor was elected and promptly decided its location was too remote, precluding community involvement which is essential to whatever rehabilitation is achieved inside. When the state abandoned the facility, the federal government took it over and 500 men confined there were as cut off from the world as a leper colony.

From the outset, we realized that to go into the prison for a week and then leave would accomplish little, even be counter productive perhaps. Community and church involvement were essential to continue Bible studies and counseling after we left. Our first job then was to line up 20 volunteers to join us.

This was a tough order. Paul spent the first few days traveling to nearby towns, all of which were many miles from Oxford. One young couple from Madison who had been visiting the prison for us shepherded Paul from church to church.

It is a sad fact of American life that even socially conscious legislators find it politically expedient to place new prisons in the least populated areas of their state. Such small communities are generally conservative bastions of law-abiding citizens who have no use for criminals or those who "coddle" them.

Inmates, too, experience trauma when suddenly removed from familiar city surroundings and thrust into rural settings. Thus, from the standpoint of rehabilitation, our system produces the worst possible combination of city-bred prisoners amid country people.

Paul encountered the expected hostility. But in Baraboo, he found the owner of a Christian bookstore willing to join up. This man led Paul to a farmer who always had had a burden for prisoners and then to a small-town pastor who had been dreaming about working in a prison. Several housewives from a local Bible study fellowship volunteered. Twenty-five people were recruited, though for most it meant at least a one-hour drive to be at the prison each day at daybreak.

Inside the prison, Paul discovered that Warden George Ralston was true to his word. A stern disciplinarian, he believed prison administrators had a "duty to provide a safe place where an inmate can be rehabilitated if he wants to be." Ralston's concern for security was as much to make life inside safe for the inmates as it was to keep them locked up.

"I told you I would open up this prison for you, and I will," he said. "Whether I'm for or against your approach doesn't matter. The inmates have a right to get what you can give." Ralston was the kind of person who laid all his cards face up on the table.

The arrangements began to fall into place. George Soltau was scheduled to present the one-week curriculum that included sessions from early morning through the evening. Permission was granted for us to eat meals with the inmates; the men attending the seminar would be excused from their regular jobs. Ralston even went on the prison's closed circuit TV to invite all inmates to enroll. Chaplain Steve Johnson was cooperative, turning the entire chapel area over to us. Since Paul and George were the only staff available, we persuaded a Christian counselor from California, John Jolliffe, to come and help out. Paul Kramer set up a temporary office in an $8 per night motel located at a highway truck stop a few miles from the prison.

Paul phoned reports to us in Washington each day where Gordon Loux took charge of pulling together the details. From the beginning the chief uncertainty was prisoner response. Our one seminar graduate inside was doing his best to recruit, but he reported powerful resistance. In every prison, religion is seen as "sissy stuff." To be involved is seen as a sign of weakness, or an attempt to win favor with the prison staff.

It was a suspenseful countdown during the last few days; what had begun as a lark, calling a hard-nosed warden's bluff was now deadly serious business. Other institutions, we learned, were sending observers; several chaplains, including some of our harshest critics, would be on hand. If the program worked, it might catch on throughout the prison system. If it didn't? Well, there wasn't time now to worry about that.

With only three days to go the outlook was anything but encouraging. Even Jackie Butner, whose upbeat, effervescent spirit always seemed unquenchable, was downcast.

"How's it going?" I asked, poking my head in the doorway of her cubicle office.

"Forty-six have signed up," she answered.

"Not too good, huh?" I smiled, trying to make the best of it.

"Not too good," she replied.

"Paul discouraged?"

"Yup, but we'll keep praying." There was nothing more to do.

Fred Rhodes was scheduled to open the seminar with an introductory session Sunday night during which the week's work would be outlined. Community volunteers would then mingle among the inmates with everyone assigned to small groups which would meet in between the lectures. I had speaking commitments in the far West all week and would not arrive until late Thursday.

The ringing in my ears was muffled and distant, then closer and more threatening. Suddenly, I threw the blanket off my head and fumbled for the alarm clock. The ringing continued. I rubbed my eyes and reached for the phone. The clock caught my eye, not quite 6 A.M. in Billings, Montana, where I'd flown the night before.

The voice was Fred's. "It was beautiful, just beautiful," he shouted into the phone. "Eighty-three inmates, thirty people from outside and the greatest spirit you've ever seen!"

Fred went on to report that Warden Ralston and the entire prison staff had greeted our party at the front gate. The chaplain was enthusiastic. When the men filed into the chapel, Fred could scarcely believe his eyes; it was almost double the number expected.

After the first day, Paul reported that the seminar was gaining strength. As word spread, other inmates began drifting in. By day's end 95 were in the chapel, almost 20 percent of the prison. From the questions asked and the many who were taking notes, it was obvious that the men were serious. Included were 10 Black Muslims who always gathered together at one table. They showed no emotion and stayed to themselves. But Soltau reported that they were following every word of his lectures.

On Thursday morning, John Jolliffe, a tall man in his early 30s with a commanding presence, was teaching. Midway through his lecture, he paused, put his notes down and stared around the room.

"You know we've been together all week and no one has asked you if you want to meet Jesus Christ in a personal way. It just struck me that it's time."

For several awkward moments Jolliffe looked around the room. The men stared back. Jolliffe had worked with us before and had considerable experience as staff counselor in a California prison. He knew the men would not risk ridicule in a hostile prison culture. Many had been "con" men on the outside and all of them knew the con game. They had been manipulated, first by the "system" on the street, later by the "system" in the prison. So an altar call can backfire, appear to be more manipulation. We often invited those who wanted to make decisions to meet with us privately after the large meetings. Many always did.

But John Jolliffe, as he explained later, felt the moving of the Holy Spirit inside that prison and a quiet confidence came over him. "Bow your heads everyone, and if you want to receive the Lord, pray with me and raise your hands." Then in a soft voice his prayer began.

As a matter of principle, many of us, Paul included, spurn head counting. We want to labor in the fields, water and till, aware that it is God who causes the plants to grow. Totaling the harvest is God's business and He doesn't need us to keep score on Him.

There can be real hazards in head counting, I had learned, like programing the Spirit right out of evangelism altogether. The night before a big city mayor's prayer breakfast, the chairman came to my room. "Tomorrow 100 people will be won to Christ," he beamed. "I've claimed it, and I know it's true. Praise the Lord." He was a short man, so full of enthusiasm that he looked like he was bouncing all the time even when he stood still. His words were so presumptuous they made me cringe: besides, though I'm sure he never realized it, he was putting tremendous pressure on me to deliver.

Sleep that night was fitful and the man's words kept parading before me. The next day's speech was a disaster. Haunted by the "goal" of 100 I stumbled and several times lost my train of thought. I gave an invitation near the end of the speech but felt no moving of the Spirit. The harder I worked, the worse it got.

When my hosts tallied up the cards turned in by the breakfast guests, only four out of 1,500 at the breakfast had recorded decisions. "The ninety-six got away," my host told me, rubbing salt in my wounds, "because you didn't quote Scripture in your invitation."

But this day, Paul Kramer couldn't resist; he quietly drifted to the back of the room and stood against the wall. As John prayed, Paul spotted a hand go up right before him, then another, then two down front. Soon hands were popping up all over the room, so many and so fast Paul couldn't keep track. Well over 25, Paul estimated.

Gordon and I arrived that evening to join a weary but happy band of Christians at the truck stop motel where our staff was staying. Joining us was a delegation of Christian businessmen from Minneapolis, headed up by Dave Rolschau, who 18 months earlier had accompanied me to Sandstone, that isolated federal prison in Northern Minnesota.

Though the response in that prison had been as icy as the arctic winds which buffeted Dave's little green and white plane, we had prayed for God to open Sandstone. Now even as Paul was making plans for the next day's closing services at Oxford, Dave and his friends were talking enthusiastically about a week's seminar inside Sandstone. We'd wait and see, I told them.

George Ralston asked me to meet with him early the next morning.

Tall, rugged as an oak and with sandy hair brushed back, Ralston looked more like a former all-American tackle turned college football coach than a warden. There was just a hint of boyish enthusiasm in his manner, as if at any moment he might say, "Okay men, let's win one for good old Oxford." Ralston was a refreshing contrast to some prison officials who seem to get squeezed into the same mold as the inmates they guard, embittered, negative and often given to vulgar language.

In Ralston's simply furnished office were pictures of the President, the attorney general, and Norman Carlson on one wall; a large, red-lettered "No Smoking" sign was on the other. He leaned across the polished desk top, empty of papers. "This has been a tremendous week. You should do this in every prison. I'll recommend it, if you want."

"We're grateful to you, Warden," I replied. "You made it possible."

"Nonsense. It's my duty to see that these men have an opportunity to better themselves. You've got something to offer, that's all."

Ralston then escorted me to the chapel where the classes were continuing. Inmates and volunteers were seated at 12-foot-long folding tables lined up side by side across the front of the large open room. A lonely guard wearing a beige blazer was leaning against the wall. Many of the tough, hardened cons were wearing brightly colored stocking caps or kerchiefs around their necks, the one item of individual clothing allowed. Well dressed, middle-aged men and women volunteers were spread through their ranks. Merely walking into the room and scanning the faces, one could instantly sense that in only one week people of the most diverse backgrounds—black and white, rich and poor—had been fused together in a way that would be the envy of many churches.

My thoughts wandered while I waited for my turn to speak. How ironic that our best efforts to get men out of here were rebuffed; and so we had come here ourselves almost reluctantly. Ralston's stubbornness, and what seemed a defeat for us, was the vehicle God used to open doors for a new ministry with a far wider potential.

When I finished my short talk, two or three gave brief testimonies of what the week had meant in their lives. One young man confessed deep anger towards God, then told how the Lord had gradually softened his heart throughout the week. Early that very morning he had been awakened; a dam inside him had burst and a flood of cleansing tears poured forth. He knew that he was a new person that day.

One of the Muslims, wearing thick, horn-rimmed glasses and a heavy blue knit cap pulled down to his ears, had shown emotion several times during my talk. Slowly he stood.

"All my life," he began haltingly, "I've been looking for something." He paused, tugged at his cap and cleared his throat. "Well, I never thought I'd find it in prison, but this week I have.

"It is love," he continued. "It is the love of Jesus Christ right here." This took courage, but a few moments later everyone in the room would be put to the same test.

One of the volunteers, an older man with a camera slung around his neck, was now on his feet. "Would everyone gather on the steps for just a minute on the way to lunch so I can get a group picture?" he announced. Taking pictures inside a prison is generally forbidden, but Ralston had given permission for this one occasion.

The inmates exchanged troubled glances. At that moment the loud-speaker announced lunch and the entire prison population began streaming into the center courtyard forming lines into the mess hall. Every man in the chapel who stood for the picture would be recording his stand in front of 400 cynical onlookers.

The official prison photographer joined our volunteer in posing the seminar group on three rows of wide, concrete steps. The catcalls began, just a few at first. Then they swept across the compound in a crescendo of discordant sounds like an orchestra warming up for a performance. "Hey, man, will this get you parole?" Some waved their handkerchiefs. The men on the steps looked pained and embarrassed.

Mercifully, the photographers were soon finished. The crowd around us dissolved and the crisis passed like the evanescent fluffy clouds of the spring sky.

A communion service was held that afternoon. The inmates and volunteers arranged chairs in semicircular rows before the altar. The Muslims, who until this hour had been as inseparable as a flight of geese, were now dispersed through the crowd. True equality, I've learned, is always experienced at the foot of the cross.

When the last hymn was finished, the orderly rows suddenly turned into clusters of rejoicing people, embracing one another, reaching over chairs to shake hands. There were tears of joy and of sadness that the week was ending.

Fred's wife, Winona, having been, as she described herself, a "very proper Presbyterian," was seated next to a tall, lean black with a bushy Afro protruding in all directions above the white kerchief tied around his forehead. He had been solemn and impassive throughout communion; now he was one of the first on his feet. He spun around, leaned down and threw his long arms around Winona, who until this day used to describe the traditional Christian greeting as "that hugging foolishness." I expected her to recoil in dismay; instead she was grinning broadly.

Two somber-faced young inmates then asked if they could see Fred and me privately. We walked toward the entrance of the chaplain's office. "This is okay," one said just inside the door and out of sight of the others.

"Look, we want to make a confession and ask your forgiveness." The man speaking was short and brawny with several scars on his face and his forearms covered with tattoos.

"This morning when all you guys were getting ready for the picture . . . well, Jimmy here and me," he pointed a beefy thumb to his taller companion . . . "well, with all the guys watching . . . well, me and Jimmy took off. We didn't want the other guys to see us in this group."

Both men hung their heads, eyes fixed on my shoes.

"I understand. Don't worry. I have been here too, remember?" I put my hand on the stocky man's shoulder.

Jimmy looked Fred and then me straight in the eyes. "Mr. Rhodes, Mr. Colson, today we failed to stand up for Jesus. It will never happen again. Never again."

The words were like cold steel. They meant it.

Preparations for the week's seminar at Sandstone, Minnesota, began immediately. My concern about Sandstone was not so much its location, nearly as remote as Oxford, but its new warden, Max Mustain. The men in Minneapolis who had been visiting the prison reported that Mustain was receptive to our work, but my memories of him at Petersburg, Virginia, were of an aloof and inscrutable man who paralyzed his own staff with fear.

The seminar at Sandstone was scheduled to coincide with the Minnesota governor's prayer breakfast at which I was to speak. Sometime during the course of my talk I mentioned that I would be going to Sandstone Prison that afternoon. Afterwards out of the crowd that gathered at the head table, a tall, dark-haired man approached me. "What time are you going to Sandstone this afternoon?"

"We're flying up around 4 P.M.," I replied.

"May I join you?"

I shook my head. "Sorry, but I'm afraid it's too late to clear anyone else to visit that prison today."

He glared at me for a moment, then his facial muscles relaxed and he smiled. "I'll get in," he said, eyes twinkling.

The chairman of the breakfast, who had been silently watching the exchange, tugged at my arm. "Do you know who that was?"

"I'm sorry, but I don't."

"That was Miles Lord, senior judge of the U.S. District Court. He is probably responsible for putting away two-thirds of the inmates in Sandstone."

I gasped. What an incredible goof!

Miles Lord, former Minnesota attorney general, good friend of the late Senator Hubert Humphrey and outspoken civil libertarian, was not someone I had expected to see at the prayer breakfast. I was told that he could be a powerful ally or an implacable foe.

We learned later that Judge Lord returned to the federal courthouse after breakfast, canceled his calendar for the day, recruited a junior judge and his own pastor as companions and ordered a car for the drive to Sandstone. The officials at the prison had no idea two federal judges would be attending our seminar until they arrived at the front gate around noon.

The visit of a judge is a major event in any prison. I've heard of prisons repainted, menus changed, and regulations rewritten in anticipation of a judge's tour.

Inmates told us later that undisguised panic hit Sandstone from the minute the nearly tongued-tied guard at the front gate called the warden's office with the stunning announcement that two judges had arrived for a visit. Lord was never one to stand on formalities either, as he strode through the prison, checking little details, stopping frequently for talks with the inmates.

"Freddie, I didn't know you were still here," he exclaimed to one of the many familiar faces.

"Yes, Your Honor, but I'm ready to get out." Freddie was an older man with a long record.

"If I let you out tonight what will happen to you? Will you end up again in my court?"

Freddie's arms hung limply at his sides as he bowed his head and mumbled, "Probably so, Judge."

"Freddie, what I want you to do is go to the chapel tonight with

Colson and those others and get your life straightened out. Then I'll send you home." With that the judge slapped him on the back and walked out.

We also heard that another inmate had told the judge that he had just mailed a motion to his court asking that his sentence be reduced. He tearfully pleaded for mercy, explaining that his wife was sick, a child had run away, and the bank was foreclosing his mortgage.

"Come to the chapel tonight. I'll decide there," the judge replied.

By 5:45 P.M. there was not a square foot of empty space in the chapel. Shoulders were pressed together in every pew; 250 men, it appeared, were squeezed into seats designed for 200. The aisles were so full we had difficulty getting down front. I had never seen such a crowd in any prison for any occasion.

Something else was different. I quickly realized the uniforms were spotless, many looked starched, and every inmate's face was scrubbed bright. The impact of the judge's presence was overwhelming. Nervously, I wondered how he would react to us.

I saw him in the fourth row grinning contentedly and surrounded by brown-shirted inmates. When the program started, I called on him to say a few words.

"Well, it is good to see so many old friends here tonight." His opening sentence was drowned out by laughter. "I appreciate the introduction by Mr. Colson. When he was in the White House I believed he was responsible for everything evil in the country, including *wounded knee.*" (A reference to Wounded Knee, South Dakota, where a shoot-out had taken place between radical Indian groups and government forces.)

Uproarious laughter followed; the inmates were eating it up.

"I went to hear him this morning, expecting to see right through this phony. But something happened and I'm not sure what. So I decided to come and hear him again."

At this point the judge swung around and pointed menacingly at me. "Now don't try to convert me, Colson. I brought my pastor along for protection."

The judge turned back to the audience, grinning. "I could issue an order cutting all of you loose tonight." Loud applause and cheers. "But it is more important for you to be right here. All I can do is save your butts."

Then he pointed at me in a grand sweeping gesture.

"He . . ." his voice rose triumphantly. "He can save your soul."

I tried to point upward to the "Him" Judge Lord was really referring to, but in one of the most startling developments of the evening, it was the warden, Max Mustain, who did it best. At the close of the program the warden stood up before the audience. I had remembered him as hard and ruthless. Over the past year a transformation had taken place in his life. His eyes were shining, his voice was filled with emotion.

"I've been around prisoners a long time," he said, "and I've tried out a lot of programs to help these men. Let me tell you my conclusion: Only God can change a man and that's the message of this evening."

It was one of the most amazing nights I've spent in any prison. The judge said he would release the man with the personal hardships and set times for hearings on other cases as he held court informally by the speaker's rostrum.

Chaplain Norm Nissen, who indicated his legitimate doubts about us during our first visit to Sandstone, was eagerly signing up inmates for our "in-prison seminar"; there were more than we could accommodate. Nissen had become a valued friend.

Later I spotted Dave Rolschau. "Are you thinking what I'm thinking?" I called to him.

He nodded. "A year and a half ago we couldn't find one Christian in this prison. Now the place is like a church. It's unbelievable."

The timing was God-sent in my own life too, fortifying me for the toughest test yet.

*On the whole the evil in the daily press consists in
its being calculated to make, if possible, the passing
moment a thousand or ten thousand times more inflated and important than it really is. But all moral
elevation consists first and foremost in being weaned
from the momentary.*

Søren Kierkegaard

24. Who Am I?

On the way back to Washington from visiting several Midwest prisons,
Mike Cromartie and I stopped in Terre Haute, Indiana. It was after
8 P.M. when we checked into the motel. Early the next morning I
was scheduled to speak at the mayor's prayer breakfast.

Mike walked to the motel desk while I chatted in the lobby with
the breakfast chairman. Mike got our keys and started toward me
when I saw the desk clerk call him back. I walked over to see what
was happening.

"Mr. Cromartie, I'm sorry but we have instructions here that I
didn't see. Mr. Colson is to be in Room 217. Let me change your
keys." Mike handed the keys back.

"Hi, Mr. Colson. Good to have you here," the friendly desk clerk
waved. Mike insisted on an adjoining room, so he was given number
215. "Remember, Mr. Colson is in 217," the clerk reminded him.

"There must be a basket of fruit for you in 217," Mike remarked
as we walked to the elevator. Friends or public relations minded hotel
managers often did that.

We soon discovered however that the two rooms were exactly alike;
there was no fruit. *Strange,* I thought. *The desk clerk was so explicit.
He wanted me in this particular room.*

Although it wasn't yet 10 P.M., Mike and I decided to go right to bed since we had an early morning call. I have never been able to sleep at night without fresh air. Although it was bitterly cold outside, I walked across the room to open the window. I released the latch and tried to push the window to the side. It wouldn't move.

I ran my fingers around the edge to locate other obstacles; there were none. I pushed again. Still no movement.

I rechecked the lock latch; it was free. The window was not frozen because I could vibrate it back and forth and it moved within its frame; it simply wouldn't budge from side to side—which was the only way to open it.

I called for Mike and we both took positions on either side of the stubborn window. *One, two, three: push.* Nothing moved despite our loud grunts. *That's odd,* I thought, *there is nothing holding this window, yet it will not open.*

"Mike, do you like air at night?" I asked.

"Not on a night like tonight."

"Then let's switch rooms."

I packed up my bag and stepped into 215 where the window worked perfectly. Mike hadn't even gathered up his things when suddenly there was a frantic pounding and shouting at the door of Room 217 which I had just vacated. Mike picked up his bags and darted through the connecting door, closing it behind him.

As I got undressed, I heard muffled voices in Mike's room for a few moments, then silence. A few minutes later Mike returned and told me what happened. When he opened the door to the hall, two women quickly pushed past him into the room.

"Can we use your phone, Sir? We're being chased," one asked with such an appealing voice it dissolved Mike's judgment. He nodded and stood watching as one girl went to the telephone while the other studied him, a puzzled look on her face.

It had happened so quickly that Mike was dazed. He remembered only a few specifics. Both women were young and attractive. Both had on overcoats which they held tightly together at the neck. They appeared perplexed over something.

The one on the phone got a number, said a few words Mike didn't catch and then slammed down the receiver disgustedly. As the woman headed for the door, Mike offered to walk them to the desk if they felt unsafe in the halls. They never answered but swooshed through the door, slamming it behind them.

Seconds later, Mike opened it gingerly and peeked out; the two girls were walking from door to door studying the numbers. If they were being chased, they were certainly calm about it.

Mike warned me not to open my outside door under any condition. I put the chain bolt on and went to bed.

The next day was so hectic that Mike and I didn't get a chance to discuss his women visitors until we had checked out of the motel and were on the plane back to Washington. The more we talked about it, the more obvious it seemed.

"It had to be a setup planned to compromise you," Mike concluded. "I was in *your* room, there's no telling what or how little those gals had on underneath their coats, and they lied to me about being chased."

Still the thing was so preposterous . . .

"Who would want to get something on you?" Mike asked.

How could I answer him? There were many old Watergate enemies, I supposed; also, people I'd crossed as Nixon's aide. Though I'd made some new enemies, hopefully no one we'd encountered in our prison work would stoop to this level.

Conversation ceased and I looked out the window of the big jet, pondering the question. How many enemies did I have? Would the hatred and suspicion ever end? "You deserve the worst that can happen to you," one critic had once written me. I fretted about that for days. Ugly mail came to me at times, and on a few occasions people angrily confronted me in public. I knew many still hated me as the symbol of Nixon ruthlessness, and I understood the depth of feelings prevailing in the country.

If I'm not careful, I thought, I could become paranoid and believe that a multitude of forces are out to get me. *I don't want to be hated*, I mused. *I yearn for affection, love and support like anyone else.* Yet trying to win the approval of everyone is obviously an impossibility. If one is to accomplish anything at all, he will meet opposition. So be it. I could only trust the Lord for protection.

Then I had a pleasant thought. "Mike, do you believe that angels sometimes guard us?"

My friend looked at me quizzically. "I guess so, why?"

"I wish we'd thought to see if the window in Room 217 was still stuck this morning. I kind of think it would have opened."

Several weeks later I had a call from Ken Adams, the young lawyer who had assisted David Shapiro in defending me during Watergate.

He reported that there was a new FBI investigation of me. A man sentenced to life in prison for a long list of crimes, including murder and perjury, had recently testified that he handed $500,000 in cash to one Charles Colson in a Las Vegas hotel room on January 6, 1973. The money was supposedly a payoff from the Teamsters Union to President Nixon for freeing Jimmy Hoffa from prison.

Any new accusation involving the Teamsters or the missing Jimmy Hoffa almost always found its way to me. Despite the sworn testimony of John Dean and Justice Department officers that they had written the conditions under which Hoffa could be released from prison without my knowledge, the press almost always linked me to it. The fact that the Teamsters later retained my old law firm gave it, they felt, a *quid pro quo* basis. Nothing I said dislodged this untruth from the continuing Watergate legend.

"It's totally untrue," I replied to Adams. "I've never been to Las Vegas in my life."

"It's routine; I think you should go ahead and testify. One quick interview will put it to rest," Ken assured me.

Two young FBI agents, wearing almost identical blue suits and somber expressions, arrived from the Detroit office. "Anything you say can be used against you in court," they warned. Even though I had been through a multitude of Watergate investigations, the words were still chilling. The familiar deadening sensation gripped me.

The senior agent, no more than 30, droned through a list of prepared questions: Where was I on January 6, 1973? Had anyone ever given me cash? Who kept my travel records? The other agent was furiously scribbling notes.

I was certain my answers were satisfying them until the questioner lifted a thick sheaf of photocopy pages out of his briefcase.

"We have examined your office diaries for this period, Mr. Colson, and there is something very strange here." He began thumbing through the pages. "On January 6 there is no entry; the page is blank."

"That was a Saturday," I replied after looking at the date. "My office diary would be blank. I was home."

"Yes, but you could have flown to Las Vegas."

"But I didn't. I've never been to Las Vegas," I answered.

"Can you prove it?" he snapped.

I couldn't do that without accounting for every hour of my time for a period of many years.

Some of their other questions seemed far off the track. When they finished, the senior agent apologized for taking my time and explained that the charges made were by someone no one really believed, but they had their job to do.

"Sorry you had to go through that nonsense," Ken chuckled afterwards, "but that's the end of it anyway." Fortunately Ken is a better lawyer than he is a prophet.

Months later I arrived in Oregon with Patty on a Saturday for a week's vacation at the Hatfield home where my decision to go into the ministry had been made in the summer of 1976. Our bags were hardly unpacked when Gordon Loux called to tell me that all three television networks wanted an immediate interview. "Some big story is about to break in *Time* magazine regarding Teamster payoffs," was all Gordon was able to learn.

Could it be the absurd charge those FBI agents came to see me about months earlier? *Impossible,* I thought. *Even those two young agents didn't seem to buy the wild accusations of a discredited and probably mentally unbalanced, convicted murderer.* The charge was so unbelievable I'd forgotten all about it.

"It can't involve me," I told Gordon. "No *Time* reporter has called me to check it out." Professional ethics require that they confirm their stories or at least get comments from their targets. We would wait until Monday to see what it was all about.

The suspense did not last long. Sunday night excited voices on radio and TV announced the news: in its editions which would be on newsstands the next day, *Time* would reveal that $500,000 was paid by Teamster thugs to Charles Colson in a Las Vegas hotel room for delivery to Richard Nixon. It would be a major exposé, *Time* promised.

There was little sleep for me that night. I had been through this sort of thing so many times in the past that my system should have been immune to the surging adrenaline inside. But I could not escape the sinking depression and the feeling of discouragement.

Would the false accusations never end? If this new one were taken seriously, it could undermine our efforts in the prisons, especially with the disagreements still going on about our program in Memphis. Another thought came through the darkness: If these charges were to be thoroughly investigated, it would have to be done by the same Justice Department which was granting us permission to go into its prisons.

Copies of *Time* arrived late the next afternoon in a local drug store. Hoping that maybe, just maybe, someone had made a terrible mistake, I hastily flipped through its pages. It was there all right, in bold headline type. As my eyes scanned the story, it was worse than I feared: "The FBI believes," the story read, "that Colson, after getting President Nixon's approval on the evening of January 3, 1973, either himself or through an associate, received the money in Las Vegas on January 6, 1973."

I wanted to scream out my denial, but only a lonely druggist who looked bewildered as he watched my stricken expression would have heard me: certainly not the 25 million people who were supposed to read *Time* each week.

Later in the text was the "corroborating" evidence: "Colson's White House calendar, obtained by Watergate investigators in 1974, is blank for the weekend of the sixth and seventh." There was one line in which the magazine took note of my denial to FBI investigators, but the tone was such that the denial sounded like confirmation of guilt.

Time editors, to whom Gordon protested when the story appeared, said their reporter had seen the FBI files (a violation of the law) and had tried to call me or Gordon but could not reach us. Charlie Morin and others in my old law firm called the Justice Department, angrily demanding an explanation and a public statement. The Justice Department refused comment, however, and so the story continued gaining momentum.

By now, every newspaper in America had republished the charges, some featuring big headlines, all unquestioningly accepting the *Time* report as truth. Radio and TV were repeating updated accounts.

Fred Graham, the prematurely gray-haired CBS reporter with the soothing southern drawl, was one journalist I had learned to trust. I called him as soon as I returned to the Hatfield home. Our conversation produced the first glimmer of light in an otherwise very dreary day.

"I probably won't even go with the story tonight unless you say something new, Chuck," Fred spoke calmly. "My friends in the Justice Department tell me that *Time's* informant can't be trusted."

CBS network news did feature a segment that night but, true to his word, Graham pointed out the flaws in the charges. The other two networks must have gotten the same information because both killed the story. NBC had given it enormous coverage earlier.

A few days later, the *New York Times* published an article exposing the unreliability of the informant and pointing out that the charges were unsubstantiated. But that story appeared on page 32.

The *Time* story sunk me to the lowest point since my release from prison. Should I file suit? Friends and some associates urged me to do so. The big newspapers and magazines, armed with many lawyers and millions of dollars, however, can tie you up in knots for years if you go after them for libel.

Fred Rhodes tried to offer comfort. In a handwritten note sent to me that week, he said he was convinced that God was saying something very specific to me: "You have no control over what they will write. They will continue to abuse you. You must trust Me to protect you! You can trust no human individual or instrumentality—you must trust Me! Therefore go ahead and pray for those who despicably use you . . . and do not let a root of bitterness grow up in you."

In my heart I knew he was right, but in my emotions I fought back. I had never been to Las Vegas, knew nothing about any so-called Teamster bribe going to Richard Nixon and was sure that if such a big sum of money had been passed to the President, the Watergate prosecutors would have uncovered it. They had traced and accounted for every cent of money in the 1972 campaign and afterwards. The White House tapes for this period had been studied and dissected by prosecutors eager to uncover any incriminating words.

Weeks later Patty found an old diary where she kept a record of our entertaining. On Saturday, January 6, 1973, it showed we had hosted members of my White House Staff. These people quickly came forward to corroborate that they had been with us, that I could not possibly have been in Las Vegas.

Despite all this, the national publicity caused the FBI to launch a fresh investigation. Media charges that someone is "under investigation" are like self-fulfilling prophecies; publicity-conscious government investigators, fearing later criticism, can afford to leave no stone unturned once a national news organization proclaims wrongdoing. Maybe you weren't under investigation, but if *Time* says you are, you soon will be.

During the weeks that followed, federal agents, though never contacting me personally, plowed through every imaginable personal record. A friend of mine who works at the bank where Patty and I have maintained our checking account for years called: "I'm not supposed to tell you this, but your bank accounts have been subpoenaed, Chuck." Then he paused and spoke in a low voice, "If you are in trouble, I'll do anything to help." I had voluntarily given all the same records to Watergate prosecutors in 1974, and they were presumably still available in some government file.

American Express formally notified me in an ominous sounding letter that all their charge account records were being furnished to a grand jury in response to a subpoena. Sometimes it takes years for one whose business is dependent on bank credit to recover from the cloud of suspicion cast over him in this manner.

Government investigators in every agency are invested with broad subpoena power; hundreds of subpoenas are typed up and routinely issued each day, often, I suspect, without any thought of the devastating impact the mere receipt of such a document can have on an individual. Or maybe some do realize this; former prosecutors I know have admitted that subpoenas are used at times to harass someone believed to be guilty, or to force recalcitrant witnesses to open up.

For me the harassment was not confined to subpoenas. Members of my old White House staff and former law partners phoned to tell me that FBI agents had visited them. To my astonishment, one agent told several individuals the nature of the charges, several times volunteering his own opinion that "there must be something in all this," and "if Colson didn't go to Las Vegas, his law partner, Charles Morin *must* have." The same agent accused my former secretary, Holly Holm, of "covering up to protect your old boss." When she stood her ground, the agent began to intimate that there was more to our relationship than simply "boss and secretary."

Several times my former law partners protested the tactics of the investigators. No one in the Justice Department would take any responsibility.

One night I sat alone in my study staring into the fire. Keeping my anger in check took every ounce of self-restraint I had. The harassment of my former secretary had been the final indignity. It was bad enough to cope with false accusations in the media and doubtful ladies trying to sandbag me in a motel, but having government investigators continuing to snoop into my life, using pressure tactics on friends and associates, spreading untrue stories reflecting on my character, was more than I could take. It would continue as long as I remained a public figure. I could see the future spread before me.

Restlessly I walked about the room, venting my resentment. I saw the helpless individual struggling against government agencies, as if confronting an army of schmoos, the fabled animal creation of the "Lil' Abner" comic strip. Only these schmoos were angry. A schmoo multiplied itself every time it was kicked or attacked. One is challenged and two others appear; another is rolled over, but its weighted bottom instantly rights it. Cut one in two and four will replace it. To battle against the schmoos, as Lil' Abner's characters discovered, is utterly hopeless.

I saw our bureaucracy as a product of the 20th century, its growth fueled not by human brains but by the computer's electronic impulses. Its programming becomes increasingly complex, eventually beyond the capacity of mortal mind to untangle. Humans serve the machine, keeping its parts oiled and its surfaces polished. But since human decisions are no longer required, no human can be found responsible for the machine's actions. Like so much of sophisticated technology its appetite is insatiable.

The citizens the machine was intended to serve are powerless to control it. The only recourse is to stay clear of it, but like Lil' Abner's characters who found the multiplying schmoos everywhere, that soon becomes impossible.

The whole wearisome ordeal deepened my despair, yet buttressed my empathy for those caught in the machine. How helpless is the individual, particularly the poor, the powerless, and the uneducated, who must stand alone before the onslaught of bureaucracy. Like a giant reaper harvesting a field of wheat, the government juggernaut grinds on unfeelingly, often incapable of discriminating between those who victimize society and those victimized by it.

Again I sat by the fireplace, my mind moving to our system of justice and how proud we Americans are of it. But I wondered if Americans realize how the fast-multiplying investigating areas are eroding the bedrock of that system? That a person is presumed innocent until proven guilty may continue to be so in the actual courtroom where the individual's rights are safeguarded; but what about the secret processes which may lead to the court? In too many cases one who is "under investigation" for all practical purposes has been adjudged guilty and stripped of his or her rights. As the government bureaucracy grows, the capriciousness and the lack of accountability can only become worse.

For a period of weeks I confessed to myself that I had been slipping into the doldrums. God seemed far away. Doubts were assailing me. My old nemesis, self-pity, was besieging me again. The same old questions arose to haunt me: Why take all this nonsense? Why put your family through it again? I'll always be a target for some crusading reporter or trigger-happy government investigator. Wouldn't Prison Fellowship be better off without me?

The Watergaters who had quietly returned to private life and stayed out of the news were spared further controversy. Was I like the moth, flying into the candle's fire, driven there by some kind of warped idealism or even a death wish? Worse yet, was this whole ministry business simply an ego trip?

The front-page stories in the Washington papers during this period had further deepened my despair. A national Christian organization was holding its annual meeting at a downtown hotel; I was one of the speakers. Each day a major story about a Christian celebrity was featured in the press. One individual was even dubbed a "saint" by the *Washington Post* headline writer. I hadn't seen such extravagant coverage of personalities since the last political convention.

One person, not invited but who arrived anyway for the press conference, was Larry Flynt, the controversial pornographic magazine publisher. Flynt had announced that he was "born again," although his subsequent actions cast doubts upon the genuineness or at least the depth of his experience. Anyone with any kind of publicized Christian experience was there for the biggest show in town, the culmination of a year of unprecedented media coverage of the born again movement.

Yet it all came across as synthetic and superficial. Was the Christian faith reduced to this—a carnival side show with sainthood determined by media coverage? Why can't Christians see that all this hoopla about celebrities merely reveals our own insecurity, as if we must prove that God still works by putting on display the latest convert? The strength of our faith rests not upon the dramatic turnaround of a corrupt politician or depraved pornographer but upon the truth of God's word.

Plunged into this trough of self-pity amidst the flowery headlines about the so-called Christian superstars brought me face to face with some hard questions about myself. I became starkly aware of something shocking: *the depth and breadth of my sinful nature.* I knew I was a sinner, of course, in the biblical sense—it's very clear in Scripture that this is man's nature—but I had never been so aware of it in a personal way. There had been all manner of mistakes and wrongdoing in my past, but like anyone I could go through a litany of self-justification when cornered.

Perhaps it took the *Time* story to sink me so far into the pit of despair that I could really see deep within myself. No, I hadn't been a bagman for the Teamsters. But yes, I was a man still filled with pride and vanity and ego and insensitivity and . . . why go on?

Jonathan Edwards, I had read, felt the same way 20 years after his conversion:

> I have had very affecting views of my own sinfulness and vileness, very frequently to such a degree as to hold me in a kind of loud weeping, sometimes for a considerable time together, so that I have been often obliged to shut myself up. I have had a vastly greater sense of my own wickedness and the badness of my heart than ever I had before my conversion . . . It is affecting to think how ignorant I was, when a young Christian, of the bottomless, infinite depths of wickedness, pride, hypocrisy, and deceit left in my heart.

St. Augustine, in his classic *Confessions,* laments the fact that he once stole pears from a neighbor's tree which he neither needed nor desired; though seemingly trivial, the incident convinced him that there was "no cause for my evil but evil itself" and therefore proof certain of the depravity rooted firmly in man's soul.

The answer to another of the perplexing mysteries of the Christian life was gradually becoming clear to me: the deeper one's commitment and the longer one struggles to follow Christ, the more distance one realizes there is to travel. A true disciple, though experiencing a deepening communion with Christ, may at the same time become increasingly sensitive to his own shortcomings even to the point of questioning the validity of his own conversion.

I began to see why many of the saints, whom modern-day Christians might regard enviously as the most godly of persons, were driven time after time to seek a deeper experience. Moody, who had evangelized two continents, struggled in his later years, yearning for a "second" experience to overcome his inadequacies. Bonhoeffer, in prison, a giant before men, comforter and pastor to the other inmates, wrote of the wrenching of his soul in the unforgettable poem, "Who Am I?"

> Who am I? They also tell me
> I bore the days of misfortune
> equably, smilingly, proudly . . .
> Am I then really that which other men tell of?
> Or am I only what I myself know of myself?
> Restless and longing and sick, like a bird in a cage . . .

As I spread apart the faintly glowing wood embers in the fireplace and headed upstairs for bed, I wondered: Who am I? What was I trying to be?

> *For many the cross is still rugged, not gilt, the gospel a solace for failures, not a legitimator for inevitable success. Some still walk through the valley of the shadow with Jesus and do not bulldoze the terrain into monotonous plains. These invisibles may help rescue or may outlast the worldly evangelicalism that now plays public relations agent to the Zeitgeist of the '70s. The Christian church will be poorer if they do not.*
>
> MARTIN MARTY

25. Out of the Valley

The next morning at the breakfast table, Patty handed me the *Washington Post*. Normally I read the news section first, but for some inexplicable reason I turned this day to the local news and the obituaries.

My eyes stopped at a headline "36 Years Aiding Daughter In Coma—Until He Died."

Holiday, Fla. (AP)—For years Louis Esposito worked three jobs to pay the medical expenses of his daughter, Elaine, who has been in a coma for 36 years.

He borrowed money to send her to Lourdes, France, looking for a cure in the healing waters. He never complained.

He was slowed by three heart attacks that forced him to quit job after job until he was unable to work. Social Security and Medicare took over. But he never complained.

He shouldered the burdens silently and put off going to a doctor for his own pains. Last week he did call a doctor after a bad cold left him hoarse. An examination found his lung and liver almost destroyed by cancer, and he was hospitalized immediately. Doctors offered no hope.

Esposito, 69, died quietly Saturday. He will be buried today in his native Chicago.

"He was a good guy, one in a million," says Lucille Esposito, his wife of 43 years. "He always wanted to do everything together. How many wives can say that? He couldn't go to the store but that he wanted me to go with him. He was a shy guy, a good guy."

Esposito's casket is adorned with roses and a banner reading "Dad" from his sleeping daughter.

Elaine was 6 when she slipped into a coma after a simple appendectomy. Doctors rushed to the waiting room to tell Esposito and his wife that something had gone wrong. Their only child would die before morning, they said.

Esposito fainted.

"I looked at my husband on the floor, my baby dying in bed with 107 temperature and I thought, 'this is the end. God give me courage,' " Mrs. Esposito remembers. "I waited that night for her to open her eyes and recognize me . . . but she never did."

Elaine never woke, lingering somewhere between life and death. She is 43 now.

Mrs. Esposito has turned her daughter every few hours each day since 1941 to keep away bedsores. She has tube fed, cleansed, applied medication and responded to the moans day and night. She never complained either. And she won't now.

Before I reached the last paragraph my vision was blurred by tears of admiration for Esposito and his lifetime of selfless sacrifice and for his courageous wife, Lucille. God had spoken to my self-pitying despair through two people I had never met.

"Of course," I muttered. "The answer is so obvious." This is the life we are called to. Service, sacrifice if necessary, obedience and faithfulness. This is the Christian life. This unknown man's life was a vastly more authentic testimony than those being heralded on the stage on Christian celebrityism.

Esposito did not enjoy the luxury of saying, "No, Lord. I don't want to put up with all this." He couldn't back away from the heavy and unglamorous cross he was required to carry. And he didn't whimper or beg for a miracle; he simply, uncomplainingly, did what he had to do. As I reflected on my own despair of recent weeks, I felt selfish and unworthy.

The last lines of Bonhoeffer's "Who Am I" also now seemed to fit into place. *"Who Am I? They mock me, these lonely questions of mine. Whoever I am, Thou knowest, O God, I am Thine."*

Over the next months, the Esposito story continued to give me fresh heart and determination. I had come to see self-pity as a form of pride—"spiritual cancer," C. S. Lewis called it—that had so blinded me all those preconversion years. The dragon I thought had been slain that night in Tom Phillips' driveway five years before had crept back into my life—and probably would keep on doing so.

My morale was further boosted weeks later by good news from Ken Adams who called to tell me that because there was no evidence, the FBI had terminated its investigation of me. The case was officially closed.

Encouraging reports flowed in from penitentiaries to which our disciples returned and from those institutions where we had conducted seminars. A woman inmate from Fort Worth, Texas, told us she had organized a Bible study fellowship of 50 prisoners. Another prisoner whose photographic memory had led him to embezzlement, had become a Christian and was applying his rare gift to memorizing George Soltau's teaching curriculum. Within a short time he was holding regular classes in his prison.

A Spanish-speaking graduate was released from prison and began his own ministry in West Texas jails and schools. Others did the same thing in Georgia, Virginia and Minnesota. We steadily heard of prisoners finding the Lord through those we had trained. God was multiplying our efforts.

The ministry at Memphis had its ups and downs for which we were not blameless. Despite his excellent preaching and lovable exuberance, Jesse Ellis was not the right person as chaplain in this sensitive post and returned to his position as adjutant of the Church of God in Christ. But the inmates continued their enthusiastic support of Chaplain Beshears and the community involvement was deepening.

For the first two years our work was mostly in the federal prisons. Then, one by one, state officials who learned of our ministry issued invitations. Three California prisons were opened to us; then Wisconsin, Virginia, North Carolina, Mississippi, Nebraska and Florida. By late 1978 invitations were arriving faster than we could respond.

As our work spread, we came in frequent contact with other prison ministries, many of which are excellent. Bill Glass' crusades bring a powerful evangelistic message to a dozen or more prisons a year. Chaplain Ray does excellent work in visitation and literature distribution. Yokefellow, the movement headed by Elton Trueblood, has built fellowships in scores of prisons. We were working closely as well with the Good News Mission where our early classes of disciples lived; the Mission now sends chaplains into many prisons and offers correspondence Bible studies for thousands of inmates.

Yet the 600 prisons and penitentiaries in America, housing 300,000 inmates, remain a largely uncharted mission field. In more than half of those we visited there had been no outside ministry before us. We began to concentrate on those and assist the other ministries where we discovered good work already underway.

Our team was growing and day by day becoming more professional. Gordon Loux proved himself such an able administrator that he was elected executive vice president with full responsibility for running the ministry. Ralph Veerman, formerly a national youth guidance director for Youth for Christ, joined us as vice president for prison ministry. We later hired Dr. Paul Morris, a clergyman with a Ph.D. in counseling, to take over education programs.

Paul Kramer's growing Christian maturity was a special joy to me. We kept giving him new responsibilities to match his developing skills. One night in 1978 he called to ask if he could stop at our home for a short visit. With him was a lovely young girl, Terry Craig. Shyly they told Patty and me that they would like to get married, almost as if we were their parents. We were overjoyed.

The wedding took place in the McLean Presbyterian Church which both Paul and Terry had joined. I was best man. While escorting Paul to the altar, I looked over a beautiful sanctuary almost filled with family and friends, the whole staff of Prison Fellowship and many ex-convicts with whom we had worked across the country. Steve Smallman, the pastor, and George Soltau—both teachers in our prison seminars—performed the service.

While standing there with surging emotions, my mind wandered back three and a half years to that first night in prison when I saw Paul, a forlorn figure in brown dungarees, almost lost in the mass of bodies in Dormitory G of the Maxwell Prison. The scars of his brokenness were painfully evident.

Terry came down the aisle, looking as beautiful and fresh as the spring flowers on the altar; her father walking beside her was smiling proudly. What an amazing journey Paul had traveled. Only the power of Christ could have so completely turned his life around.

Paul's eyes met mine during the service as he turned to take Terry's ring from me. In his look was inexpressible joy. How proud I was of him!

The ministry's spread has touched others as well. Max Mustain, the stony-faced warden I'd first met in Petersburg, Virginia, had indeed undergone a profound experience in his own life. Under his leadership—and Chaplain Nissen's—Sandstone, Minnesota, had become a center of Christian fellowship with as many as 75 men attending Thursday night Bible study and the chapel packed for many services. To cap it all, Mustain told us on one of our visits to his prison that he had decided to enter full-time Christian service. His plan was to take an early retirement and join a Missouri-based prison ministry.

George Ralston, warden at Oxford, Wisconsin, whose refusal to send inmates to the Washington seminar led to our first in-prison classes, was transferred to the Terre Haute Penitentiary. Once a skeptic, Ralston was now a supporter, inviting us to bring our team to Terre Haute. When I spoke to a Christian businessmen's prayer breakfast there, Ralston was one of those who marked a "decision card" that he wanted to become involved in Christian work.

Judge Miles Lord, the federal district judge in Minneapolis, continued his personal interest in improving conditions at Sandstone Prison and then began visiting other prisons in his jurisdiction. At Stillwater he was horrified by the subhuman conditions he discovered in the dreaded "hole," the solitary confinement cells that had so repelled Fred Rhodes and me during our visit there in early 1976. Men were confined there for a minimum of 12 months straight; some went insane. Lord faced down the warden with an ultimatum: "Close it today or I'll issue an order when I get back to my court." The "hole" was promptly shut down.

In every prison I visit I always ask to tour the "hole"; the inmates there seldom see anyone from the outside and are the ones most in need of help. Sometimes we discover that God's agents have been planted even there in the bowels of the world.

One turned up when I was touring "solitary" in a southern prison on a hot summer day. Guiding me through was a young corrections officer whose spit-shined shoes, close-cropped blond hair and military bearing would have qualified him for the honor guard at Parris Island. "Right this way, Sir," he commanded crisply, swinging open the second barred gate leading to the labyrinth of cell doors and dark corridors. He stood, quiet and erect, to the side of each cell as I managed a conversation through the narrow slits in each door.

When we passed the last cell, he stopped, looked in both directions and leaned toward me, whispering, "Can I see you alone, Mr. Colson? Right over here." He pointed to a shadowy area around a bend in the corridor which was out of range of TV monitors beamed down the main walkway.

"I'm a Christian," he spoke excitedly. "Do something to help these men. It's awful in here. I'm new and I'd lose my job if I said anything, but you can help. Please help, Mr. Colson." The officer went on to tell me that the men had no reading materials of any kind; for lack of anything to do many were going stir-crazy.

Later that day the warden agreed to our supplying books and magazines to the "hole." The next day we found some Christians in town to help; Bibles, religious books, some old westerns, a stack of magazines were handed out. Gradually in subsequent meetings with the warden other changes were made.

The Lord is never without a witness we know from the writings of Paul and Luke. Still it is a surprise sometimes to find His people so strategically placed in some of the most forlorn outposts. We encountered one at the Terre Haute, Indiana, penitentiary, where nearly 150 inmates and 30 volunteers took part in our seminar.

During the closing hymn, "Amazing Grace," I could see faces of inmates in the front row begin to glow in the reflection of the stage lights. Tough, hardened cons were singing at the top of their lungs. The angriest expressions melted in the warmth of the song. Tears began to run down the cheeks of the man nearest me; then other eyes began glistening. The words "a wretch like me" were sung with richer meaning in this home for killers and thieves than any place I'd ever heard it.

Afterwards, I threaded my way through the crowd, heading for the front door. A tall, well-dressed man thrust his hand toward me, clutching my arm firmly.

"Mr. Colson—wait, wait!" he commanded. His taut face features and thin black mustache made him look almost sinister in the yellowish light of the fluorescent lamps high overhead.

Probably a community volunteer who didn't like something I said about prisons, I thought. This is no place for an argument. The man's dark eyes were piercing, adding to the appearance of anger. "I'm a guard here," he said slowly, "and for 17 years I've prayed every day that God would send someone like you here." Suddenly the man burst into tears, his whole body heaving. His wife, who stood nearby, put her arms around his waist as if to support him. "No, John, no. People are watching." she whispered.

"Thank God, thank God," he kept muttering between sobs.

I thought often about that guard in the days that followed. What a dreary, seemingly hopeless existence they have—for some a lifetime of long days invested inside cold, gray walls, surrounded by hate and violence. Perhaps he found fulfillment doing things each day to make life a little more bearable for the 1,500 inmates; or perhaps he was stationed there just to pray persistently against the powers of darkness completely overrunning the place. I knew nothing about the man, but I was convinced that God must have put him there, right in the middle of what has to be one of Satan's favorite hunting grounds. The Kingdom is full of unsung heroes like that guard—and like the Espositos.

The more I mingled with the poor, the disadvantaged, the mistreated people of our society, the more I saw the raw evil of injustice. I saw suddenly why episodes such as the *Parade* and *Time* stories were probably necessary for me to experience. It wasn't so much to balance off the times when I had dealt despicably with White House foes as to show me what it felt like to be defenseless.

As I studied and groped for more truths about my Christian faith, I made another discovery about myself. My contempt for the "fuzzy-headed liberals" who have marched so often to protest discrimination and injustice was lessening. In fact, though it was painful, I had to admit that on occasion I even felt some grudging admiration for their courage in taking unpopular positions. That, after all, is what Peter and John had once done.

"Chuck, are you planning to be in this area sometime today or tomorrow?"

It was Myron Mintz, calling from his office in my old law firm.

"I'll be down there late this afternoon," I told him.

On the way to see Myron, I wondered what news he had for me. Could he be serious this time about becoming a Christian? No, he had ducked that one too many times in the past.

There had always been something to stop him from taking this step. Only a week before Myron and Nancy had come for dinner, their first night out since their son, Robert, had been born. Len LeSourd, my publisher, was in town and joined us. It was a memorable evening.

Patty had drawn the English print drapes, which made the dining room, lighted only by two candles, warm and intimate. The conversation had wandered over a range of subjects: Myron's law practice, our prison work, the making of *Born Again* into a movie. Abruptly, Myron changed subjects.

"Well, Chuck, when are you going to talk to me about being a Christian?" Myron peered at me through thick, wire-rimmed glasses, just the hint of a smile on his face. I almost dropped my fork. Patty at the other end of our dining room table stopped her conversation with Nancy in midsentence to stare at Myron.

"Tonight, after dinner," I suggested.

"Why not now?"

"Okay, now."

"You see, Chuck," Myron continued, "I already believe in Christ. Because of my Jewish background I've read the Old Testament which stops a few hundred years before Christ. If Jesus weren't the Messiah, wouldn't God go on revealing Himself as He did before? The way I figure it, the Old Testament stopped because Jesus is the Messiah."

Myron's mind never failed to amaze me. I'd given him a dozen arguments for believing in Christ, but he came up with one I'd never thought of.

"More than believing in Him is necessary, Myron," I pressed. "The devil knows there is a God."

"Well, what more do I have to do to be a Christian, Chuck?"

Nancy, who is a Lutheran, watched with wide-eyed delight as Len and I took turns explaining: genuine repentance of sin, asking Christ in as Lord, then the importance of telling another person. The last point bothered him.

"Why do I have to tell anyone?" he asked, and I sensed that visions of standing on a platform giving his testimony were flashing across his mind.

"Because Christ says so," Len answered. "He told us: 'Everyone who shall confess me before men, I will also confess him before My Father who is in Heaven.'" (See Matthew 10:32.)

Myron ate a few bites of food and then continued his questions. "Do I have to join a church? I'm not sure I'd want to. There is a lot of hypocrisy in the church," he added.

I have learned that this is the argument most often used as a cover for a person not wanting to make a commitment of his life to Christ.

"You don't have to join one, but you should," I answered.

"Why haven't you joined a church?" Myron fired back. Myron didn't realize it but the question stabbed as sharply as if he had thrust a dinner knife into my stomach. I'd been struggling with the question for months.

"I have an Episcopalian background," I answered feebly. "But I just haven't found a church I really want to join."

A fine example I'm setting, I grumbled to myself. I believed that every Christian needs the fellowship, accountability, and nurturing of a home church. Yet if I didn't belong to one, how could I lead others? And now Myron, on this point, was wriggling off the hook as well.

After dinner Myron and I talked alone in my library. It wasn't long before he came to the subject where he was hurting most: If God is a loving God why do the innocent have to suffer as so often they do? The memories of Meredith's death were still painful for Myron.

Through my studies with theologian R. C. Sproul I had come to grips with some hard questions including the question of God's justice. Taking a deep breath, I plunged in with Myron.

"Let's begin with the book of Genesis, Myron. You've studied it carefully, you told me. You remember that God created man and woman in a perfect setting, but man was disobedient. God had made it clear that the penalty for this was death."

Myron nodded and asked me to continue.

"If we believe the word of God then, sinful man has no *right* to live; that we do live at all is by His mercy alone and that is therefore the most powerful proof of His loving nature."

I went on to point out how simple this logic was for lawyers to follow: man broke the law, the sentence was prescribed, so he has no right to complain. When the disciples complained of the unfairness of Roman soldiers massacring innocent Galilean pilgrims who were offering sacrifices in the temple, Jesus didn't smile benignly and say, "We can't understand the mysteries of God's ways." He understood God's law full well and said, "Unless you repent you will all likewise perish." (See Luke 13:1–5, RSV.)

How foolish and pitiful we must look to God when we complain about His justice. In truth, God has spoken clearly, though in words even the most committed believer prefers not to hear.

"Those who can't understand or see this have a poor alternative if they think about it, Myron," I continued. "If there is not a sovereign God, then events are a matter of pure chance; our life is like a roulette wheel, with tragedy and death striking randomly whenever the wheel happens to stop on our number.

"Since our universe is so perfectly ordered to the most minute detail, vastly more carefully programmed than the most sophisticated of man's computers, why should anyone think that life is a random chance? For me, it could not be. God has indeed proven He is sovereign in my life."

Myron listened attentively but said nothing, obviously not ready to commit himself.

Later I wondered if I should have been so blunt in discussing God's justice and the "hard" teaching of Jesus. Would it sound like a calloused rationalizing of his daughter's death? No, he knew I cared.

I hoped Myron would respect my honesty in dealing openly about some of the hard questions. The truth is, there aren't always easy pleasant answers to every question about the Christian faith and I was sick of hearing Christians make it sound like there were. If one is to submit to the authority of Scripture, the bitter must be taken with the sweet; it isn't *easy* to be a Christian and better we stop selling people a phony bill of goods.

I parked my car, entered one of Washington's newest office buildings and took the elevator to the top floor. The receptionist waved me by the large glass doors of the law offices, and I took a shortcut through the firm's library to the open door of Myron's office.

Inside Myron was in shirt sleeves, his back to the door, leaning backwards in a visitor's chair, feet outstretched atop his desk. One of his partners was standing over him, arms folded across his chest, listening intently to Myron. I couldn't hear what was being said. When I knocked on the open door, Myron slowly turned in the chair and peered up over the tops of his glasses. "Hi there, Boss." He was casual as always.

"What are you doing?" I asked.

"What am I doing?" he chuckled. "Just telling Arthur here how I accepted Christ this weekend, that's all." He never changed the dry tone of voice; it was as if I *obviously* should have known.

My mouth dropped open. I wanted to shout for joy, but Arthur probably thought we were a couple of odd ducks already, and an outburst from me would only have made it worse.

Myron slowly got up out of the chair. "You look surprised, Boss. I'm only doing what you and Len told me. 'Tell another person,' you said, and so I decided to tell Arthur," he grinned.

Regardless of what Arthur thought, I threw my arms around Myron and hugged him.

A few days later, I took a long walk in the woods behind my home, sniffing the fresh, spring air and seeing the first shoots of green poke through the crusted brown earth. It was that day that a dream began to take form. It had been vague and drifting at times over the past months, but this morning it seemed so clear: In it was the church—healed and vital and alive—preaching the Lordship of Jesus Christ and at the same time holding out a cup of cold water in His name to those who were thirsty.

In the three years I had spent traveling the country, over and over had I been struck by the tragedy of a church divided. Fundamentalists, evangelicals, charismatics—the labels were often misleading and the delineations blurred—were on one side, while the liberal, social-action Christians were on the other. The division, some thought, could be traced to the Moody era when this great evangelist became so convinced of Jesus' imminent return that he felt the only thing that counted was saving souls—and fast. Other Christians, led by a compassionate pastor, Walter Rauschenbusch, began to see Moody followers as indifferent to the suffering of humanity. Distrust grew between the succeeding generation of disciples and the gulf widened.

If men of vastly different political persuasions like Hughes, Cleaver and me could come together loving one another as brothers, then why could not those who have different theologies but follow the same Christ lock arms, one with another, for the glory of God? Christ heals Republicans and Democrats, Jew and Gentile, black and white; why not His own Church?

As a part of this dream I saw Prison Fellowship going into prisons with the help and cooperation of *all* the churches in the surrounding community. There was no magic wand to wave which would instantly cement back together a vast church which had fragmented over a century, but at least we could do our part in the places we went.

At the same time I was being convicted about my own role in the church. I had to take an individual step before I could expect our Fellowship to take a corporate step. God was speaking to me forcefully this quiet spring day.

My work with Dr. Lovelace and the reading I'd done independently, convinced me that genuine revival in America would come about only through the renewing of the church. Yet *a Gallup poll showed that one out of five Americans attended prayer or Bible meetings outside of church at least once a week*. This was understandable in the light of my own experience. I would frequently rearrange my schedule to be at Tuesday morning breakfasts with Harold Hughes, Doug Coe, Graham Purcell and Al Quie, but I often skipped church on Sunday mornings. The result was that I belonged to a small prayer group, not a community of believers. Like much of the rest of America apparently, my spiritual nourishment was coming from small, nonchurch, private meetings. That met my selfish needs, but if everyone did it, there would be no church—and without a strong church there would be no Christian impact on society. Prayer groups, I saw, were very important, but not as a substitute for the church.

Yes, I concluded that sunny spring day, I was part of the problem—and in addition to being a poor example for Myron and others, I was missing a lot in the process. The early church, we learn from the book of Acts, was the place for fellowship, the apostles' teaching, breaking of bread and prayer. That there is strength and power in that simple formula is evident from the vigorous history of the first-century Christian church.

As I presented to God my own needs and views of Scripture over the next days and weeks, He helped me to a decision. I would join Columbia Baptist Church in Falls Church, Virginia, where Pastor Neal Jones had become such a close and admired confidant. There was warmth in the church and Neal's preaching always nourished me. While I understand and respect the views of those whose reading of Scripture leads them to another conclusion, for me the desire to be baptized by full immersion became compelling. I wanted to experience it as Jesus had—to perform an outward sign in affirmation of what had happened inwardly—the death of the old as I dipped into the water and the resurrection, fresh and new, as I rose out of it.

Myron Mintz decided to join me in this baptism for what has become a treasured moment of my young Christian life. Dressed in white cotton robes, I followed Myron to the baptistry. Just before we reached the three steps leading down to it, where Neal was waiting, he turned toward me, smiled and stuck out his hand. His gray-speckled, curly hair was tousled, shooting out in all directions. His face was aglow and standing barefoot he looked exactly as I imagined the Hebrew disciples of the first century must have looked.

For an instant, I was there with those early Christians, feeling their excitement over a step in faith, sharing the fellowship. The soft sand was under foot and the Jordan River lay before us.

How unchangeable are His ways, I thought. The church may be sadly divided, but Jesus Christ is the same yesterday, today and always.

> [*A belief in the second coming does not preclude*]
> *work for the future within the limits of ordinary mo-*
> *rality and prudence. For what comes is judgment.*
> *Happy are those whom it* [*the second coming*] *finds*
> *laboring in their vocations, whether they are merely*
> *going out to feed the pigs or making good plans to*
> *deliver humanity a hundred years hence from some*
> *great evil. The curtain has now fallen. Those pigs*
> *will never in fact be fed, the great campaign against*
> *white slavery or government tyranny will never in*
> *fact precede the victory. No matter; you were at your*
> *post when the inspection came.*
>
> C. S. LEWIS

26. Life Sentence

Kirk Schenk was on the phone. "Shay, Chuck," his voice trailed off, then struggled back. "I need hep . . . shay, Chuck." He sounded like he had a mouth-full of marbles and for Kirk it was an all-too-familiar sound. Every time he called, we followed the same procedure: humor him on the phone, find out where he was and call one of our friends in Minneapolis who would take him somewhere to sober up.

What made it so discouraging was that when Kirk was sober, he was a hard and conscientious worker and a dedicated student of the Bible. Trouble was that every few months he would fall and fall hard. Kirk had been out of prison two years now, and I had felt especially close to him ever since our first meeting at Stillwater Prison when we learned that he had been sentenced to 10 years for a $20 unarmed robbery.

His problem with alcohol was what got him into trouble in the first place. Son of a successful businessman, Kirk had been a model youth until he hit the bottle; then he would go berserk. His conversion in prison was genuine, I am convinced, because behind bars where no liquor was available he was a spiritual powerhouse.

We all fail, I had to keep reminding myself. The myth that we can achieve perfection in this world is what so often makes us afraid to admit our faults—especially to other Christians. It was so clear to me now; covering them up only makes them worse, denying us the chance for help and understanding when it is most needed, and from the people best able to give it to us.

I've found myself not wanting to talk about the imperfections of the prisoners we work with for fear it will make people think they weren't really converted or that our discernment and training were deficient. As a matter of fact, there were times when we found Kirk an embarrassment. I must also admit that our worry was whether Kirk would get into more trouble with the law, resulting in publicity which would reflect on Prison Fellowship.

Thus we always waited anxiously for a call back from Minneapolis that would tell us Kirk was in safe hands. This time the news came the next day. One of our friends found him passed out in his room; he was sobering up and had agreed to undergo alcoholic treatment. Kirk needed professional help.

For the next few months there were no calls, only a note from Kirk telling us of the excellent progress he was making, first at a treatment center, later in out-patient care. He was determined to kick the problem.

A second note written in high spirits in early spring brought the good news of Kirk's engagement; later in the year he and his fiancee would be married. Our friends, too, reported that Kirk was settling down. His long nightmarish ordeal with alcohol, which in 10 years had taken him from a fine suburban home to the gutter and then to prison, might finally be over.

In June of 1978, however, Kirk's name kept popping into my mind. Not that I was being given any guidance or direction; at least I didn't sense that God was trying to tell me something. Simply at odd moments, I'd find myself thinking of Kirk or seeing his face. When this happens more than once, it is my practice to pray for that person. That month I prayed often for Kirk.

Then on June 24 I wrote Kirk a short note: "I've been thinking about you a lot lately and wondering how you are doing. Drop us a line, Brother."

Kirk never answered; instead a few weeks later a note came from a friend who had gone to Kirk's rescue many times. "I'm sorry to have to be the bearer of bad news," he wrote, "but Kirk Schenk is dead."

It was as if a blast of furnace air had hit my face and a flood of conflicting emotions washed over me: grief for Kirk, anger at myself, then guilt.

We failed him. God forgive us. We failed him, were repeated over and over in my mind.

A newspaper clipping explained the tragedy. Kirk had gotten drunk, threatening suicide. Apparently no one took him seriously. So one night Kirk climbed over the guardrail and crawled to the outer steel ledge of the St. Paul Bridge; there he sat down, his feet dangling out over the churning waters below. Then he began to scream.

Cars stopped, people gathered. Someone called the police, while others pleaded for him not to jump. The police arrived along with Kirk's mother-in-law-to-be. When she began to reason calmly with Kirk, he seemed to slowly regain his senses.

As is so often the case with those whose lives are filled with despair and rejection, suicide may be attempted merely as a means of getting attention. Kirk, I am convinced, wanted attention—not suicide. Timidly he began to step back from the edge. The woman kept pleading, talking softly. Slowly Kirk took a few more steps along the steel superstructure back toward the rail and safety. Then he stopped and glared at the police who stood nearby. Memories of uniformed prison guards would still be fresh in his mind. The woman kept talking. Kirk took another faltering step. He was almost within her reach. Then another step, his body moving unsteadily.

Suddenly someone leaned over the rail, grabbing for Kirk's body. Startled, Kirk jerked away; one foot slipped and he was gone. His body hit the water but did not come up. For hours police floodlights illuminated the river but Kirk's body was not found, then or ever.

I closed the door of my office and sat alone with old memories and fresh pain. My mind wandered back over two and one-half years, recalling all the late night calls, the letters, the ups and the many more frequent downs. Could this have been foreseen, I asked myself? No, Kirk Schenk had never before displayed suicidal tendencies. That was not his intent now, I was convinced. Walking out on the superstructure of the bridge was yet a more dramatic way of seeking help.

Had God been trying to warn me to do something about Kirk when his name kept flashing before my mind? If so, what more could we have done?

Then I remembered Jerry, a young man in a lumberman's jacket, who stood up near the end of a Prison Fellowship meeting in Peoria,

Illinois. Jerry reported that he had been visiting prisoners in the local prison for three years. He befriended a young Christian inmate, assuring him that, as his brother, he'd stand with him anywhere. Months later, the inmate was released and turned up on Jerry's doorstep. Jerry took the young man in, bought him a suit of new clothes, gave him a bed and stuffed him with home-cooked food. The man stayed for several weeks, eventually getting a job and then his own apartment.

Jerry seemed pleased with himself as he told the story that day in Peoria. He put his index finger to his tongue and then chalked up number one on an imaginary blackboard. One success, he seemed to be saying. Everyone in the room smiled. Without changing his expression, Jerry then told how the man was arrested eight months later and was now back in jail. Jerry then made a quick erasing motion over the spot where seconds earlier he had marked the number one.

"So," he said, putting his hands in his pockets and shrugging his shoulders, "I'm back to zero, but I'm still going into the prison because that's where God wants me to be."

At the time I had felt uncomfortable, a little sorry for him, in fact. There was no applause when he sat down. After all, three years is a long time to work with no apparent success. Earlier in the meeting when I had told of growing Christian fellowship in scores of prisons, the 100 or so people in the room exploded with applause.

Why would I remember Jerry now? I had been to a hundred or more meetings just like that one. Yet Jerry's face and his story were as vivid in my mind's eye as if he were standing before me in my office telling it all over again. Was it his honesty? He was surely honest, painfully so, confessing his own weakness.

Feelings of guilt suddenly bored deeply into my soul. Not so much over Kirk's death as over my own feelings. I had never been able to face the truth about Kirk Schenk or, for that matter, the half dozen or so other problem cases like him. Whenever we learned of a disciple slipping, we spoke in hushed tones, wanting to shove the whole mess in the nearest empty closet, slamming the door and then forgetting all about it. There was not a speech or a newsletter or an article or an interview I could ever remember when I had acknowledged a failure.

I couldn't do it. Anything done in the name of Christ must produce positive results. That's what other Christians and the world expect. To admit that this doesn't always work would be like saying that God's word isn't true or we are not really spiritual enough to draw on God's power.

The mind-set that I had embraced is what theologians call "triumphalism," claiming complete and perfect success for everything done in God's name. It is nothing less than prideful arrogance, no less offensive to God or obnoxious in the sight of our fellow-man than the man-can-do-anything hubris which caused us to swagger, drunk with illusions of power, through the corridors of the White House.

For three years I had studied the Bible faithfully, listened to learned scholars, prayed, read all the books I could get my hands on, tried to be humble by working in dark holes of prisons, constantly reminding myself of how vulnerable I was to pride and ego. I had given away my money, felt my values being transformed, and yet now I could see that all the while, unknowingly, the sin of pride, cleverly cloaked in the respectable disguise of spirituality, had nearly recaptured my values and personality. It was a second lesson in a matter of months about the insidious ways of pride.

How weak and vulnerable we are! No matter how hard we try, I guess we always will be. We are susceptible to the cunning of the devil, who slyly can invade us in the name of humility, Christian service and noble good works as easily as he can in the name of worldly power and avarice.

What is the answer? In a rare moment of awareness I saw it—the frank acknowledgment of our nothingness and total dependence on Jesus Christ, the search for truth not through ourselves but through Him, and obtaining strength for service through the indwelling power of His Holy Spirit. Jerry put it well: we do what we do out of obedience to Jesus.

There is no heresy in Christians' openly acknowledging their humanness and failures. Nor is that a reflection on the truth of God's word; the weakness is in man not God.

Sometimes people discover God's truth and the transformation is swift; occasionally slow. Much depends on the rebelliousness of our flesh. Sometimes too, experience is genuine, other times it isn't. Some people fall away to return later. But we Christians should not pretend failure doesn't happen; that it does is not a denial of the veracity of His word or an undermining of His power. If God depended on our perfection, He would be the captive of His creation and not God at all.

The death of Kirk Schenk helped us to an awareness of the dangers of triumphalism in our prison work. This has been a major turning point for Prison Fellowship. Failures would be a recurring part of the work. We needed to accept this. Our goals would remain the same: the redemption of mixed up lives through the power of Christ. We would expect every prisoner to have this transformation, but we would not avoid or shy away from the failures no matter how often they occurred.

Acknowledging our inadequacies helped us in other ways as well. We were learning how futile it sometimes is to rely on our own cleverness or skills, that to penetrate the formidable, walled fortresses of American prisons requires a powerful assist from God's Spirit. One night at the Atlanta, Georgia, federal penitentiary vividly brought that home.

For two years the agony of the Atlanta Prison spilled out of its rock wall confines into grisly headlines, congressional hearings and TV specials. The grip of organized crime reached through the prison's iron gates and clutched the very innards of life inside. Death struck swiftly, often and with impunity.

Over a period of 16 months 10 men were brutally murdered, gangland style. One was burned alive in his sleep; others savagely slashed or beaten. Prison officials tried to clamp down, but the terror continued as 2,000 inmates lived in fear for their lives. Guards recoiled at the prospect of walking along cellblock corridors; visitors were banned.

Jack Hanberry, as fair and decent a man as ever walked through the gates of this hundred-year-old fortress, had been named warden in the middle of the carnage. Hanberry knew the Atlanta Penitentiary; he had been stationed there as a chaplain in the mid-1960s when he won the respect of both inmates and staff. Then he switched to administration, was transferred out, quickly moved up the ladder and now had returned to the post of warden at the Atlanta institution. The inmates immediately put him to the test; there were two killings, a string of assaults and 24 fires in the cellblocks during Hanberry's first two months on the job.

The week Jack Hanberry became warden, Paul Kramer called to offer our help. To Paul's mild surprise, Jack quickly accepted. An in-prison seminar was scheduled for the following month.

"Are we ready to tackle Atlanta?" I asked as Paul told me what he and Hanberry had agreed to.

"We should do something," Paul insisted.

"There is no hotter spot right now," I warned.

"That's where the Lord would go, isn't it?" Paul replied.

Still there were tough problems to work out. The security of getting 30 community volunteers inside was the chief one. Also we did not know what to expect from inmates. Paul and I had gone there twice to meet with the prison's Christian fellowship which numbered eight inmates out of 2,000.

Two prisoners had been furloughed to come to our second seminar in Washington, but both were among our disappointments, through no fault of their own. "Slim," the tall young black, was the one who later had escaped when his life was threatened. The other had returned to prison, stayed in his cell through fear for his life and soon was transferred out. Three men were scheduled for the next Washington class, but their potential for leadership was unknown.

Fortunately, our coordinator in the Atlanta community was a young, enthusiastic, sandy-haired Presbyterian pastor named Tom Roddy. The prison chaplain, Charlie Riggs, a moon-faced, energetic Southern Baptist, whose faith was strong as steel, and Father Tim Ondahl, a tall, bearded man affectionately known as "the hippie priest," were solidly with us.

Riggs' dynamism paid off. He recruited, astonishingly, 150 inmates for the seminar. Since the facilities would accommodate only 75, we could for once be selective.

Still, tension built as the date for our seminar approached. It was an especially hot summer, and day after day fierce sun baked the penitentiary's unshaded buildings. The cellblocks, ventilated only by antique fans, were like furnaces. Most prison riots, we knew, erupt in the "dog days" of late summer. We had not only chosen the toughest prison, we had chosen the worst time of the year.

Paul Kramer left early to begin the seminar. I would arrive later in the week to address the inmates on my way from an appearance on the PTL network in Charlotte, North Carolina, which was scheduled that same day.

All through the interview that morning, thoughts of what lay ahead weighed heavily on me. PTL had just moved into a new studio, one of the largest and best equipped in the world. As I studied the giant cameras, electrically operated sets and other marvels of modern technology, my mind wandered to the Atlanta prison's paint-chipped concrete, its slimy latrines, and slow-moving iron gates. I looked at the smiling, white, scrubbed-clean faces of the audience, handsomely dressed, the ladies with puffed up coiffures that looked like spun candy; but my mind saw expressionless men in dirty brown, marching in cadence along steel and concrete ramps. For me, this was reality, I realized, as I pushed aside my thoughts of the conflicting worlds where we attempt to live our faith.

Paul was somber when he met me late that afternoon at the gate of the Atlanta penitentiary. There was not a whisper of a breeze. Inside, the walls would be like the fires of hell.

"The seminar is going fine," he told me. "That's the good news. But things inside are pretty tense; that's the bad." Warden Hanberry had taken the unusual step of opening the evening meeting to the entire prison population. Nothing like that had happened in a long time.

The prison complex is located in a rundown neighborhood in the heart of Atlanta. It would have been closed years ago but for the strong political influence of Georgia's congressional delegation. The main penitentiary building, which was designed for 1,200 inmates but now houses more than 2,000, sits back a few hundred yards from the street. A gentle, sloping, green lawn separates the prison from the entrance gate. Gray brick with three-story-high, barred-over glass windows, the exterior of the massive building looks like any other institution. But all likeness ends at the electrically operated control gates just inside the door.

Jack Hanberry, in his shirt sleeves with sweat running down his smiling, round face was waiting there to greet us. His gentle manner and hound-dog eyes belied the tough core inside. "Hard but fair," is the way the inmates spoke of him. "He cares about us," was another description frequently heard.

Jack and the two chaplains escorted us through the maze of gates into the main center corridor with its high ceiling and drab, concrete walls. Our heels clicked on the hard floor. Four cellblocks were connected like spokes in a wheel to this one common hub. Guards controlled traffic by opening and closing the gates leading into each block like floodgates in a network of canals. For most inmates the center corridor, along with their cell and the mess hall, is all of the world they see.

As we passed hundreds of peering, curious eyes, Chaplain Riggs told me that eight brothers, the small core group of the fellowship which Paul and I had met with before, were waiting in his office for prayer before the meeting began. Riggs led us up a long flight of steel stairs to the second floor and the chaplain's office, surrounded like everything else by steel gates and bars.

It was a joyous reunion for us and I've never seen warmer smiles from men who had so little to smile about. There was "Sunshine," a tall, handsome young man in his early 30s; and Cal, square-jawed with three teeth missing, who had once been a gospel singer; and Carl Bistrom, a smiling, bespectacled old man with thinning gray hair slicked straight back, who had spent nearly 40 years in prison; and Don Taylor, studying for the ministry by correspondence, a blond-haired young man with eyes as clear a blue as tropical waters, who was almost four years into a 40-year sentence for kidnapping. How much these men meant to me! How much inspiration I drew from their faith!

We took chairs in a circle. Cal, who was an unofficial leader for the group, spoke first. "We're sure glad you're here, Chuck. The betting was two to one you wouldn't show."

"Why wouldn't I be here?" I answered.

"Because it's hot here. Man, it is hot."

"It's hot in another way too," Sunshine explained, drawing his hand across his throat.

"Look, Chuck, things are bad. The men are very tense," Cal continued. "I don't want to alarm you, but some dudes are expecting a little trouble here tonight."

I tried to act calmer than my stomach felt. "We'll be okay. This is the Lord's night."

"There's another thing," Cal frowned. "You can't preach or talk about Jesus here tonight. The men won't take it. No religion, okay?"

His words were accompanied by a chorus of "right, man," and "amen."

"The trouble is, Chuck," Sunshine continued, "that the men feel you're out to con them. The warden's been saying good things about you and . . . the men are suspicious. But they'll be there tonight. Maybe a thousand."

A thousand inmates in one room in Atlanta on a sweleteringly hot night! I shook my head. After those lonely nights in the dormitory at Maxwell when I'd heard that someone wanted to kill me, I had never again known fear inside any prison. But I began experiencing it now. Doubts, too, about whether we should have come.

"Maybe you could talk about prison reform, Chuck," Don Taylor chimed in. Carl Bistrom nodded, "That would be good. Everybody is for that."

I looked over at Chaplin Riggs, standing against the wall, arms folded. He was nodding agreement.

"I came here to tell these men what Christ can do for them," I said. But the fire was gone from my words; the men knew this place better than I.

"Some other time," Carl said softly.

We prayed together, joining hands in our circle. The prayers were filled with claims for God's promises, but the circle seemed very tiny, a little spot of light in a vast sea of darkness.

I asked the men to leave me alone so I could make notes for a speech on prison reform. Minutes later Charlie Riggs knocked on the door. "The auditorium is filling up fast. Let's go," he announced. My mind was churning and my heart was pounding as we headed toward the auditorium.

There were 800 to 900 inmates spread throughout the hall which we entered from the rear. Sitting near the front were the community volunteers and our staff, 30 in all. Their clothes seemed garish by comparison with the rows upon rows of brown through the auditorium.

As I walked the long corridor to the front of the room, heads snapped, eyes stared. A few nodded, but most faces were grim. The heat was unbearable. Tension was crackling in the air like static electricity.

I took a seat down front next to Jack Hanberry. That was probably a mistake since all wardens, even the best, are suspect and so are their friends.

Jerry Potter, a Minneapolis businessman who volunteered a year of his time to work in our ministry, was speaking. Jerry is good at warming up an audience, but this night he might as well have been Demosthenes, the ancient Greek orator who used to stand on the shore and address the sea. The only response was sullen restlessness.

Next the "hippie priest," Tim Ondahl, marched to the microphone. For the first time I felt a lifting of the oppressive atmosphere as the priest opened the evening with a simple but eloquent prayer.

"We thank you, Father, for the fine people here this evening to share with us. They bring dimensions to us that we never dreamed possible. They don't even expect a payback. And, for us that is unreal; or maybe, we should say simply Christian.

"We are a mixed bag, Father. And we are coming from a lot of different places, traditions and experiences. But, we are happy to know that your message fits us all. Help us in our belief, but even more, help us to practice the teachings of your Son, our Brother, Jesus Christ. Amen."

Nancy Honeytree who often accompanies us into prisons, was next.

With her granny glasses, baggy coveralls and a railroad man's cap perched atop pigtails, she is always able to charm her audiences. But the crowd this night seemed distant throughout Nancy's performance.

My own anxieties were climbing as fast as the temperature in the room. It was hot enough to ignite the notes in my hand and suffocatingly close. There were no fans.

Nancy finished and there was polite applause. When Paul walked forward and began to introduce me, I bowed my head to say one last, pithy, crisis prayer. As I moved to the microphone it was so stifling that I took my jacket off and threw it on the floor beside me. The mild applause had long since died out, replaced by an uncomfortable silence. In a way the quiet was more unsettling than the raucous outburst at Attica. Every face in the room, even inmates I knew to be friendly, appeared stern. I tried a quick joke but there was little response. *Lord,* I thought, *if I've ever needed Your help it's now.* Then I drew a deep breath and Ondahl's prayer paraded across my mind. "For us it is unreal, these people coming here. Or maybe we should say simply Christian." That was it. They couldn't figure why we are here!

"I know what many of you guys are thinking," I began. "What is Chuck Colson doing here? What's his game? Is he here to make money? There's got to be an angle, right?"

Heads nodded all over the hall.

"And look at these nice people from town," I continued. "Why are they here? Is it just to go back to their nice churches in the nice part of town and tell the nice people they've done something good? They went to see a prisoner."

There were even more nods now. I didn't know where the words were coming from, because this wasn't what I had planned to say at all.

"Well, let me tell you why I am here and why these people in front are here. Because we have committed our lives to Jesus Christ and this is where He calls us to be." Down front I saw Cal wince. This is what my friends feared would set the crowd off.

By now I had folded up my "prison reform" notes and stuck them in my pocket. If I was sure of anything, it was that tonight I would talk about Jesus Christ.

The crowd seemed intent as I traced the history of Prison Fellowship. They laughed when I told them of neighbors around Fellowship House confusing congressmen and convicts; there was scattered applause once or twice when I talked about our vision of bringing men and women out of prison into training sessions.

The heat in the room was overpowering. By now every stitch of clothing on my body was wet through; I'm sure I looked like I'd just come in from the rain. This should have brought weakness but instead came strength. Words and sentences I'd never said before flowed out of me, as if they were raised up from the inner recesses of my spirit. I talked on about my own decision to go into prison work full time, about the amazing love that Jesus has for those of us who have fallen.

"Jesus Christ came into this world for the poor, the sick, the hungry, the homeless, the imprisoned. He is the Prophet of the loser. And all of us assembled here are losers. I am a loser just like every one of you. The miracle is that God's message is specifically for those of us who have failed.

"Jesus rode into Jerusalem on a donkey," I said at the end. "He did this so that people would know that He came from the dirt and the mud, that He had been with weak and ordinary people and those who hurt and suffered.

"The message of Jesus Christ is for the imprisoned—for your families, some of them who aren't making it on welfare on the outside. Christ reached out for you who are in prison because He came to take those chains off, to take you out of bondage. He can make you the freest person in the entire world, right here in this lousy place.

"Jesus, the Savior, the Messiah, the Jesus Christ I follow is the One who comes to help the downtrodden and the oppressed and to release them and set them free. This is the Jesus Christ to whom I have committed my life. This is the Jesus Christ to whom I have offered up my dream and said, 'Lord, I want to help these men because I have lived among them. I came to know them, I love them. There is injustice in our society, but we can change it. Yes, God, we can change it. I give my life to it.'"

What happened next can only be explained as an extraordinary outpouring of the Holy Spirit. Men were not only standing throughout the auditorium, they were getting up on their chairs, clapping and shouting. The change in the faces was awesome. They were warm and smiling. There were tears in the eyes of many where before there had been distrust and hate. It was the ultimate for me in learning how to be used of God; I was the wheel—He the Potter.

For over an hour I stood in one corner of that auditorium praying with some, counseling others and simply holding out a friendly hand to many. Several met Christ that night; we didn't count, but a year later would find nearly 400 men in chapel programs.

A black man, tall and lean with ugly scars on his neck and arms, came up to talk to me but couldn't. He simply leaned his head on my shoulder and cried like a baby.

Another, tough-looking white man, a three-day, wiry, black stubble on his cheeks and chin, said, "My whole 39 years were a waste, 20 of them in joints like this. But they were only a preparation for this night. It's all turned around tonight. God bless you."

Still another handed me a penciled note, asking that I mail it to his wife. Scratched on the notepaper in faint pencil without punctuation was the most touching message I've ever seen. It went something like this: "Darling everything will be all right now because I am at peace finally with the Lord this night like you are and have been telling me and so we will be closer than ever even though we are apart please tell the kids its all going to be fine at last. I love you all."

Joe, the "Butcher," as he introduced himself, was the most colorful. His title had nothing to do with his working in a meat market. Short and stocky with curly black hair all over his head and chest where his shirt hung open, he put two beefy hands on my shoulders.

"Mr. Colson, I'm gonna do something I ain't never done before," he announced. "I'm gonna apologize. But wait a minute. I want my friends to be in on this."

Joe turned, waving and shouting to several men nearby: "Pete, Harry, come here," he commanded. No one argued with Joe, who had been a well-known Mafia chieftain. They quickly joined us. "Over here, Fink. Yeah, you too; get over here," Joe kept fingering his pals. Soon there were more than a dozen standing in a half circle around us.

"Okay, now," Joe continues, "Mr. Colson, I thought you was a phony. I told these guys that. Told 'em not to listen. Well, Mr. Colson, I was wrong. You are our friend and so is Jesus."

Then the "Butcher" prayed for Jesus to come into his life. He asked forgiveness for his sins, thankfully not listing them all since the night was short. Many of Joe's buddies followed him. The angels in Heaven must have sung an especially joyous chorus that night over Joe and his friends.

Before leaving the prison, I walked back to Chaplain Riggs' office with the eight Christians who would soon find their ranks increased by hundreds of new believers. They were wearing the kind of smiles that looked like they'd last at least forever. We got on our knees and thanked God for this one remarkable night. It was difficult to keep the prayers going around the circle because so many were choked up.

As I stood at the head of the stairs leading back to the central corridor, saying good-by, Chaplain Riggs moved from one foot to the other. "Hurry up or we'll all be in the hole."

Cal stuck out his hand for a last farewell. "I wish I could stay here with you guys," I said as tears filled Cal's eyes. Funny thing is, I meant it. I didn't want to leave these men behind.

Suddenly, so much came into focus right here in the most dreaded of all prisons: I really loved these inmates. These were indeed *my* brothers. It was here in Atlanta and in dark holes all across America that I experienced the richest, most meaningful fellowship. I could easily understand why Jesus went to people like these and places like this. Mysteriously and inexplicably, here one could sense the presence of God, the unspeakable joy of all joys.

Now I was understanding myself, finally, and maybe understanding God, too, as I had not really before. I'd seen in my young Christian life a lot of phoniness, but this was authentic, made up for all else, in fact.

Tears filled my eyes as I stood on those stairs looking into the faces of Don, Carl, Cal, Sunshine and the others. They said so much in those few seconds of silence it would take volumes to write it all down. Cal reached over the railing and put his hand on my shoulder. "Go, Brother," he said calmly. "Go, because we need you out there. While there are people outside who care, we have hope. Go and God bless you."

Then I hurried down the stairs and along the granite corridor. I couldn't help stopping for a moment to look up into Cellblock A, five tiers high, catwalks surrounding the rows of tiny cages into which, in minutes, hundreds of men would be herded. Men like Don, and Joe the Butcher. Other men too, some I would never meet. "God help them," I muttered, "God help them."

What a torture, I thought. *These men come back from the spiritual high of this meeting and then live in this hell. But this, too, will change. I know it will. When Christians see what this is all about, they will do something, I know,* I told myself. And with God's leading, it will change because it must.

My friends were waiting in the lobby. There was Tom Roddy, our local leader, and Paul, my ever-faithful brother, and Jerry Potter and Nancy Honeytree. There were a half dozen others from the community waiting, who were all smiling, not like the guys upstairs—it was different—but big smiles just the same.

We started down the long driveway away from the big building and toward the gate. It was nearly ten. Though still very hot, the air outside was refreshing compared to the sweltering auditorium. The moon was full and its light flooded over the concrete in front of us and the grass to either side. We were all emotionally spent and walked slowly. I was taking very deep breaths.

Suddenly there was a clatter behind us, a knocking sound and some muffled shouts. "Pray that it isn't trouble. Not tonight," someone said. I looked back at the darkened building silhouetted in the moonlight. The noises grew louder. I squinted to see.

The three-story-high windows of Cellblock A were brightly lighted. The towering dark bars covering them had a golden hue. A few small windowpanes were open—that's where the sound was coming from. Then I made out the shadow figures of men standing on the inside ledges of the windows behind the bars; there were many figures, perhaps 30 or 40.

"They're waving," Honeytree exclaimed. "And they're calling goodby to us!"

That is what it was, all right. It was not trouble in this cellblock where so many men had died in recent months. All we could see were silhouettes and waving arms. These men, many with life sentences, were peering through narrow window slits and shouting at us. I heard "God bless you" and "Thank you."

We all stood and stared at the amazing sight. *How, God,* I asked quietly, *could I have taken so long to figure out where You wanted me?* I knew this night, as I had not known it before, that I was "at my post," and that for me it was a life sentence.

As we turned to walk away, Paul muttered, "This place will never be the same."

"I'm afraid it will be, Paul. For a while anyway, but we won't."

Cal's words were ringing in my ears as they do today, "Go, Brother. Go, because we need you out there. While there are people outside who care, we have hope."

Yes, go in your thousands into prisons across the land.

With Gratitude . . .

If this book accomplishes what it was written for—to encourage and challenge others—it will be first because of answered prayer, and second because of the labors of many. In writing it, I experienced once again one of the richest rewards of the Christian life, the unstinting and unselfish support of other believers. *Life Sentence*, both the book and the experiences it relates, was made possible because a team—family, friends and co-workers—joined together in a common task.

Patty's partnership in my life and ministry has grown more important and meaningful to me with each passing day. As with *Born Again*, she took dictation, typed draft after draft, rescued me from my ill humor when the frequent frustrations of writing overcame me, and spent many lonely evenings while I was closeted in my library. Without her sacrifices, this book would not have been possible. Not many could ask for more than this remarkable woman has freely given.

The same team from Chosen Books which edited *Born Again*—Leonard LeSourd, with an assist from Elizabeth Sherrill—devoted their extraordinary energy and talent to this manuscript. We followed the same system we developed with *Born Again:* I wrote, Len cut. I wrote more, Len cut more—something like sawing a thick tree limb with a two-man saw. In time I was forced, though reluctantly, to conclude that Len's efforts were more creative than mine, that less is more. Though I still grieve for some of the flowing prose that died under the merciless assault of his pencil, remarkably we all ended up closer than ever after a year of working together.

Mike Cromartie, the young man who researched, wrote, critiqued and even occasionally warded off chocolate pies tossed my way, deserves much credit—not only for his work on this manuscript, but for the larger task of providing much of the intellectual stimulus for my own Christian growth. Mike's memos on every subject from civil religion, to criminal law, to predestination, were often brilliantly insightful and always provocative.

As is obvious in *Life Sentence,* Fred Rhodes has been my trusted spiritual counselor and close friend from the first days of my Christian life. Countless times he steadied the course. In 1977, Fred began writing a book about his experiences and the beginnings of this ministry. When the manuscript was well along, Fred abandoned it for fear its publication might interfere with this book. That decision was consistent with Fred's selfless commitment to me as his friend, and our ministry as his calling from God.

What is recounted in this book is the story of the Prison Fellowship team. God has raised up a truly remarkable group of gifted people, headed by Gordon Loux. Gordon not only shouldered his own burden, while I was preoccupied with writing over several months, but shouldered mine as well. He has not only become a superb manager but my trusted and valued confidant. I am deeply grateful to him and the others on the staff, whose loyalty and friendship I treasure.

Prison Fellowship staffers—Carolyn Bonker, Nancy Niemeyer, Jeanne Hurley, and Sara Drexler—all pitched in to type, check, edit, and proof manuscripts and galleys. Sara's final editing was a great contribution.

To Richard Lovelace, James Houston, and R.C. Sproul—three gifted theologians—I owe a special debt of gratitude. The countless hours of tutoring I have enjoyed from these men of uncommon intellect have been the most renewing experience of my Christian life. All three gave inspiration to this book; Dr. Lovelace and Dr. Sproul also offered their time to critiques of the last draft.

At various times in the preparations of the book, I consulted other friends and professionals as well; sometimes their comments got my derailed train back on track, other times a word or suggestion came at just the right moment. I am grateful to each of the following for their unique contributions: Carl Henry, Paul Henry, Frank Gaebelein, Doug Coe, Harold Hughes, Wes Michaelson, Jim Wallis, Francis Schaeffer, Dave Cauwels, Jim Millen, James Hurley, Clayton Brown, Nick Wolterstorff, Jay Kesler, David Kucharsky, George Sweeting, Paul Robbins, Clark Pinnock, Neal Jones, Myron Augsburger, Ted Engstrom, Pat Robertson, Sherwood Wirt, George Wilson, Robert Walker, Lloyd Ogilvie, Stephen Board, Martin Marty, Joe Bayly, Dick Halverson, Mark Hatfield, Jack Hayford, Vernon Grounds, Wes Pippert, Foy Valentine, and Os Guinness.

Through the generosity of Phil and Marrianne Wheeler, Mark and Antoinette Hatfield, and Charles (Jiggs) and Jackie Davis, Patty and I had three lovely and quiet homes, one on the East Coast, the other two on the West Coast, to which to retreat and write. Our thanks to these, our good friends.

Because of the publisher's deadlines, an index of names was not included in the hardcover edition. A Prison Fellowship volunteer, Marilyn Smith of Highland Falls, New York, noted the omission and offered to prepare the one which appears in this copy. I am grateful for her most important contribution, characteristic of the marvelous enthusiasm of so many of our workers across the land.

Then there are hundreds of others, too numerous to list here, whose friendship has encouraged both Patty and me in our Christian experience. Many of them are leaders in many walks of life, in all corners of the world; many others are inmates, deeply committed disciples, who live in the squalid holes we call penitentiaries.

It is to the latter group, with whom I shall always feel a special closeness, that I say a special thanks. Your courage and your faith spurred me on to live the experiences of this book and then to write it. I thank God that we will continue to serve our life sentences—together.

Since Then

Following that memorable night in Atlanta, Chuck Colson's work in the prisons has continued, the ministry expanding across the country and to other continents as well. The Prison Fellowship staff of 100 now harnesses the efforts of more than 6,800 volunteers in scores of communities from churches of all denominations.

Prison Fellowship now has a full-time director in each of 23 states and plans to have directors in all states by the end of 1983. More than 30 classes have graduated from the Washington, D.C., seminars with no major incidents! Nationally, 9,000 inmates have graduated from in-prison programs; 8,000 more are scheduled for 1981. Many governors have endorsed the ministry, and teams are now teaching in more than half of the state prisons. Job banks are being organized for released prisoners. Counseling and assistance are being provided inmate families.

Long overdue, the assault by Prison Fellowship is the first full-scale one in this century by the Christian church on America's prisons.

Though Colson and his co-workers thought the task of reaching America's 600 penitentiaries was overwhelming enough, God had even more in store for them. Christian leaders in England invited a proposal. At first, Chuck was reluctant, but after he and Gordon Loux met in November 1978 with 200 pastors, government officials, and prison workers in London's historic Church House, the conclusion was inescapable. There was an urgent need in England's Victorian-era prisons, and a Prison Christian Fellowship was organized there.

On a trip "down under," Chuck and Gordon toured Australian prisons. What happened in England was repeated. The ministry is now operating in Australia, New Zealand, and Canada as well. Early in 1981, Chuck made visits to the Bahamas, Japan, and Korea to determine needs in those countries. Ireland, France, Puerto Rico and Columbia, among others, are close to receiving their charter for Prison Fellowship.

Although Chuck Colson's own Christian growth continues through setbacks and frustrations, he will probably remain one of the most enigmatic and controversial figures among American Evangelicals. At press conferences, he is often sharply challenged. Some who knew him well in government can't comprehend why he would lose himself in prison work.

After the recent funeral of his one-time boss, U.S. Senator Leverett Saltonstall, Chuck was stopped in the Harvard College Yard by John Kenneth Galbraith, former ambassador and famed economist. The lean, lanky professor greeted him warmly, "Good to see you back in these parts, Chuck. What are you doing these days?"

"I work in prisons now, Mr. Ambassador," Colson replied.

"Oh," Galbraith replied, nonplussed. "Well, cheer up, better things are ahead."

Shortly thereafter in an overcrowded Colorado prison, known for its violence and brutality, a young prisoner of Spanish ancestry grasped Colson's arm. "I have no family, no friends, and I've been here seven years," he said, his voice strained. "I wrote you a few months ago, and you put a family in Colorado Springs in touch with me. They write me and visit me. I just want you to know that for the first time in my life I have hope and a reason to live."

Hope and a reason to live for the "least of these." Others may continue to doubt and wonder, but Chuck Colson is a man who understands well why this is his Life Sentence.

CAN YOU HELP?

If God has used this book to touch your heart, you may wish to join thousands of other Christians who make up Prison Fellowship around the world.

Perhaps you would like to correspond with an inmate. Maybe you would like to lead a Bible study inside one of our federal, state, or local prisons. Perhaps you feel a burden to do what you can to ease the plight of a family whose parent is incarcerated.

If you feel God is calling you to join us at Prison Fellowship, as a volunteer or as a financial supporter, please write to me now. We can work together in fulfilling the biblical command to minister to inmates as if we were prisoners at their sides.

Charles W. Colson

☐ I'm interested in learning more about Prison Fellowship's ministry.

☐ I'm interested in writing to a prisoner; send me details on how to go about it.

☐ I'm interested in other specific volunteer activities, such as visiting prisoners and working with ex-offenders and families.

Prison Fellowship
P.O. Box 17500
Washington, D.C. 20041-0500
703-478-0100